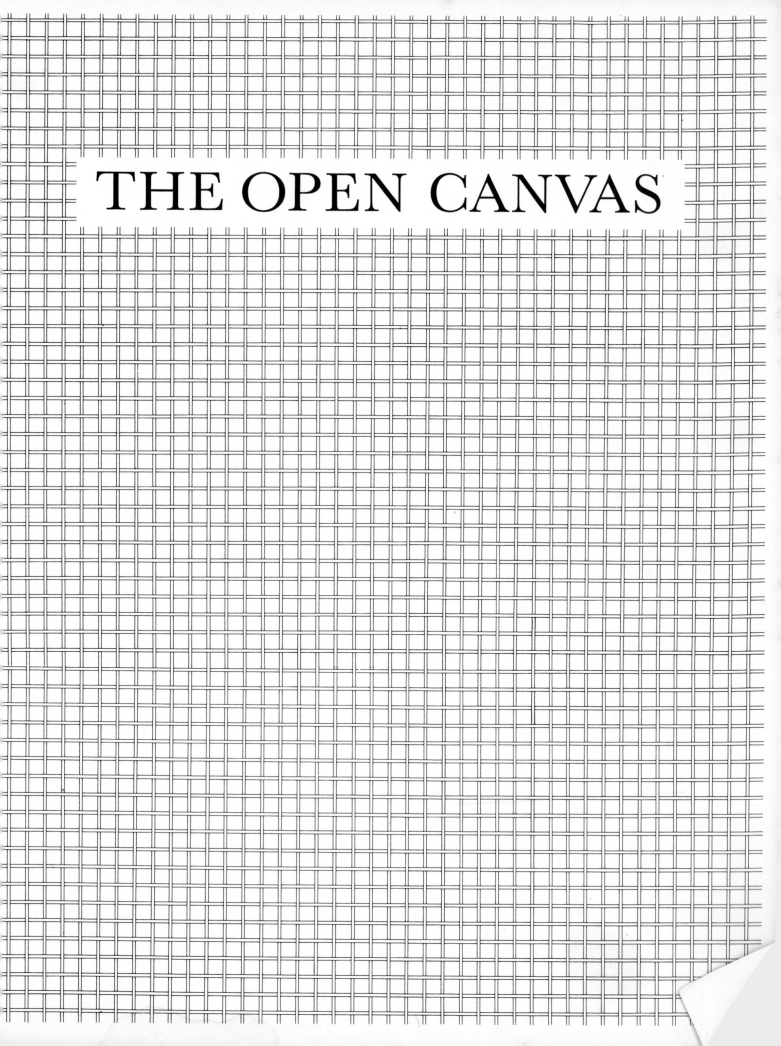

THE OPEN CANVAS

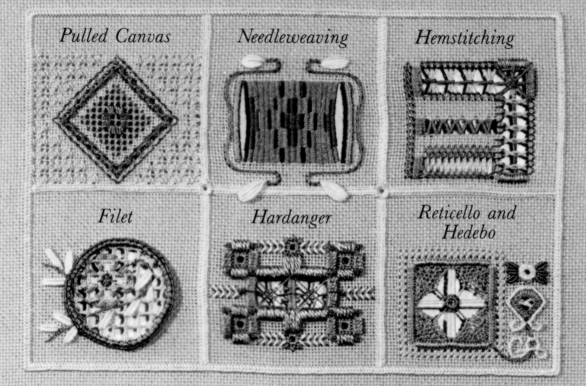

CAROLYN AMBUTER

THE OPEN CANVAS

Illustrations by Patti Baker Russell
Photographs by Jerry Darvin

WORKMAN PUBLISHING, NEW YORK

Library of Congress Cataloging in Publication Data

Ambuter, Carolyn.
The open canvas.
Bibliography: p.
1. Canvas embroidery.   I. Title.
TT778.C3A496   1982   746.44   82-60066
ISBN 0-89480-170-8   ISBN 0-89480-171-6 (pbk.)

Cover design: Paul Hanson
Book design: Barbara Huntley

Workman Publishing Company, Inc.
1 West 39th Street, New York, N.Y. 10018

Manufactured in United States of America
First printing October 1982
10 9 8 7 6 5 4 3 2 1

FOR AMANDA

ACKNOWLEDGMENTS

As I sit here, after all these years of work, I know I cannot possibly thank all those who helped bring this book to life. So many helped in one way or many ways—like Patti Russell, whose art and needlework graces these pages, and who has also graced my life. Family and dear friends offered advice, sympathy, physical labor, support, and encouragement. I have studied so many embroidery books, attended so many workshops and seminars, taken (and given) so many private lessons—where can I start and how can I end my thanks? I must at least include those who were involved with the actual production of *The Open Canvas*—Peter Workman, Sally Kovalchick, Paul Hanson, Jerry Darvin, Louise Gikow, Barbara Huntley, and Amy Gateff. I thank you all.

CONTENTS

INTRODUCTION

WHY *THE OPEN CANVAS?*

Needlework is an art that is as old as painting and sculpture, but it has only recently received recognition as such in this country. Classified as fiber art, it now demands that embroiderer and artist be one and the same. This raises several questions. How expressive can needlework be? Can an accomplished embroiderer employ color and design to project thoughts or emotions with needle and thread? Can a fine artist develop enough technical embroidery skills to employ needlework as a means of expression? In this volume, I have explored some open-work techniques from the past with the object of aiding embroiderers who wish to become artists, and artists who wish to become embroiderers. I have chosen canvas as a foundation fabric because its even weave, open mesh squares, and starched elements are an excellent framework on which to learn.

WHY OPEN WORK?

The field of embroidery can be divided into three almost literal levels: surface, raised, and open work. Surface work includes techniques that embellish or cover the foundation fabric, including all counted-thread techniques (canvas work, blackwork, darning and cross-stitch), crewel work, and free stitchery. Raised work includes those techniques in which another distinct plane is added to the work, such as couching, appliqué, trapunto, quilting, smocking, and soft sculpture. Open work involves deflecting, withdrawing, or cutting the fabric, securing it, and then filling the open spaces. Many fine books have surveyed the fields of surface and raised work, bringing them up to the present. However, at the time I began thinking about it, there was no volume devoted to open work, a subject that I think is the most exciting field of all for fiber artists.

THE VOCABULARY

Every field of endeavor has its own precise language, and embroidery, open work in particular, is no exception. I have made an effort to incorporate the latest academic terms without losing the charm and flavor of the past.

The phrases *drawn thread, drawn fabric,* and *deflected-element work* all describe *pulled canvas work,* but I have generally stuck to the latter for the sake of simplicity. The threads of the canvas are referred to as *elements,* and embroidery thread is called the *working thread.* When describing the size of the canvas mesh, a number with a slash mark and the word *inch* is used—for example, 18/inch (18 canvas elements to the inch).

The words *stitch* and *stitch unit* are probably the most used in these pages, although there are very few "single" stitches—most are units of several straight, slanted, looped, or knotted ones worked together. In each of the books of this volume, you will find stitches grouped in closely related families.

Do not tax your memory learning them all. Rather, try to understand what each accomplishes and where it would be appropriate. You can always refer back to this book for help. A glossary has been provided as well; refer to it when needed.

WHY SAMPLERS?

In this "instructional encyclopedia of open-work techniques" I have chosen one or two samplers to illustrate each family of stitches. Samplers have a long and interesting history, having provided learning experiences long before embroidery books were written; and they can still be used to practice on, allowing the embroiderer to experiment with many techniques. They can also be displayed as pictures, or laced together with fabric or canvas of the same size to produce pillows, tote bags, and the like. You might want to work them in bits and pieces and slip them into a notebook, just as the photographs of these worked samplers have been cut up to illustrate each stitch. Best of all, samplers need never be finished and can be expanded almost indefinitely.

HOW TO USE THIS BOOK

The Open Canvas is actually six books in one. Although it proceeds in order by gradually opening the canvas, each book is a completely independent unit. If you want to study any of the fields covered, you need not refer to another. Old, reliable friends such as buttonhole, chain, or four-sided stitches are repeated as needed, so that skipping about is not necessary. Reference is made to other books, however, so that you can see different examples if you so desire.

Each of the six books is a series of lessons that progresses along with the samplers, which are completed with the last lesson. These lessons can be formally taught, they can be a group experience, or they can be followed independently. Use them in any way that suits you. Both pattern diagrams and stitch diagrams are often provided for each stitch. Pattern diagrams are used to locate the stitches on the canvas, and descriptions of the work accompany them. Stitch diagrams actually show the techniques employed; they are usually illustrated without tension, to avoid distortion. The little photographs show the stitches as they appear in the sampler, actual size. Advanced embroiderers need only study these pictures and diagrams; intermediate students can refer to the captions for additional information, and beginners will probably want to read the entire text.

Although specific numbers of elements and stitches are shown in the diagrams, the embroiderer should learn to vary them. There are limitless possibilities within each technique. These books should serve as introductions only; the rest is up to you.

BOOK ONE

PULLED CANVAS

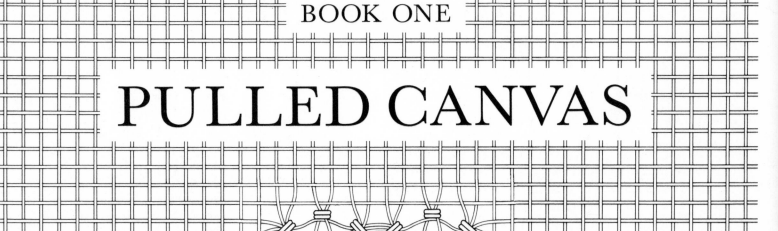

Selected elements are forced out of alignment by pulling the working thread with various degrees of tension. This creates patterns in both the positive and negative spaces.

CONTENTS

INTRODUCTION

The lessons that follow are designed to examine and expand upon basic pulled work techniques. From the great wealth of existing patterns, a limited number that best represented the stitch formations were selected to illustrate each technique. It takes two samplers to cover this material. Sampler I provides a thorough introduction to pulled techniques. Sampler II offers supplementary methods and fillings. Also included is a floral composition that uses pulled fillings and couched outlines as well as other techniques from *The Open Canvas,* to give you a chance to employ a nongeometric design for pulled canvas.

Both the samplers and the floral design should be worked in sequence with the lessons. Begin by preparing the canvas, following the instructions in Lesson 1. You can either employ the master patterns or drawings or work independently, in which case the samplers will serve as illustrations for the stitches and fillings. Along with the photographs and keys to the two samplers are lists of materials required to make them as shown.

Take a few minutes before you start to familiarize yourself with the history of pulled work, overall procedures, and essential materials.

A THIMBLEFUL OF HISTORY

The principal examples of pulled work are to be found in the white open-work embroidery that reached a peak of delicacy during the eighteenth century in both northern Germany and Denmark. It has been described as drawn muslin lace and referred to as Dresden work, Dresden point, and Tonder work. Most of this work was deflected-element or pulled work, though some of it was used in combination with withdrawn-element work. Designs of leaves and flowers were worked in a great variety of filling patterns with strong outlines of couched threads, called cordonnets. The cordonnet stood in relief to the fillings and the ground, which was often filled with yet another pattern.

Dresden work ornamented women's caps, fichus, sleeve falls, and aprons, and men's waistcoats. It was originally a more practical, time-saving decoration than the more costly and fash-

ionable *punto in aria* true laces, which were made without any ground fabric. However, exquisitely delicate Dresden work soon rivaled needle lace, and became greatly desired by wealthy Europeans. As a result, it spread rapidly through the Low Countries, France, Russia, England, and America. The subsequent nineteenth- and twentieth-century development of Ayrshire work, broderie Anglaise, Russian and Greek drawn grounds, and Danish Samenntraekssning all evolved from this eighteenth-century Dresden work.

SOME NEEDLE POINTS

In this section of *The Open Canvas,* reference is made to positive and negative spaces. The term *positive spaces* refers to the canvas elements and stitches. *Negative spaces* are the openings left where the stitches have pulled the canvas elements out of alignment or where the elements have been completely withdrawn—that is, cut away. Traditionally, pulled work, employing tiny white stitches of fine white thread on delicate white foundation fabrics, focused on the negative spaces exclusively. The stitches were not meant to be seen; the pattern was made by the shapes of the open spaces. But in our treatment of pulled canvas, the focus shifts from purely negative space to a relationship between the two kinds of space. Stitch techniques, color, and design must be reconsidered. They are already critical to the other traditional techniques discussed in *The Open Canvas,* in which the embellishment supplied by the stitches was always as important as the open spaces.

A canvas foundation fabric has coarse, stiff elements with a very open weave that results in obvious patterns in the positive spaces and clear definition of negative space. Therefore, extra care must be taken with stitch formation. The pulled canvas stitch diagrams are designed to conceal connecting threads on the backface and to regulate the slant of stitches on the frontface. Positive space is usually light and negative is dark, unless the canvas is lit from behind. Now that we are focusing on positive space, colored canvas and working threads become useful. It is a good idea to employ lighter colors to provide contrast with the dark openings. The density of the patterns also affects the color; closely packed stitches create darker values than sparsely worked stitches. Consider, too, the direction or movement made by the stitches as well as that of the openings. Some fillings are static; others move left, right, or diagonally. Place them where they can make a contribution to the total design concept.

When you begin a pulled canvas work, you must make a decision about technique: whether to outline the filling patterns before or after they are completed, or whether to outline them at all. When you outline first, you provide yourself with a convenient place under which you can bury connecting and fastening threads. However, you do limit the possibility of extending the pattern. If you set the fillings in first, you can anticipate their edges, which will enable you to bury working thread under the outline. In Sampler I, I have resolved the outlining question by outlining both before (see Master Pattern, Sampler I), and after (see Lesson **12**). In Sampler II, a more contemporary and more challenging method is employed. Some of the work is set in without outlines (see Master Pattern, Sampler II), and some of the fillings are outlined after they are set in (see Lesson **12**). All of these methods are suitable for geometric designs that follow a master pattern. If you are working from a drawing that you want to develop and refine in the process of stitching, you should work the fillings first, spotting and balancing them carefully. When they are all set in to your satisfaction, you can consider and work appropriate outline stitches.

The pulled work itself is easily mastered. Pull on the thread, not the needle, or the thread in the eye of the needle will break. At the uppoint, make a single even pull, up and toward the space that will serve as the downpoint (see Glossary). At the downpoint, make a single even pull, down and toward the space that will serve as the uppoint. The amount of tension you exert determines the size of the openings as well as the size of the stitch itself. Tension should be tight for most work, but it can be medium or light, particularly for satin stitches. In the lessons that follow, use a tight tension unless otherwise noted. If the pressure of the working thread hurts your hand as you exert tension, you can dampen the canvas lightly to make it more pliable, using a moist sponge or swab. There may be occasions when it is difficult to bring the connecting thread from one row to another and achieve the desired stitch slant. In this case, you can take short, straight stitches over a single canvas element that will barely show. You should use a waste knot (see Glossary) whenever possible for fastening on or off; but you will still often need to use a sharp or crewel needle to bury ends on the backface.

WORKBASKET SUPPLIES

CANVAS

Mono canvas with its simple one by one basket-weave construction is the only variety that allows you to pull the elements out of alignment with any degree of ease. Use only the best quality, because the tension you must employ for this work can break the weak elements of a poor quality canvas.

Select a mesh size that is appropriate for your design and comfortable to work. In pulled work, exposed warps and wefts become an integral part of the patterns, so notice the weight of the elements, which is determined by the number of elements to the inch. The more elements to the inch, the finer their weight. Traditional work is usually done on sixteen elements to the inch or finer, which produces light, lacy work. Do not, however, neglect larger meshes for contemporary effects. Try washing the canvas first to soften it, although it should be completely dry when you begin to work. You can achieve some original unstructured effects combining the fillings in *The Open Canvas* with your own variations.

Mono canvas is available in different colors and fibers, in addition to the usual white cotton. Apricot toile, various colors of congress canvas, cream linen, and tan cotton mono canvases are all good choices. You can also experiment with a softened washed interlock canvas. Avoid canvas of manmade fibers, as they are too slippery.

THREADS

Strong fibers with little texture are what you look for in selecting working threads for pulled canvas. The strength of the working thread must match the strength of the canvas elements or one of them will break. Since the stitches are usually pulled taut, it is best that they have neither hairs nor a high luster. Textured threads can be used to embellish the work, however, for overstitching or outlining. The thickness of the working thread should be either the same as the thickness of the canvas elements or finer. If you are using working thread of more than one ply, be sure to separate and align the plies when threading the needle, and maintain them that way as they are drawn into stitches. Plies of silk or cotton floss, silk twist, pearl cotton, cutwork and embroidery thread, fine crochet cotton, and linen are all good choices.

FRAMES

You can use interlocking wood strips or a rotating frame with tapes. The work stays on the frame throughout, but it is frequently turned for fastening off and on.

NEEDLES AND OTHER TOOLS

You will need tapestry needles in sizes that suit the working threads, and crewel needles for fastening off and on. If you employ couched outlines (see Lesson **12**), you will need an appropriately sized chenille needle for sinking, and sharps for sewing the couched thread on the backface. You will also need beeswax if you are couching down metal with silk. An awl is helpful for preparing the eyelet holes, counting the elements, and tracing the movements of the working threads when studying some of the stitch diagrams.

KEY TO STITCHES AND THREADS
Sampler I

Pulled Canvas Sampler I is worked with silk threads on 17/inch linen mono canvas. The finished size is 10¼ inches by 14 inches. See the accompanying key to identify the stitches and threads. The bold numbers with letters refer to the lesson where each stitch or pattern is located in *Pulled Canvas*. The bold italic numbers refer to the threads listed under Materials Employed.

1A Backstitch Outline: use *3* for entire outer frame, except for final edge use *1*; outline inner shapes with *1*
2B Small Ringed Back Filling, *6*
3A, 3B Overcast Grounds, *7*
3C Whipped Satin Ribbing, *8, 11*
3D Coil Filling, *6*
3E Coil and Satin Filling, *8, 2*
3G Reed Border Variation, *1*
3H Freely Made Satin Filling, *2*
4B Basket Filling Variation, *6*
4E Flat Step Filling, *6*
4F Framed Cross Filling, *2*
4G Cobbler Filling, *2*
5A Eyelet Stitches, *1*
5B Diamond Eyelet Filling, *8, 12*

5C Square Eyelets, *8, 12*
5D, 5E Eyelets, *2*
5F Eyelets, *1, 3*
5G Eyelet Ground, *3*
5H Freely Worked Eyelets, assorted colors, *1, 2, 3, 5*
6B Double Wave Filling, *2*
6C Window Filling, *2*
6G Cable Filling, *4*
6I Honeycomb Filling, *2*
6J Turned Honeycomb, *8, 2*
7A Single Faggot Filling, *8*
7B¹ Double Faggot Ground, *4*
7B² Double Faggot Ground, *5*
7C Diagonal Drawn Filling, *4*
7D Satin and Faggot Filling, *5, 7*

7E Reverse Faggot Ground, *5*
7F Reverse Faggot Ground Variation, *8*
7G Pulled Russian Ground, *4*
7H Diagonal Chain Border, *8*
8A Diagonal Cross Filling, *4*
8B Diagonal Cross-Stitch, *8, 4*
8C Diagonal Raised Band, *2*
8D Open Trellis Filling, *5, 8*
8E Checker Filling, *4*
9A Square Cushion Filling, *2*
9B Double-Back Filling, *7*
9C Finnish Filling, *1*
9D Diamond Filling, *7*
10A Italian Cross Filling, *5, 8*
10B Mosaic Filling, *2*
10C Coil and Cross Border, *3 or 8*
10D Four-Sided Border, *3 or 1*
10E Dropped Four-Sided Filling, *5, 7*
10I Indian Drawn Ground, *1*
11A Spaced Buttonhole, *3*
11B Buttonhole Eyelet, *1*
11C Quarter Buttonhole Eyelet, *3*
11D Buttonhole Eyelet and Whipped Satin Band; Satin Diamond and Cross, *4*
11E Greek Cross Filling, *4*
11F Loop Stitch Filling, *2*
12A Tent Stitch, *9*
12C Whipped Chain Outline, *10*
12E Outline Stem, *8*
12G Four-Sided Edging Variation, *1*

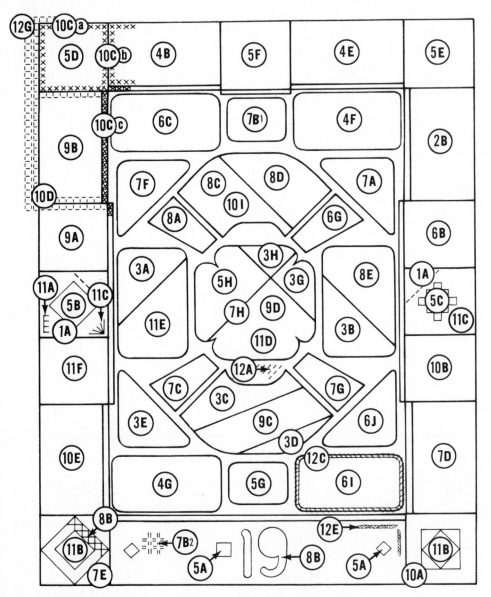

MATERIALS EMPLOYED
CANVAS
17/inch cream linen; 14 inches wide by 18 inches high; edges bound
THREADS
1 Kanagawa Silk Twist, 158 yellow gold
2 Kanagawa Silk Twist, 175 peach
3 Kanagawa Silk Twist, 161 green
4 Kanagawa Silk Twist, 162 green
5 Kanagawa Silk Twist, 106 light blue
6 Kanagawa Silk Twist, 104 medium blue
7 Kanagawa Silk Twist, 798 dark blue
8 Kanagawa Silk Twist, 797 turquoise blue
9 Au Ver A Soie Silk, 531 ivory
10 Au Ver A Soie Silk, 622 orange gold
11 Globo Rayon Floss, 140 peach
12 Globo Rayon Floss, 30 gold
NEEDLES
Tapestry 22, 24   Crewel 8
STRETCHER STRIPS
1 pair 14-inch   1 pair 18-inch

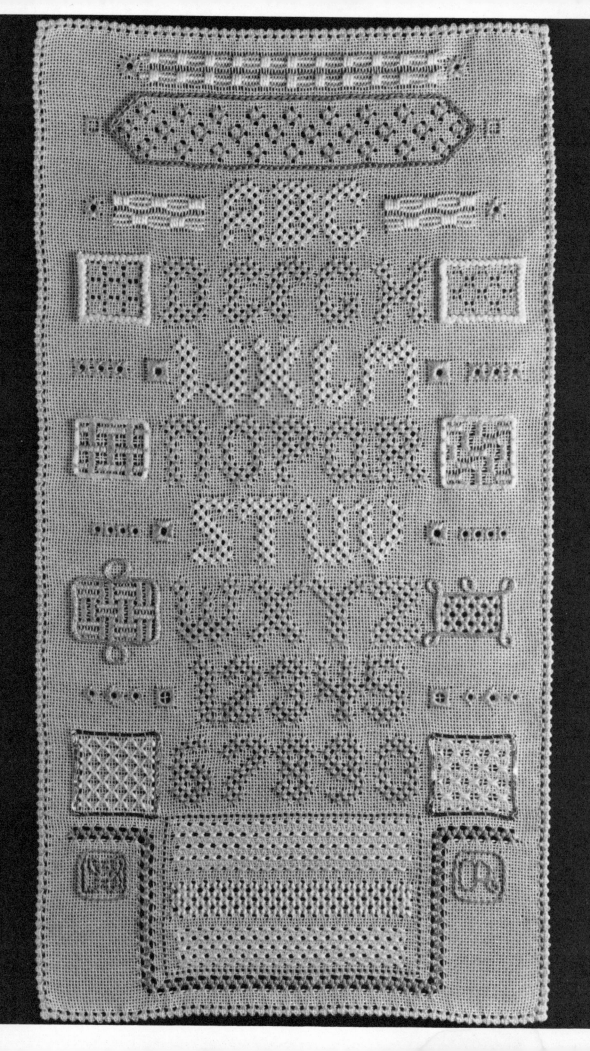

KEY TO STITCHES AND THREADS
Sampler II

Pulled Canvas Sampler II is worked with cotton, silk, rayon, and metal threads on 23/inch light blue congress canvas. The finished size is 7 inches by 13¾ inches. See the accompanying key to identify the stitches and threads. The bold numbers with letters refer to the lesson and diagram where each stitch or pattern is located in *Pulled Canvas*. The bold italic numbers refer to the threads listed under Materials Employed.

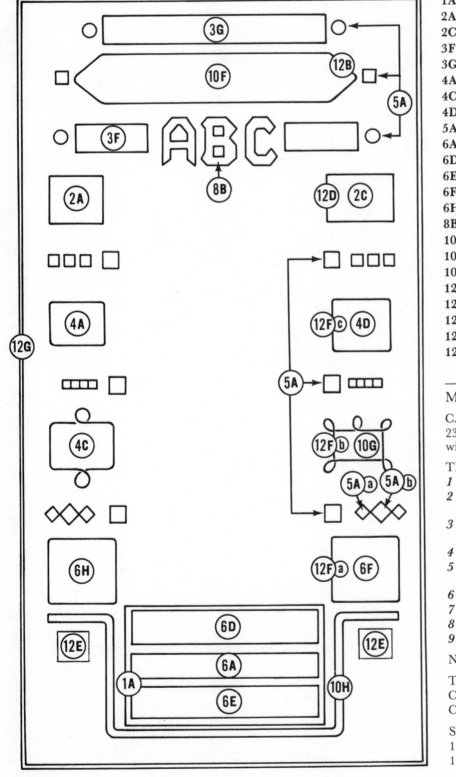

1A Backstitch Outline, *3*
2A Ringed Back Filling, *5*
2C Festoon Filling, *5*
3F Reed Border, *1*
3G Reed Border Variation, *1* with *5*
4A Basket Filling, *5*
4C Small Chessboard Filling, *5*
4D Step Stitch Filling, *5*
5A Eyelet Stitches, *5*
6A Wave Filling, *1*
6D Reverse Wave Filling, *1*
6E Pebble Filling, *1*
6F Reverse Window Filling, *1*
6H Waffle Filling, *1*
8B Diagonal Cross-Stitch, *2, 3, 4*
10F Detached Square Filling, *3*
10G Three-Sided Filling, *5*
10H Three-Sided Border, *4*
12B Chain Stitch Outline, *4*
12D Double Knot Outline, *1*
12E Outline Stem Stitch, *3*
12F Couched Outline **a**, *8*; **b**, *7*; **c**, *6*
12G Four-Sided Edging Variation, *3*

MATERIALS EMPLOYED

CANVAS
23/inch light blue congress, 9 inches wide by 16 inches high; edges bound

THREADS
1 DMC Pearl Cotton, size 5, white
2 DMC Cordonnet Crochet Cotton, size 30, white
3 DMC Cebelia Crochet Cotton, size 30, 799 blue
4 DMC Pearl Cotton, size 8, 318 gray
5 Au Ver A Soie Silk, 921 rose, 2- or 3-ply
6 Lotus Dori Rayon Cord, white
7 Lumiyarn Cord, #1 silver
8 Japanese Couching Silver, size 10
9 Silk Sewing Thread, gray

NEEDLES
Tapestry 20, 24, 26
Chenille 18
Crewel 10

STRETCHER STRIPS
1 pair 9-inch
1 pair 16-inch

KEY TO STITCHES AND THREADS
Basket of Flowers

The Basket of Flowers tray cloth is worked with cotton, linen, silk, and metal threads on 23/inch beige congress canvas. The finished size, including the border, is 14⅞ inches by 9⅞ inches. See the accompanying key to identify the stitches and threads. The bold numbers with letters refer to the lesson and diagram where each stitch or pattern is located in *Pulled Canvas*. The bold italic numbers refer to the threads listed in Materials Employed. The sculptured leaves are described in *Needleweaving*. A border shown in the color photograph of this design is described in *Hemstitching*.

2A Ringed Back Filling, *2,3*
3A Overcast Ground, *5*
4C Small Chessboard Filling, *6*
4F Framed Cross Filling, *1*
4G Cobbler Filling, *1*
5B Diamond Eyelet Filling, *1*
5C Square Eyelet Filling, *1*
6A Wave Filling, *1*
6D Reverse Wave Filling, *1*
6E Pebble Filling, *1*
6G Cable Filling, *4*
6H Waffle Filling, *1*
6I Honeycomb Filling, *3*
7A Single Faggot Filling, *1*
7B Double Faggot Ground, *1*
8A Diagonal Cross Filling, *3*
10G Three-Sided Filling, *6*
12B Chain Stitch Outline, *6*
12F Couched Outline

MATERIALS EMPLOYED
CANVAS
23/inch beige congress, 18 inches wide by 13 inches high; edges bound
THREADS
1 DMC Pearl Cotton, size 8, white
2 DMC Pearl Cotton, size 8, 754 coral, light
3 DMC Pearl Cotton, size 8, 352 coral, dark
4 Silk Twist, dusty rose, light
5 Silk Twist, dusty rose, dark
6 Swedish Linen, size 16/2, 237 rust
OUTLINE THREADS
Japanese couching, size 10, gold
Lumiyarn Cord, #1 gold
Lotus Dori Rayon Cord, white
Silk Twisted Cord, dusty rose
NEEDLES
Tapestry, 22, 24
STRETCHER STRIPS
1 pair 18-inch   1 pair 13-inch

LESSON 1

CANVAS PREPARATION

MASTER PATTERN, SAMPLER I

MASTER PATTERN, SAMPLER II

MASTER PATTERN, BASKET OF FLOWERS

A BACKSTITCH OUTLINE

THIS lesson deals with the first stage of pulled canvas, which involves establishing a master pattern of the main outlines and then transferring the pattern by various means onto a stretched canvas. The two samplers provided here involve simple geometrics that have been chosen to illustrate the variety of stitches in the lessons that follow.

Flowing floral patterns are also very typical of pulled work, so examples of these are provided in the Basket of Flowers design; also included here is a master drawing for its pulled canvas areas. Even unstructured abstract designs should be based on line drawings that establish the major pattern, which can then be developed further with filling stitches.

The method for outlining with the backstitch that follows is a safe and practical way to transfer any pattern. It enables you to study and revise a layout as needed before working the fillings. By outlining in evenly spaced backstitches, you can both provide yourself with a guide for secondary stitches and allow a sufficient number of elements for each counted filling.

MASTER PATTERN, SAMPLER I

Whether you are outlining the pulled geometric sampler provided here or one of your own design, it is necessary to follow an accurately graphed master pattern like this one. It is not necessary, however, to graph the entire shape of a centrally balanced design; graphing a little over a quarter of it, as shown here, is sufficient. Simply mark the center of the proposed design on the plan, and put the two center lines of the graph onto the canvas with large basting stitches. Then give the canvas a quarter turn to work each segment.

It is important in a geometric sampler to organize the filling shapes in the central portion first, so that you will be able to fit them in comfortably before being limited by a boundary line. In this plan, the heavy broken lines in the central portion are drawn over two grid lines; they represent outline backstitches over two elements. See Pat-

tern and Stitch Diagrams **1A** to design and work the outline backstitches.

Next enter the outlines for the outer shapes, which in this sampler are square and rectangular. They are indicated by heavy broken lines drawn over three grid lines, representing backstitches worked over three elements. Notice that at the middle of the sides of the piece (at the lower left of this pattern diagram), the lines are drawn over four grids to indicate a longer stitch (which also affects two border stitches, making them rectangular as well). This was done to make the pattern come out evenly.

Work only the heavy broken lines to prepare the canvas for the fillings that follow. Enter the fillings in sequence with the lessons, which progress in order and build upon one another. Symbols for coil and cross borders and four-sided stitches are indicated on this pattern, but you should not work them until Lesson **10**, which contains stitch diagrams for them. They are only here for placement. The four-sided finished edge shown on the plan is worked in Lesson **12**, which completes this sampler and the pulled canvas lessons.

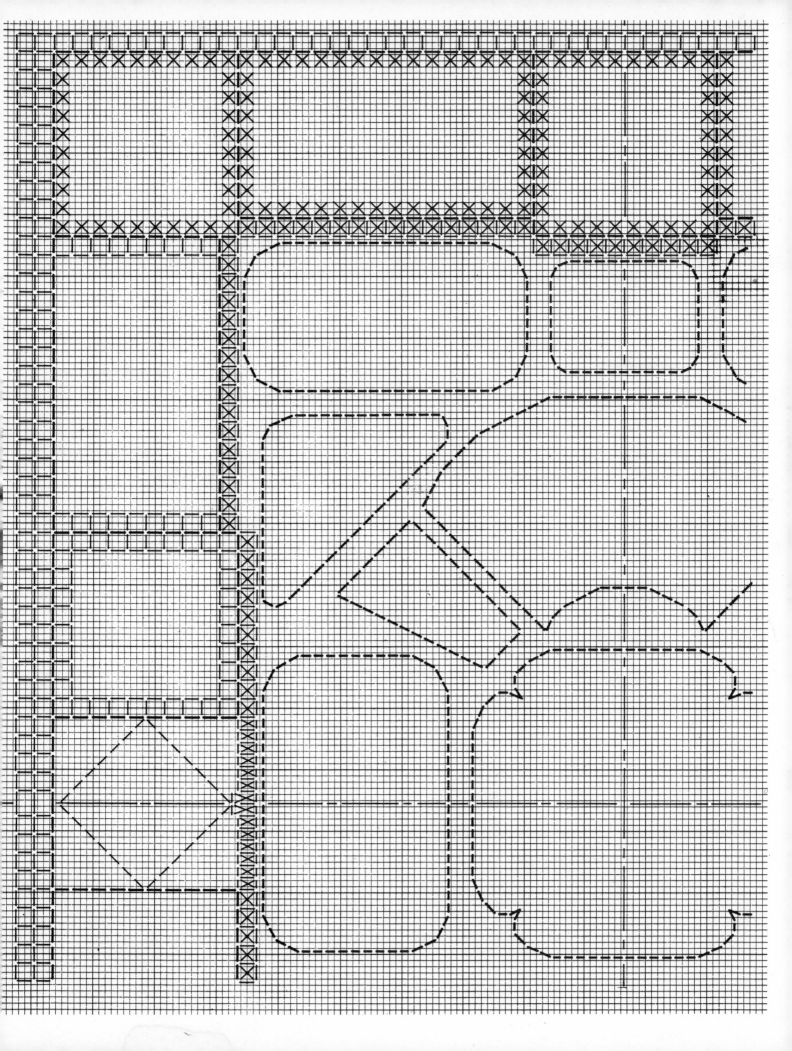

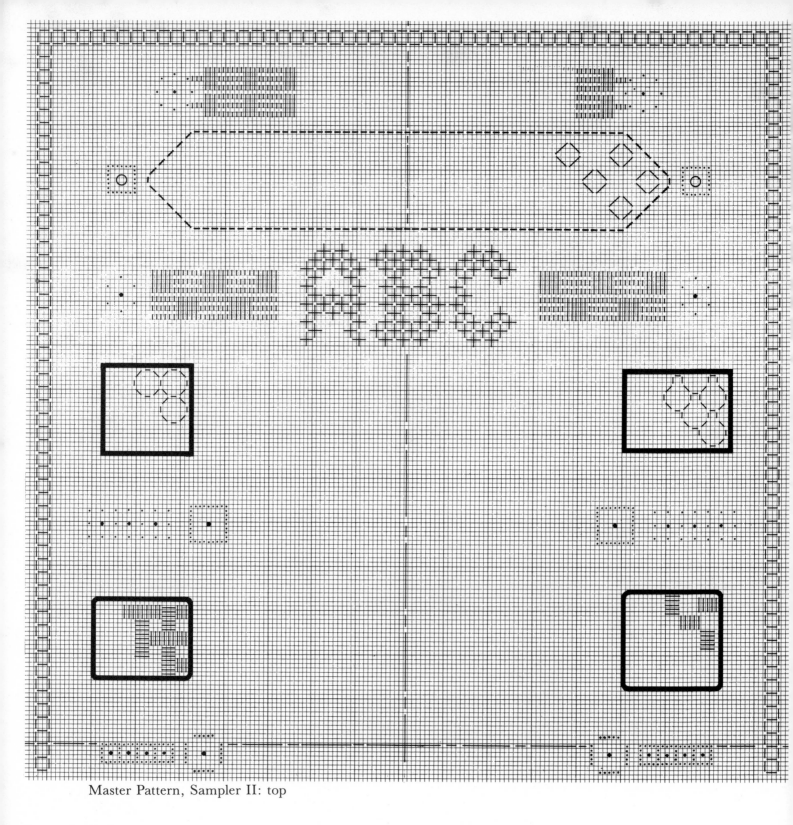

Master Pattern, Sampler II: top

MASTER PATTERN, SAMPLER II

To work a pulled geometric sampler without outlines, it is necessary to follow a master pattern such as this one, which has the placement of stitches and fillings indicated on it. Since this design was planned as an alphabet sampler, the letters for the central portion were planned first. There is a complete pattern diagram for the alphabet in Lesson 8. The fillings were placed symmetrically around the alphabet. However, this is not

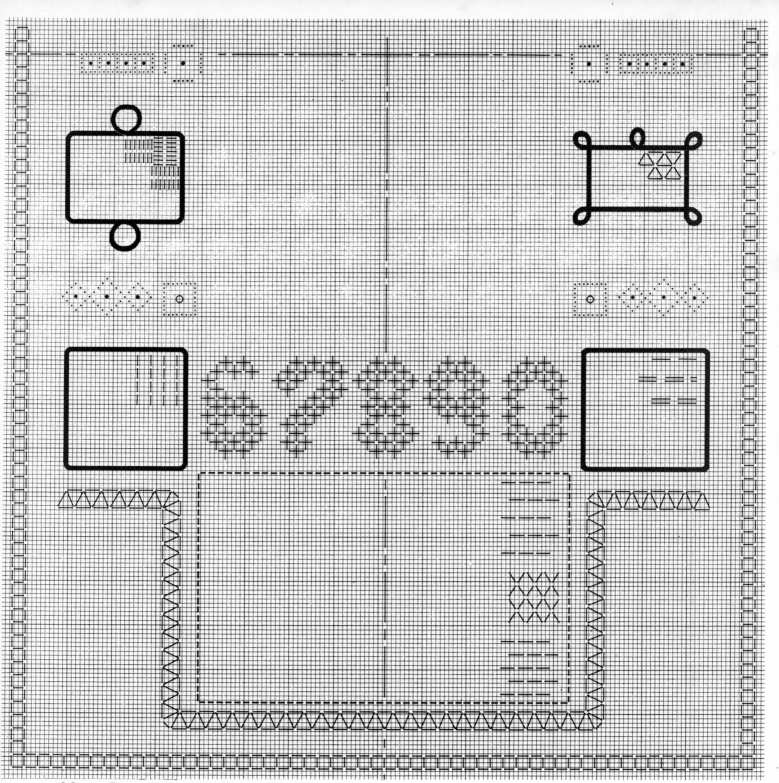

Master Pattern, Sampler II: bottom

the order in which to work the sampler. Start the work by marking the two center lines on the canvas with a long running stitch, which will be removed later. Counting the grid lines as canvas elements, locate each of the eight fillings on either side of the center line and baste their positions on the canvas. Once you have established these loca-tions, you can easily position the other patterns. Start the sampler with Stitch **1A**, the backstitch outline. Follow the sequence of the lesson numbers and letters, completing the sampler with the four-sided edging in **12G**.

Master Pattern, Basket of Flowers

MASTER PATTERN, BASKET OF FLOWERS

There are two methods for transferring a non-geometric design onto canvas, both of which require a carefully scaled inked drawing of the basic lines and shapes. You can trace the lines directly onto the canvas with disappearing ink; or you can trace the lines onto a sheet of tissue paper first and then, with small basting stitches, sew the tissue to the canvas over the pattern lines. Carefully rip away the tissue as you work the fillings within the guidelines. Remove the basting wherever it interferes with the work. If you are working the Basket of Flowers, do not baste the outlines for the needlewoven leaves. Work the fillings and then the couching; then you can add the needlewoven foliage. See *Needleweaving* for this technique. The hemstitch border is diagramed in *Hemstitching*, which also shows the elongated buttonhole stitch and coral knots that make up the butterfly.

STITCH 1A
BACKSTITCH OUTLINE

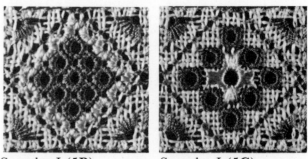

Sampler I (**5B**)   Sampler I (**5C**)

The backstitch is extremely useful for outlining shapes on an even mesh fabric such as canvas. You can travel in any direction following the angles and curves of all simple shapes. You can backstitch in slants of three different degrees.

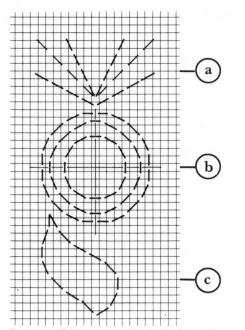

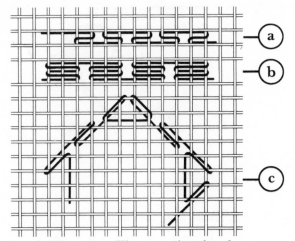

Pattern Diagrams: *Backstitch outline can be worked evenly over paired elements and will conform to any simple shape.*

Stitch Diagram: *The connecting threads on the backface fall alternately on the inside and the outside of the shape.*

(**a**) Backstitches can slant over the elements in two directions with three slants.

(**b**) Backstitches can make nicely rounded circles and curves if you gradually change the slant of the stitches.

(**c**) Backstitches can conform to curving shapes.

(**a**) Emerge, directing the needle to enter the backface in the opposite direction from that in which the row is traveling. By alternating the positions of the connecting threads on the backface, you can make the threads less noticeable on the frontface when there is no overstitched border pattern added when the fillings are completed. In Sampler I, you backstitch all of the outlines in the Master Pattern, employing tension where it is recommended. Never employ tension where outlines of embroidery or couching are to be worked over the backstitches.

Sampler II

(**b**) Work backstitches twice in each location for a border; this improves the tension and enlarges the holes. In Sampler II, a double backstitch outline frames three stitch patterns at the bottom. Although this stitch diagram shows stitches over three elements, the backstitches are made over two elements in Sampler II.

Pattern Diagram: *The backstitch outline creates the diamond shapes in Sampler I that are later filled with other stitches.*

(**c**) Backstitches are made at 45-degree angles to create the diamond shapes in Sampler I that are filled with Stitches **5B** and **5C**.

LESSON 2

BACKSTITCHES

A RINGED BACK FILLING

B SMALL RINGED BACK FILLING

C FESTOON BORDER OR FILLING

I N this lesson, backstitches travel across the canvas in waving lines; not until the return journey do they become complete patterns. (The technique of stitching half a pattern on one journey and completing it on the second is fundamental to many stitches in *The Open Canvas*.) Three fillings are shown. In the first two, each backstitch is worked twice; in the third, all but the horizontal stitches that join the rows are worked twice. The arrows on the pattern diagrams show where the first half of the journey begins. These fillings are similar to Holbein work (see Glossary), in which a route is charted first; the pattern emerges on the return trip.

STITCH 2A
RINGED BACK FILLING

Sampler II

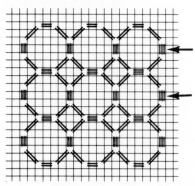

Pattern Diagram: *There are twice the number of stitches where two rings meet.*

Each complete pattern unit or ring of backstitches is six elements in height and width. Begin a row of ringed back filling with the two vertical stitches marked with an arrow at the right side of the pattern diagram. Complete the row, and return to

the same location for the second pair of vertical stitches. Drop six elements to begin another row of the filling.

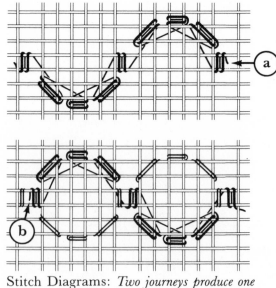

Stitch Diagrams: *Two journeys produce one row of the pattern.*

Start on the right side. After the two vertical stitches, backstitch a waving line across the area to be filled **(a)**, making half circles above and below the two central elements. Return from the left side with a waving line that closes the waves and makes rings **(b)**. Work each stitch twice; there will be four of them (vertical or horizontal) wherever the rings meet. If the pattern gets too crowded, work one stitch in each location. In Sampler II, only a single strand of thread is used so that the four stitches will fit on the 23/inch mesh. Pull gently when using fine thread.

STITCH 2B

SMALL RINGED BACK FILLING

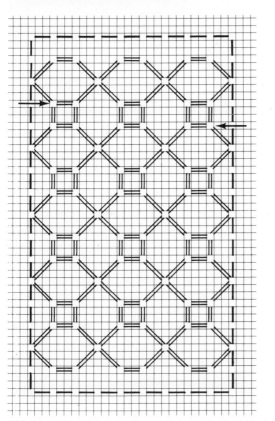

Sampler I

Pattern Diagram: *There are only two stitches in each location.*

To follow this pattern diagram, start the first half of the journey at the arrow on the right; the return journey is made from the left. Each new row of pattern begins on the right, nine elements below the preceding row. The stitches in the diagram that appear above the first row of the pattern and below the last are compensating ones (see Glossary). Work these compensating rows after completing the pattern.

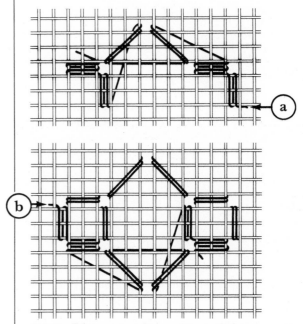

Stitch Diagrams: *Pairs of backstitches produce even tension with large, clear negative spaces.*

The first journey (**a**) works half of each stitch unit; the second journey (**b**) completes the unit. Although all the up- and downpoints are shared, none of the stitches is duplicated on the return journey.

STITCH 2C

FESTOON BORDER OR FILLING

Sampler II

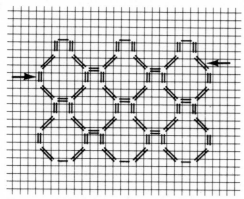

Pattern Diagram: *Festoon (see Glossary) from the right; scallop from the left.*

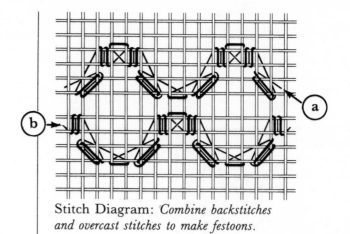

Stitch Diagram: *Combine backstitches and overcast stitches to make festoons.*

Start a festoon row at the arrow on the right of the diagram with a pair of diagonal backstitches. Start the return at the left with a pair of vertical stitches. Each completed row of the pattern occupies eight rows of elements. Drop eight elements to begin a second row.

If you want to make a festoon border, follow the first line of stitches in the diagram (**a**). To make a filling, place the returning row as shown in the diagram (**b**). Note that the horizontal stitches are worked just once in each journey, but two stitches emerge where the journeys meet.

LESSON 3

SATIN STITCHES

A STRAIGHT OVERCAST GROUND

B SLANTED OVERCAST GROUND

C WHIPPED SATIN RIBBING

D COIL FILLING

E COIL AND SATIN FILLING

F REED BORDER

G REED BORDER VARIATIONS

H FREELY MADE SATIN FILLING

THIS lesson deals with a group of satin stitch fillings that change through the use of alternation (see Glossary). The placement, sizes, and number of stitches create the various patterns. The emphasis here is on the stitches rather than on the negative spaces. Some of the satins are worked with a little tension; these should be carefully laid with several plies of a light-reflecting thread.

STITCH 3A
STRAIGHT OVERCAST GROUND

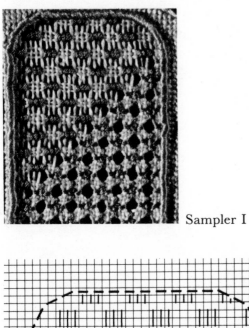

Sampler I

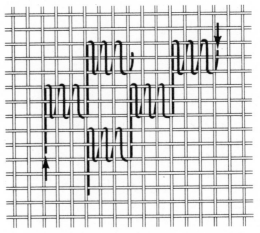

Stitch Diagram: *Alternate the direction of the rows for smooth stitching.*

By working an overcast ground of straight satin stitches in descending and ascending diagonal rows, you produce straighter stitches than if you worked the satins in horizontal rows. Reverse the position of the uppoint in alternate rows to have an identical stitch slant on both the front- and backface of the work. Obviously, a single row of straight satin stitches, as in the basket border of the Basket of Flowers tray cloth, must be worked horizontally.

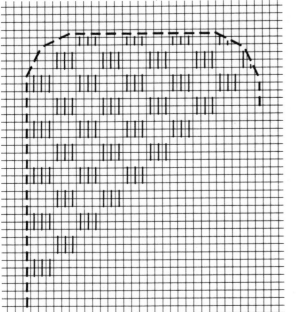

Pattern Diagram: *An overcast ground is composed of units of straight satin stitches.*

Work three straight satins over three canvas elements, and travel in descending or ascending steplike diagonal rows.

STITCH 3B
SLANTED OVERCAST GROUND

Sampler I

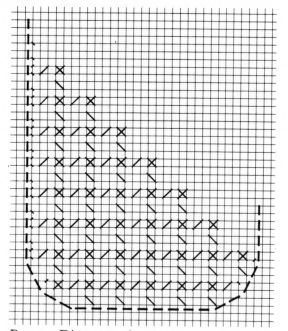

Pattern Diagram: *An overcast ground is made with rows of slanted satin stitches.*

This neat pattern of alternately crossed stitches is a particularly good ground to employ when the positive space is as important as the negative space.

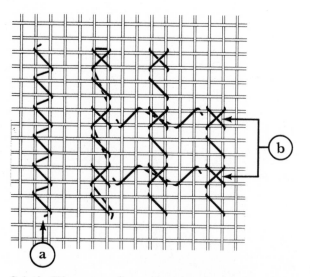

Stitch Diagram: *Cross alternate slanted satin stitches in vertical rows first.*

Work the vertical rows first. Start with an ascending row (**a**). Stitches on the frontface slant over two canvas elements. Then descend with a return journey that crosses every other stitch. Skip two vertical elements between the vertical rows. Finally, work horizontal rows across the crossed stitch rows (**b**).

STITCH 3C
WHIPPED SATIN RIBBING

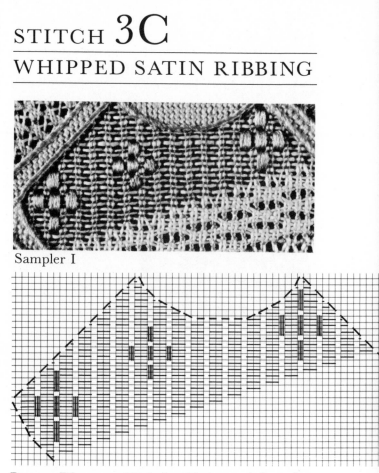

Sampler I

Pattern Diagram: *Work the ribbed ground first, then the large satin spots.*

There are several pulled fillings that provide handsome grounds on which to superimpose other stitches. This whipped satin ribbing with large satin overstitching is one of them. Two others are double and reverse faggot stitches, both diagramed in Lesson **7**.

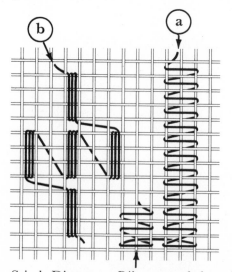

Stitch Diagram: *Ribs are made by pulling or whipping (see Glossary) columns of satin stitches.*

Work vertical rows of horizontal satin stitches with tight tension to create a vertical ribbing (**a**). The canvas wefts make a strong horizontal pattern in the negative space. Deliberately reverse the direction of the connecting threads on the backface from row to row to avoid a static pattern. Manipulate the connecting threads at the base of the rows to hide the transition from one row to the next. The secondary pattern (**b**) is stitched *over* the whipped satins using no tension and a high luster thread.

STITCH 3D
COIL FILLING

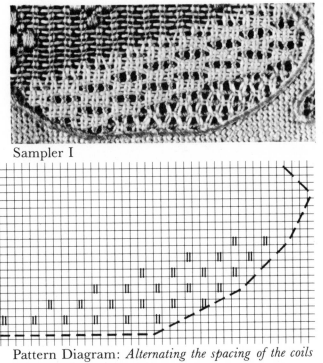

Sampler I

Pattern Diagram: *Alternating the spacing of the coils creates vertical movement.*

This simple coil filling creates an unusual undulating pattern. This is achieved by centering coils in one row between the coils in the row above.

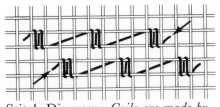

Stitch Diagram: *Coils are made by whipping units of satins between pairs of elements.*

Work units of two whipped satins snugly between two canvas elements. Alternate these units with an even number of canvas elements. Center the units in the subsequent row under the unworked canvas elements in the row above. Work in consecutive horizontal rows, alternating the position of the uppoint as diagramed.

STITCH 3E
COIL AND SATIN FILLING

Sampler I

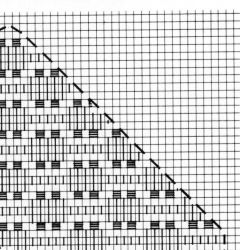

Pattern Diagram: *Two satin fillings are combined to make a rich open ground.*

Use a different color or texture for each of the two opposing striped patterns to achieve a dense but open ground.

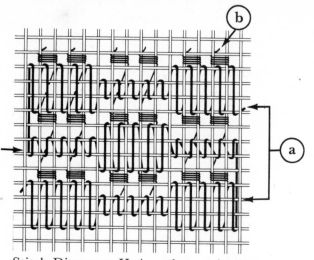

Stitch Diagram: *Horizontal rows of satins are striped by vertical rows of coils.*

Work the horizontal rows, composed of two sizes of satin units, first (**a**). Then work vertical rows of coil stitch units in a contrasting color (**b**). Alternate the direction and slant of the straight satin rows. The vertical coil rows can be worked in either direction, but be sure to maintain the same stitch slant.

STITCH 3F
REED BORDER

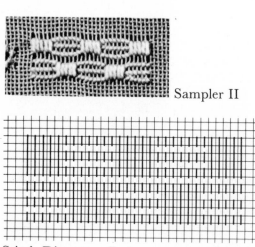

Sampler II

Stitch Diagram: *Each row consists of short and long stitches.*

Alternate three narrow bands of seven short whipped satins with five tall satins for each row of a reed border. The seven-stitch reeds are centered

under five tall satins in alternating rows. The reed border diagramed here is the same as in Sampler II, where two rows are worked.

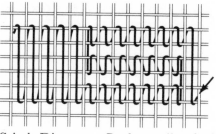

Stitch Diagram: *Reeds are ribs of whipped satins.*

Work five tall satins with light tension. Continue to work from right to left with seven whipped satins over two canvas elements. Travel back for the second row of reeds and from right to left again for the third. Use a tight tension for the whipping. Alternate the tall satins made over six elements with the three narrow rows of reeded satins. You can easily vary this border by changing the stitch count.

STITCH 3G
REED BORDER VARIATIONS

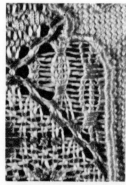

Sampler I

Sampler II

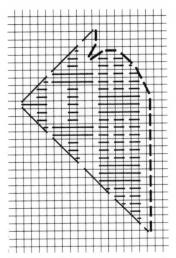

Pattern Diagram **a**: *In this shape from Sampler I, notice that different reed borders can be made by changing the stitch count—even within a single space.*

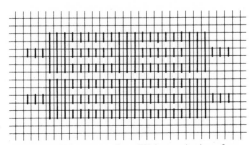

Pattern Diagram **b**: *This variation from Sampler II consists of two rows of reed border with gracefully curving reeds which occur when the elements are deflected.*

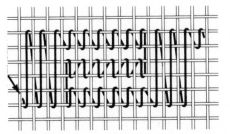

Stitch Diagram: *Use a continuous working thread and vary the stitch count within a shape, or vary the working thread and maintain the same stitch count.*

Use a continuous thread to work the reed border in this stitch diagram and in Sampler I. Use the same pattern with two different working threads for the reed border in Sampler II.

STITCH 3H

FREELY MADE SATIN FILLING

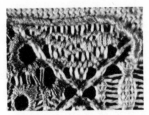

Sampler I

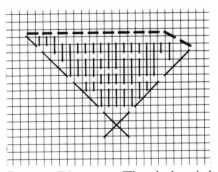

Pattern Diagram: *Though the stitches are freely made, they gracefully fill the shape.*

Pulled canvas can be worked freely. Although most of the patterns in these samplers have been carefully counted, they can just as easily be set free. The satins shown in this lesson and the eyelets of Lesson **5** particularly lend themselves to free expression.

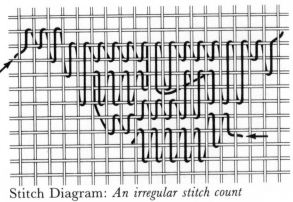

Stitch Diagram: *An irregular stitch count can make a rhythm.*

This filling has neither a regular stitch count nor repeating patterns. Varied tension, spacing, and stitch sizes create its rhythmic movement. Experiment with your own freely worked fillings.

LESSON 4

SATIN STITCH VARIATIONS

A BASKET FILLING

B BASKET FILLING VARIATION

C SMALL CHESSBOARD FILLING

D STEP STITCH FILLING

E FLAT STEP FILLING

F FRAMED CROSS FILLING

G COBBLER FILLING

THE first group of five fillings in this lesson is composed of a family of patterns in which like size units of straight satin stitches appear to weave like fabric elements. There is always an odd-and-even relationship between the height and width of the units in order to center them or make them work. Two unrelated fillings appear at the end of the lesson; they are included because they employ straight satin stitches. Framed cross and cobbler are only concerned with negative spaces and they relate more fully to the wave stitches in Lesson **6**.

STITCH 4A

BASKET FILLING

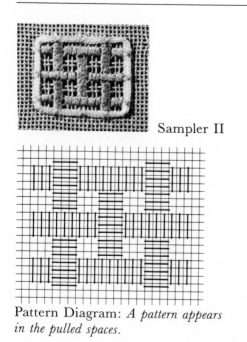

Sampler II

Pattern Diagram: *A pattern appears in the pulled spaces.*

This filling imitates the even weave of the foundation fabric on which it is worked. However, the medium tension of the satin stitches pulls the underlying canvas elements together, and a little open checkerboard results.

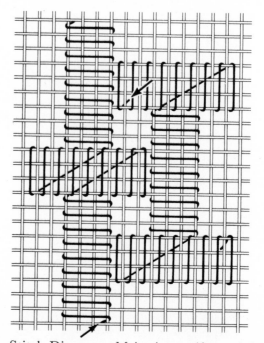

Stitch Diagram: *Maintain a uniform stitch slant.*

Work the units, composed of nine satins over four elements, perpendicular to each other and in vertical rows. You can travel in alternating directions, descending and ascending, but be sure to reverse the position of the up- and downpoints of the satins. In this filling, it is important to have the stitch slant of all the units match. Use medium tension and a working thread that reflects light.

STITCH 4B

BASKET FILLING VARIATION

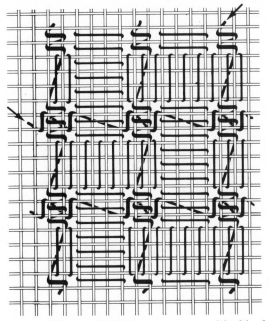

Stitch Diagram: *Cover the canvas with this dense variation of basket filling.*

First, work a basket filling as in the previous stitch diagram **(4A)**. Then work vertical and horizontal rows of whipped satins over the remaining pairs of elements. The little checkers disappear from the pulled spaces and larger openings result. This variation is particularly suited to canvas work, where it is often desirable to cover the canvas elements completely.

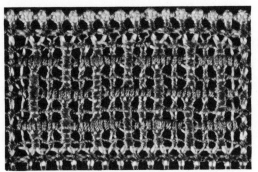

Sampler I

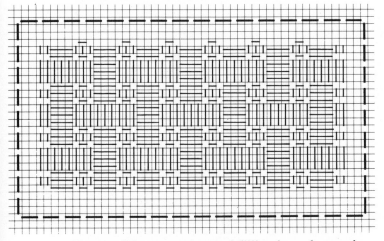

Pattern Diagram: *A second filling is made over the remaining elements of a basket filling.*

In this pattern, almost no canvas shows. There is good contrast between the solid positive spaces and the open negative spaces.

STITCH 4C

SMALL CHESSBOARD FILLING

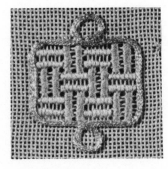

Sampler II

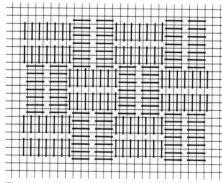

Pattern Diagram: *This filling looks like woven ribbons when it's worked.*

A square unit of horizontal satin stitches alternates in block formation with a square unit of vertical stitches, creating a chessboard effect.

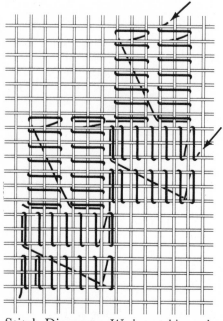

Stitch Diagram: *Work matching columns in step formation.*

Starting at the top and descending, make two vertical columns of seven horizontal satin stitches, each over three elements, to form a large square unit. Travel in steplike diagonal rows, beginning each new square unit to the left. Pass under three additional elements when you begin a new unit. Alternate rows of vertical columns with rows of horizontal columns. To work a large chessboard, as in the Basket of Flowers, make the square units in three columns of ten satins each.

STEP STITCH FILLING

Sampler II

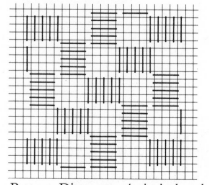

Pattern Diagram: *A checkerboard remains in the unworked canvas.*

Step stitch filling is another simple pattern with movement in both the positive and negative spaces.

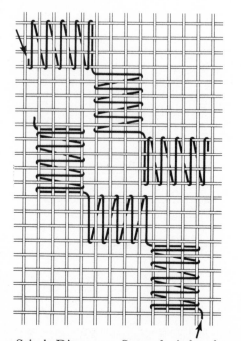

Stitch Diagram: *Steps of stitches descend and ascend in diagonal rows.*

Work these units of five satin stitches in steplike diagonal rows. Alternate the direction of the rows. Notice how the last stitch of each unit shares a hole with the first stitch of the next unit. Use medium tension.

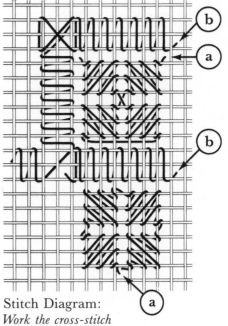

Stitch Diagram:
Work the cross-stitch as you descend the steps.

STITCH 4E
FLAT STEP FILLING

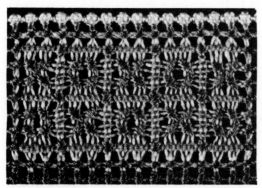

Sampler I

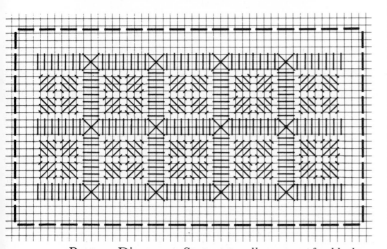

Pattern Diagram: *Steep steps allow space for blocks of flat stitches.*

Positive and negative spaces are equally decorative in this pattern, which employs step, flat, and cross-stitches. Notice that the slant of the four flat stitch units within a block makes a pattern and that there are two different styles of blocks that alternate directions.

First work the large blocks composed of four flat stitches (**a**). Flat stitches are units of graduating slanted satin stitches. Use medium tension. Fasten off each block as you complete it by weaving under the four units on the backface. Then, with slightly more tension, work the step stitch filling (**b**). Make a cross-stitch as shown in this diagram as you move from a horizontal step to a vertical one.

STITCH 4F
FRAMED CROSS FILLING

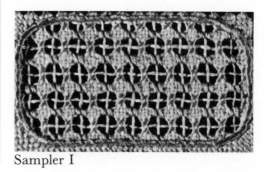

Sampler I

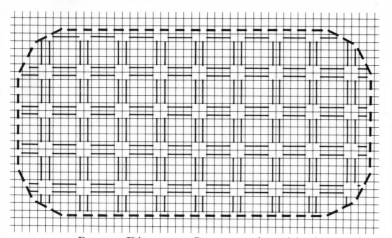

Pattern Diagram: *Crosses are framed in the negative spaces.*

This stitch is named for the pattern of crosses in the negative spaces, which are framed by pairs of satin stitches. A secondary pattern occurs in the positive spaces achieved by the satins, which slant one way in the horizontal rows and another way in the vertical rows.

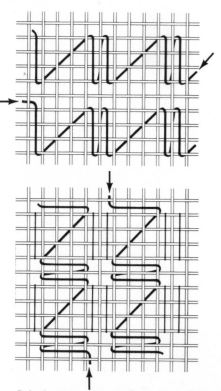

Stitch Diagrams: *Complete all the horizontal journeys first, then the vertical ones.*

First work a horizontal row from the right with the uppoints of the pairs of satin stitches at the base. Then work the next row from the left with the

uppoint of the stitches at the top. The connecting threads will match in both rows, making all the stitches slant in the same direction. Notice that there is one vertical canvas thread between the two satins; then four are skipped. Leave a horizontal canvas element between the rows. Work the vertical rows in exactly the same way.

STITCH 4G
COBBLER FILLING

![Sampler I photograph]

Sampler I

![Pattern Diagram showing double crosses]

Pattern Diagram: *Double crosses appear in the negative spaces.*

A busy secondary pattern occurs in the positive spaces because the slant of the stitches changes with each vertical and horizontal row. Cobbler filling can also be worked so that all rows of stitches maintain the same stitch slant.

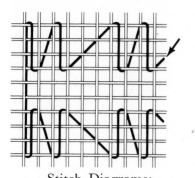

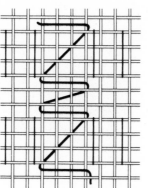

Stitch Diagrams:
Cross horizontal rows with vertical rows to make cobblestones.

Work this filling by leaving two canvas elements between pairs of satin stitches and then skipping four canvas elements. The single cross of the framed cross filling (**4F**) becomes a double cross. To further alter the pattern, change the stitch slant in consecutive rows to slant in opposite directions. Accomplish this by beginning the rows on alternate sides, with all the uppoints of the stitches at the base. After completing the horizontal rows, work the vertical ones in exactly the same way.

LESSON 5

EYELETS

A EYELET STITCHES

B DIAMOND EYELET FILLING
WITH EYELET SCALLOPS

C SQUARE EYELET AND EYELET CROSS

D SQUARE EYELET WITH RIBBING

E SQUARE EYELET WITH RIBBING

F EYELETS WITH OVERCAST GROUND

G EYELET GROUND

H FREELY WORKED EYELETS

E YELETS are units of consecutively made satins that emerge on the frontface around the perimeter of a shape and enter a common center hole. You can make large, round, even holes by preparing them first, gently spreading the canvas elements apart with an awl, stiletto, or even the pointed end of a small embroidery scissors. Eyelets are used in many embroidery techniques and appear in the *Hardanger* and *Reticello and Hedebo* sections of *The Open Canvas*. But essentially, they involve pulled or deflected elements, requiring tension to make large, clear holes. The lessons that follow illustrate many styles of eyelets; later on, in Lesson **11**, another variation of eyelets appears with buttonhole edges. Do not overlook the freely made eyelets at the end of this lesson; if you feel like working in a less restricted manner, you may find this exercise a liberating one.

STITCH 5A

EYELET STITCHES

All these eyelets appear on Sampler II.

ROUND

Make the horizontal and vertical stitches long and drop one element for each of the diagonals.

FRAMED DOUBLE CROSS

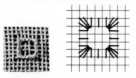

Leave two by two elements bare in the center. Emerge from every hole around the perimeter of the square; only corner stitches share holes.

DOUBLE-STITCHED SIMPLE ROUND

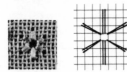

Work two stitches in each of the six locations. Omit the horizontals.

LARGE SQUARE

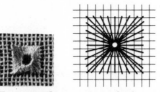

Emerge from every hole around the perimeter of a large square.

SIMPLE SQUARE

Emerge from only the straight or 45-degree-angle stitches.

CROSS

Omit the three corner stitches of a large square eyelet.

SQUARE

Emerge from every hole around the perimeter of a small square.

FRAMED CROSS

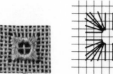

Leave two crossed elements bare in the center. Emerge from every hole around the perimeter of a large square.

DIAMONDS

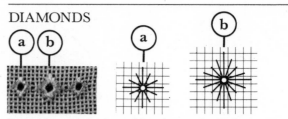

Pass the vertical and horizontal stitches over one more element than the diagonals.

Stitch Diagram: *Always emerge around the perimeter and converge in the center.*

Start with a straight satin stitch over the desired number of elements; the stitch diagram here is for a diamond eyelet, but the technique applies to all eyelets. Make all downpoints into the center hole and emerge around the eyelet perimeter. Use medium tension; try not to lose the rhythm of the satin stitches. Produce a large, clear center hole. End the eyelet on the backface by passing the needle around and under all the stitches. Since eyelets are units of many stitches, you can prevent overcrowding by employing fewer plies or a finer working thread than for other stitches.

STITCH 5B

DIAMOND EYELET FILLING WITH EYELET SCALLOPS

Sampler I

Pattern Diagram: *Eyelet scallops are compensating units of diamond eyelets.*

Use a high luster working thread in a constrasting color, as in Sampler I, to emphasize the scalloped edge. Notice that each scalloped eyelet shares all of its uppoints with another eyelet.

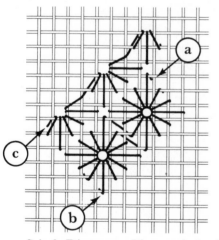

Stitch Diagram: *First work the diamond eyelet filling, then the eyelet scallops.*

Stitch the diamond eyelet filling in diagonal rows. There are two ways to do this. This stitch diagram illustrates a system of working half of each stitch in a descending row and then completing it in an ascending row. Start with the top stitch (**a**) and work the other five on the left side of the unit. Descend to the next unit and begin at the top once more. Complete the row. To ascend, start with the bottom stitch (**b**) and work the five on the right side. Complete the row. Or, you can follow the

system described in Stitch Diagram **5C** (square eyelets), where complete eyelets are worked one at a time. When working scalloped eyelets (**c**), pass the thread from one to the other as shown.

STITCH 5C
SQUARE EYELET AND EYELET CROSS

Sampler I

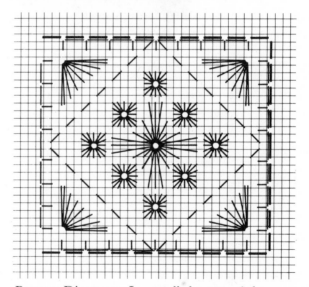

Pattern Diagram: *Locate all the center holes first with an awl or stiletto.*

The square eyelets share corner holes with each other as they move around the center cross. They also share holes with the center cross. To make this cross stand out, use a high luster thread with many plies. The corner fan-shaped buttonhole eyelets are described in Lesson **11**.

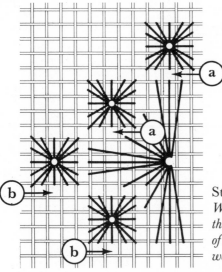

Stitch Diagram: *Work the cross first; then start at the base of the top eyelet and work clockwise.*

Complete the large center eyelet cross first, making the more vertical and horizontal arms of the cross long and the diagonal ones shorter. Then work the square eyelets in diagonal formation around the cross. Start descending rows with the first stitch of each eyelet at the base of the unit; start ascending rows with the first stitch at the top of the unit (not illustrated). You can turn this diagram if you like. Work eyelets that are on diagonals angling to the left in a clockwise direction (**a**); eyelets that are on diagonals angling to the right are worked counterclockwise (**b**).

To work a solid filling of square eyelets, you can also stitch half of each square in a descending diagonal row; complete them in ascending rows. Emerge for the top right diagonal stitch and enter the center hole, working clockwise to the opposite diagonal stitch in each unit.

STITCH 5D

SQUARE EYELET WITH RIBBING

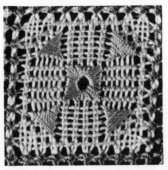

Sampler I

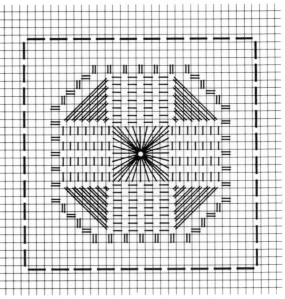

Pattern Diagram: *A large square eyelet is enhanced by various satin stitches.*

This motif is composed of a large square eyelet, four half flat units (see Glossary), ribs of whipped satin, and a border of satin coils.

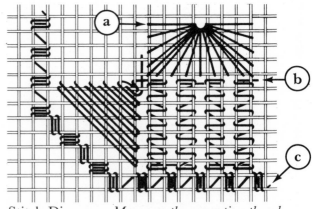

Stitch Diagram: *Maneuver the connecting threads to keep the negative spaces open and clear.*

This diagram shows the lower left quadrant of the pattern diagram. Turn the diagram and the work to complete each quarter. Work the entire large square eyelet first (**a**) and fasten it off. Then begin the satin ribs. The first rib descends (**b**). While making the first stitch in the adjoining ascending row, hold the connecting thread above the down-point of the needle so that it is securely above the open space when the stitch is drawn. Reverse this procedure at the top of the third rib. After completing the ribs in this quarter, work the first corner in a half flat stitch. This consists of twelve diagonal satin stitches that increase in length. Work six (from small to large) and then return, working six more, sharing the same canvas holes. When you return from the sixth stitch to the first, you are in position to begin the next series of satin ribs. When working the return journey of the half flat unit, carefully align the pairs of satin stitches. Use medium tension for the square eyelet and the half flats. Work the coil border (c) after all four quarters are completed.

STITCH 5E

SQUARE EYELET WITH RIBBING

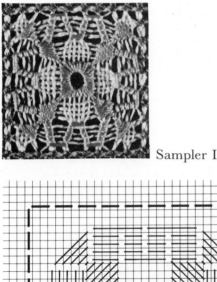

Sampler I

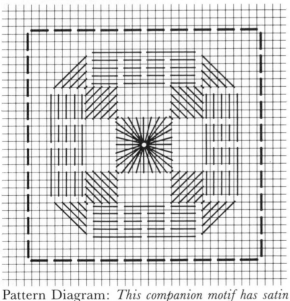

Pattern Diagram: *This companion motif has satin ribs that move around the large square center eyelet.*

This variation of Stitch **5D** combines a large square eyelet that has the four corner stitches omitted with flat and half flat units and satin ribs.

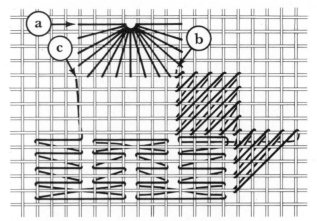

Stitch Diagram: *A flat and a half flat move easily into satin columns, concealing the connection.*

This diagram shows the lower right quadrant of the pattern diagram. Turn the diagram and the work for each segment. Work the entire large square eyelet first (**a**), omitting the four corner stitches, and fasten off. Descend, stitching the flat and half flat (**b**). After the half flat is complete, carry the working thread on the backface so that when it comes to the frontface for the first satin, it shares a hole with the lower left corner of the flat unit. Work the first satin with the downpoint above the connecting thread to conceal it. Complete the column with a long stitch two columns wide. Secure the connecting thread under the working thread as you draw the working thread taut to make the first satin stitch in the ascending column. Complete the four ribs in this manner and emerge in position to begin the flat of the second quarter, at the corner of the large eyelet (**c**). Use medium tension for the eyelet and the flats.

STITCH 5F

EYELETS WITH OVERCAST GROUND

Sampler I

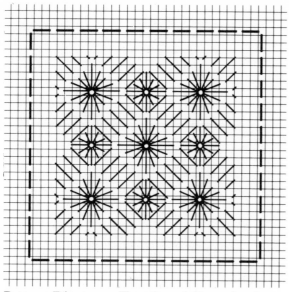

Pattern Diagram: *Two sizes of diamond eyelets are surrounded by an overcast ground.*

This is a composition of diamond eyelets framed with a pattern of slanted satin stitches referred to as an *overcast ground*. The overcast ground would be more obvious if this motif were extended into a filling. To do this, complete the compensating stitches and keep repeating the sequence.

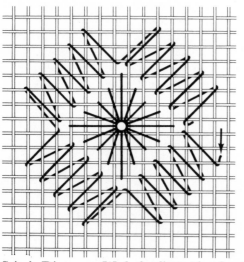

Stitch Diagram: *Work the diamond eyelets first to set the placement of the satin stitches.*

Locate the center holes for the two sizes of eyelets, following the pattern diagram, and work the eyelets. Satin stitch around the center eyelet first (illustrated); then do the compensating satins around the perimeter. Use medium tension for all. To use this pattern as a filling, work long diagonal rows of five-stitch satin units. Complete the rows

heading in one direction first; then finish the others. Skip elements for the eyelets. Then work the eyelets in the unworked diamond-shaped spaces.

STITCH 5G
EYELET GROUND

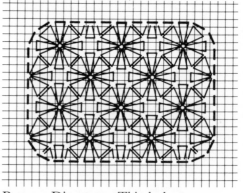
Sampler I

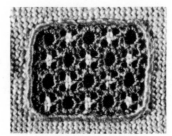

Pattern Diagram: *This looks more complicated than it is.*

These eyelets, which resemble wheels with spokes and rims, are worked in diagonal rows as a filling. All the rim stitches are singles; the spokes are double. The diagonal rims butt against neighboring rims, however, and therefore appear to be double.

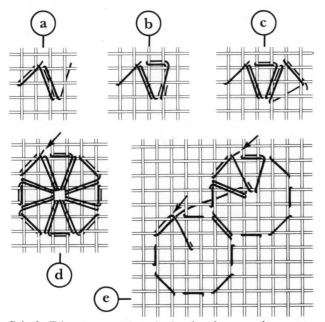

Stitch Diagrams: *The wheels of eyelet ground connect in diagonal rows.*

Locate and enlarge all the center holes first. All of these holes are eight elements apart horizontally and vertically, and four apart diagonally. Make a single diagonal backstitch for the first rim stitch (**a**), then two stitches into the center hole for a spoke. Work a second rim and spoke (**b**), then a third (**c**). Continue to make a wheel (**d**). Start the next wheel (**e**). Work in diagonal rows.

STITCH 5H

FREELY WORKED EYELETS

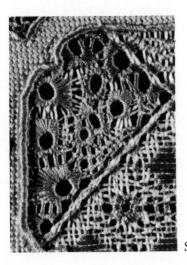

Sampler I

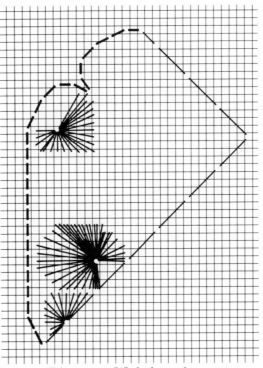

Pattern Diagram: *Work these, then try some of your own.*

Only three freely made eyelets are shown here; space is left for the embroiderer to plan more of these irregularly shaped eyelets, or they may be stitched directly onto the canvas.

Stitch Diagram: *Design your own eyelets.*

Work square, diamond, or round eyelets around off-center holes. Then try some eyelets with irregularly shaped perimeters. Connect some of them with freely made ribs of coil stitches (see photo).

LESSON 6

WAVE FILLINGS

A WAVE FILLING

B DOUBLE WAVE FILLING

C WINDOW FILLING

D REVERSE WAVE FILLING

E PEBBLE FILLING

F REVERSE WINDOW FILLING

G CABLE FILLING

H WAFFLE FILLING

I HONEYCOMB FILLING

J TURNED HONEYCOMB FILLING

THE wave stitch fillings in this lesson belong to a large family of closely related patterns in which the stitches rise and fall on one face of the work and have horizontal connecting threads on the other. In fact, the front- and backfaces of a stitch are shown as two stitches in several places—when the backface becomes the frontface and the stitch name is preceded by the adjective *reverse*. In all but one of these stitch patterns, the second row of stitches is a mirror image of the first row. They are all worked with the rows traveling in alternate directions.

STITCH 6A

WAVE FILLING

Sampler II

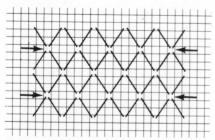

Pattern Diagram: *The diamond shapes of this diagram turn into undulating waves when stitched.*

Emerge at the arrow on the right to work the first row, and at the arrow on the left to work the second row, which reverses the pattern of the first row. Drop three elements to start the third row. Repeat the first two rows to produce a filling. You can work wave filling over four horizontal elements if you like, but you must always have an even number of vertical elements between the slanted stitches to center each stitch unit around a single pulled space.

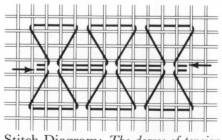

Stitch Diagram: *The degree of tension determines the wave and the opening.*

The pattern of waves is made by a slanted stitch on the frontface that pulls the elements out of alignment as it passes around the warps to emerge on the frontface again. The tighter the tension, the straighter the stitch and the larger the opening. This stitch has a pleasant sewing rhythm and is therefore a good choice for large backgrounds.

STITCH 6B
DOUBLE WAVE FILLING

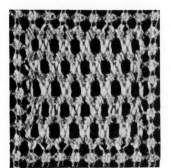

Sampler I

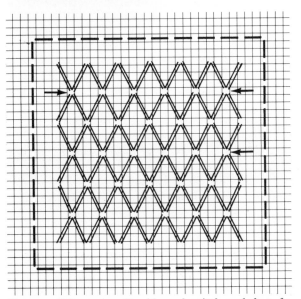

Pattern Diagram: *Double each stitch and drop four canvas elements for each row.*

Double wave filling is the same as wave filling except that the stitches on the frontface are worked twice in each position. Notice that this diagram shows the stitches taken over four elements in height. The connecting stitch on the backface must pass under an even number of elements in order to center each row of work.

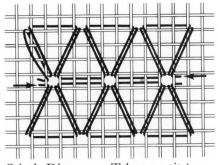

Stitch Diagram: *Take two stitches on the frontface and one connecting stitch on the backface.*

Produce larger, squarer holes in the canvas with double stitches that tighten the tension and hold the stitches firmly in place. Notice that the double row of stitches on the backface is caused by the single connecting thread from two rows of work.

STITCH 6C
WINDOW FILLING

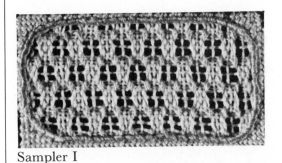

Sampler I

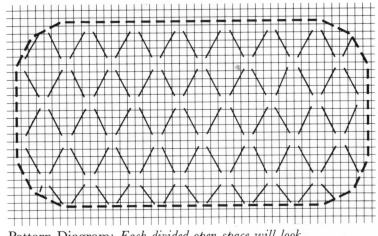

Pattern Diagram: *Each divided open space will look like four windowpanes.*

The negative space is neatly divided into four squares by changing the spacing of the stitches to an odd number and skipping an element between the rows.

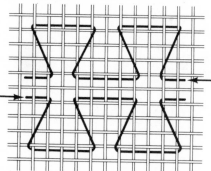

Stitch Diagram: *Skip an element between the stitches and between the rows.*

A single unworked vertical element is left on the frontface between the stitches; the connecting stitch on the backface is under five elements. A long horizontal element is left between the rows. When the stitches are pulled, the single elements between the stitches and rows divide the openings into four squares, or windows. There must be an odd number of elements between the stitches to center the unworked elements.

STITCH 6D
REVERSE WAVE FILLING

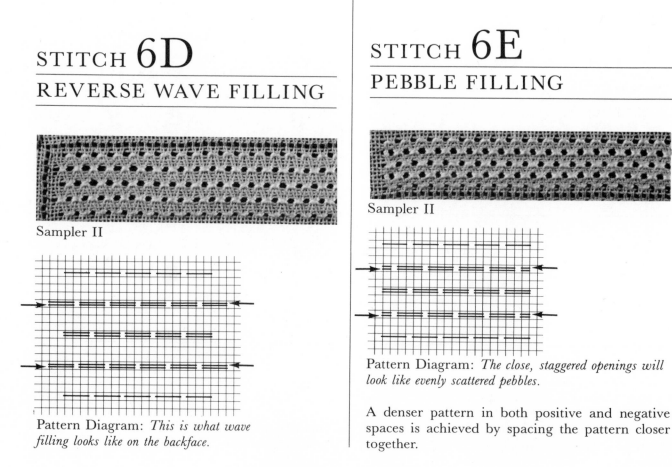

Sampler II

Pattern Diagram: *This is what wave filling looks like on the backface.*

Reverse the stitch formation of wave filling from the backface to the frontface and a pattern of double horizontal stitches appears, laid in brick-like formation.

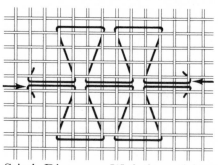

Stitch Diagram: *Work the straight connecting stitches on the frontface and the slanted stitches on the backface.*

Start the first row with a horizontal stitch over four canvas elements. Enter the backface to make a diagonal stitch and emerge on the frontface to make another horizontal stitch. Work rows of mirroring pairs, reversing the direction of travel and sharing the same holes for the horizontal stitches.

STITCH 6E
PEBBLE FILLING

Sampler II

Pattern Diagram: *The close, staggered openings will look like evenly scattered pebbles.*

A denser pattern in both positive and negative spaces is achieved by spacing the pattern closer together.

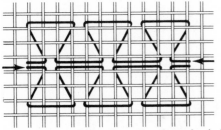

Stitch Diagram: *Pass the slanted stitches under three elements to narrow the openings.*

Work pebble filling in the same manner as reverse wave (**6D**), except that the diagonal connecting threads on the backface are taken over three horizontal elements instead of four.

STITCH 6F
REVERSE WINDOW FILLING

Sampler II

Pattern Diagram: *The backface of window filling is lighter and airier than the frontface.*

As in window filling, an uneven number of canvas threads is required for the horizontal stitches that make the windowpanes. Very little of the working thread appears in this pattern. Match the thread to the canvas for a light, open filling.

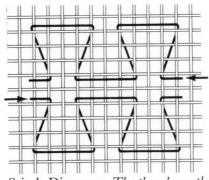

Stitch Diagram: *The threads on the backface wave, and the horizontals on the frontface create the pattern.*

Reverse the stitch formation of window filling by taking horizontal stitches on the frontface and diagonal connecting stitches on the backface. Skip an element between the horizontal stitches and between the rows.

STITCH 6G
CABLE FILLING

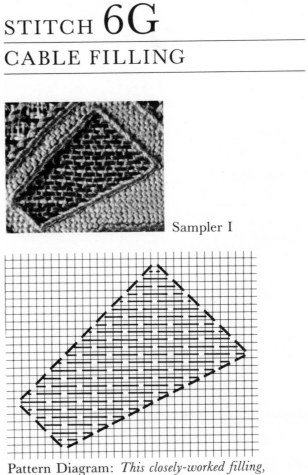

Sampler I

Pattern Diagram: *This closely-worked filling, which resembles bricking, makes a dense ground.*

There are many variations of wave fillings. However, this is the only member of that family of fillings in which all the rows of pattern are worked identically. There is no mirror image row in cable filling.

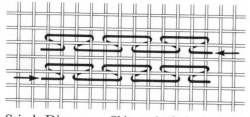

Stitch Diagram: *Skip a single horizontal element between these closely-worked wave stitches.*

Work horizontal stitches on the frontface over four canvas elements. Slant the connecting thread on the backface over one element in height and two in width. Leave a single long element unworked between identically worked rows that alternate only in the direction of the work.

STITCH 6H
WAFFLE FILLING

Sampler II

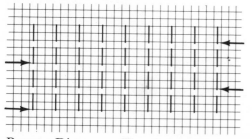

Pattern Diagram: *The stitches make a pattern of diamond shapes when pulled.*

With tension, these stitches, which appear straight in the pattern diagram, become slanted. It is interesting to note that in pulled work, the straight stitches become slanted, and the slanted stitches become straight.

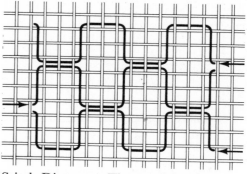

Stitch Diagram: *These straight stitches slant when they are pulled.*

Straight stitches are worked on both the front- and backface in this wave stitch variation. The stitches in the diagram rise over three horizontal and pass behind three vertical elements, but they can also employ an even number of elements. Each row mirrors the previous one; where the straight stitches rise and fall in one row, they fall and rise in the next.

STITCH 6I
HONEYCOMB FILLING

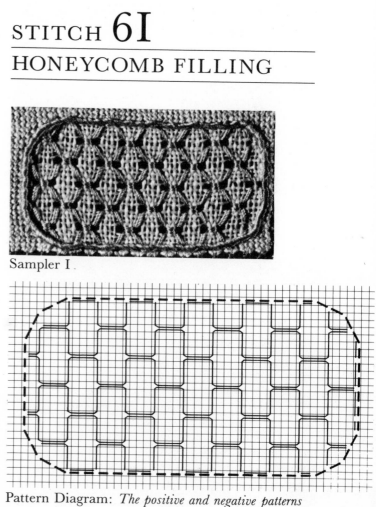

Sampler I

Pattern Diagram: *The positive and negative patterns are equally pretty.*

A backstitch is added to waffle filling (**6H**), which pulls the canvas elements together at the top and bottom of each stitch. A graceful honeycomb pattern results. Although this particular honeycomb filling occupies four by four canvas elements, any number of elements could be employed in either direction to change the size of the honeycomb.

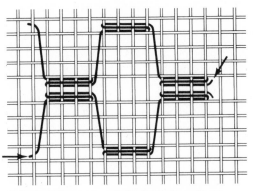

Stitch Diagram: *A backstitch pulls the upright stitches into rounded peaks.*

Work a single horizontal backstitch on the front-face over the four canvas elements between the vertical stitches. The backstitches from each row share elements with another row.

STITCH 6J
TURNED HONEYCOMB FILLING

Sampler I

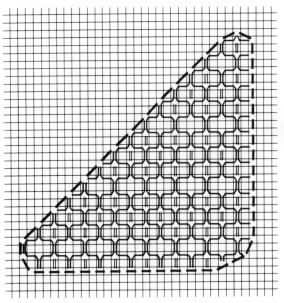

Pattern Diagram: *Use this pattern for a busy, colorful effect.*

This little repeat pattern begins with a honeycomb filling made over two canvas elements with the canvas turned on its side. The color and texture of the working thread add further detail.

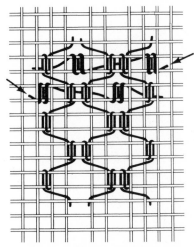

Stitch Diagram: *Complete the honeycombs first; then turn the work and stitch the coils.*

After working the entire ground in a honeycomb filling with the canvas turned on its side, return the canvas to normal position and work rows of coil stitches between the rows of honeycomb units (see pattern diagram). Skip a row before continuing the coil stitches. In the sampler, a single ply of fine silk is used for the honeycomb pattern and two-ply silk for the coils.

LESSON 7

FAGGOT STITCHES

A SINGLE FAGGOT FILLING

B DOUBLE FAGGOT GROUND

C DIAGONAL DRAWN FILLING

D SATIN AND FAGGOT FILLING

E REVERSE FAGGOT GROUND

F REVERSE FAGGOT GROUND VARIATION

G PULLED RUSSIAN GROUND

H DIAGONAL CHAIN BORDER

THIS lesson deals with eight closely related faggot patterns. All of them travel in diagonal journeys that resemble flights of stairs. Like the family of wave fillings, the front- and backfaces of faggot fillings are equally handsome and useful. They are therefore treated as separate patterns. Faggot fillings blend well with almost any embroidery technique; they can be a little tricky, but mastering them is well worth the effort.

One journey of reverse faggot stitches results in two lines of work with a space of two or three elements between the lines. However, the next journey butts against one of these lines of stitches, giving the impression of a double row. Since this can be confusing, the term *row* is not employed for faggot stitches. One route of work is referred to as a *journey*.

STITCH 7A

SINGLE FAGGOT FILLING

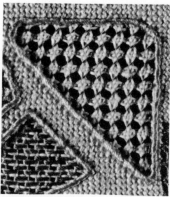

Sampler I

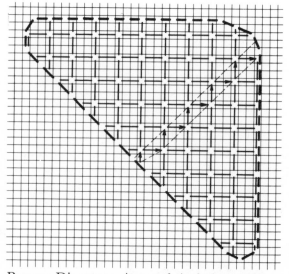

Pattern Diagram: *A row of single faggot filling is made up of horizontal and vertical stitches on the frontface and diagonals on the backface.*

In this diagram, all of the stitches are made over three elements except the compensating ones at the edges. It is easier to begin with a journey that does not start with a compensating stitch. Each hole is shared four times in two journeys, making large rounded openings.

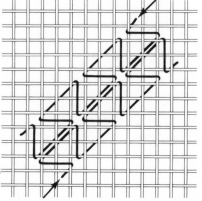

Stitch Diagram: *When a single journey is completed, it resembles a flight of stairs.*

Ascend and descend in alternate diagonal journeys. It is the diagonal stitch, which in single faggot is on the backface, that heads in the direction in which you are traveling. The steps and risers are like backstitches that head away from the direction of travel. Notice that the uppoint of each stitch in a journey is shared by the downpoint of another stitch. Each of these holes is also the uppoint and downpoint of the next journey.

STITCH 7B

DOUBLE FAGGOT GROUND

Sampler I (**7B**¹)

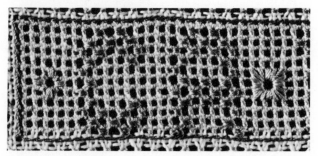

Sampler I (**7B**²)

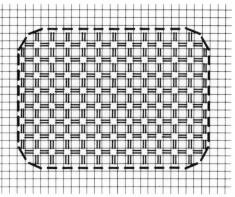

Pattern Diagram: *Use the double faggot as a filling or as a background for other stitches.*

This fine, dense, geometric filling makes a perfect ground for a secondary stitch pattern (**7B**²). The ground of double faggot filling is completely finished; the eyelets and the diagonally cross-stitched initials and date are then worked over it. See **5A** for the eyelets and **8B** for the diagonal cross-stitch alphabet.

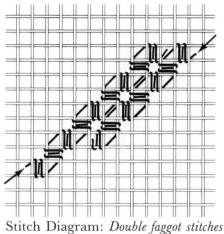

Stitch Diagram: *Double faggot stitches make a square stitch pattern with a round opening.*

In this diagram, two stitches are made over two elements in two directions. Once you have mastered it, this double faggot filling works very quickly and becomes a very useful addition to a stitch vocabulary. On the *Hardanger* collar, it is used as a filling that surrounds a festooned web.

STITCH 7C

DIAGONAL DRAWN FILLING

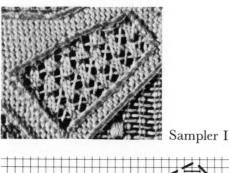

Sampler I

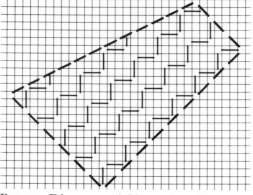

Pattern Diagram: *Achieve a lot of pattern with little stitching.*

The deflected elements make a wonderful asymmetrical pattern, achieved by very few journeys. Use this filling when a light, lacy pattern is needed.

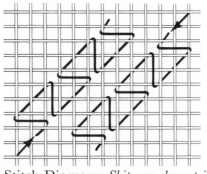

Stitch Diagram: *Skip one element in each direction between the journeys.*

Work one journey of single faggot filling. Then work succeeding journeys, leaving one horizontal and one vertical canvas element between the horizontal step stitches. Remember that the stitches on the frontface head away from the direction in which you are going.

STITCH 7D

SATIN AND FAGGOT FILLING

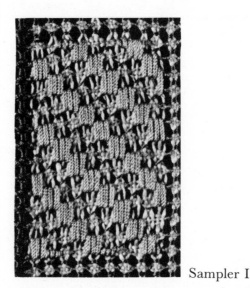

Sampler I

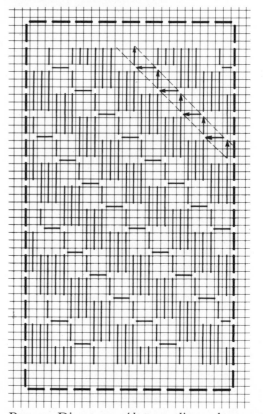

Pattern Diagram: *Alternate diagonal rows of satins with journeys of single faggot stitches.*

Good contrast exists in this pattern between the dense, light-reflecting satin stitches and the dark openings of the single faggot stitches.

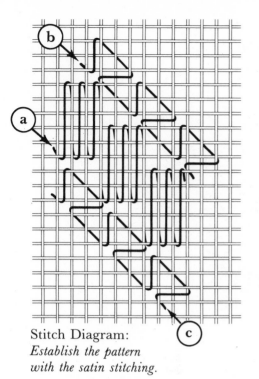

Stitch Diagram:
*Establish the pattern
with the satin stitching.*

Completely work all of the satin stitch units (**a**) in the space to establish the position of the single faggot journeys. Then work the single faggot journeys. In the diagram, a journey begins at the upper left (**b**). Emerge with a vertical stitch at the top of the rightmost stitch of a satin unit. Enter the same stitch hole with the next horizontal stitch. Descend in this manner. Ascend (**c**), occupying the stitch holes at the bottom of the leftmost stitches of the satin units.

STITCH 7E

REVERSE FAGGOT GROUND

Sampler I

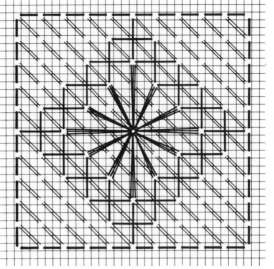

Pattern Diagram: *A strong diagonal ground is achieved by working single faggot stitches in reverse.*

A reverse faggot filling produces an even open ground with a strong diagonal direction. The stitch can be worked to the left or right. In this diagram, the stitches slant from lower right to upper left, and are taken over three elements. In Pattern Diagram **7F**, they slant in the opposite direction. The overstitched diamond shape of diagonal cross-stitches employs the stitch holes made by the reverse faggot filling. See **8B** for the diagonal cross-stitch. The large central buttonhole eyelet in the center is in **11B**. Completely cover the area with the filling stitch before working the other stitches.

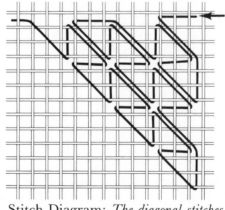

Stitch Diagram: *The diagonal stitches head in the direction of travel; steps and risers head away.*

Produce pairs of diagonal stitches on the frontface by reversing the single faggot filling. The pairs of stitches sharing the same stitch holes are from separate journeys. Remember: the diagonals that are now on the frontface still head in the direction in which you are traveling, and the horizontals and verticals on the backface head away. At first, this filling may seem difficult, but as you establish a rhythm, it will become quite easy.

STITCH 7F
REVERSE FAGGOT GROUND VARIATION

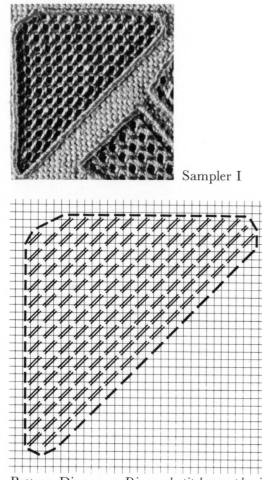

Sampler I

Pattern Diagram: *Diagonal stitches emphasize the diagonal shape.*

This is a variation of the reverse faggot pattern in the previous diagram. The stitches now slant in the opposite direction. The stitches also occupy

fewer canvas elements, making this pattern darker and denser.

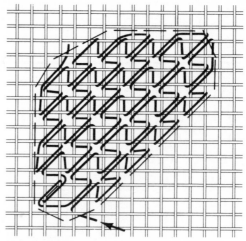

Stitch Diagram: *Use compensating stitches to fill the shape.*

This stitch diagram shows the first journey starting at the lower corner where it can follow the diagonal shape quite easily. Each journey of reverse faggot stitches makes two lines of spaced stitches on the frontface. The rightmost line of diagonal stitches in the first journey is worked to fall along the backstitched line of the sampler shape. This diagram demonstrates how the journeys connect at the edges to avoid constant fastening off and on. These connecting stitches appear awkward in the diagram, but in the pulled work they fall rather neatly in place.

STITCH 7G
PULLED RUSSIAN GROUND

Sampler I

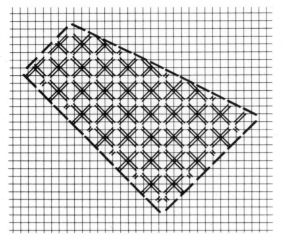

Pattern Diagram: *Reverse faggots worked in both directions makes a trellis.*

The positive space is filled with a handsome close trellis pattern and the negative one with large square holes. The pattern can be made lighter and less dense by working the stitches over more elements and making the journeys further apart.

A stitch diagram for pulled Russian ground would be far too complicated and discouraging, since it would have to be composed of one complex diagram superimposed on another. Follow Stitch Diagram **7E**, noting that it employs three canvas elements and pulled Russian ground employs only two. Completely fill the space with this reverse faggot filling, which slants in one direction, then turn to Stitch Diagram **7F** and fill the shape with reverse faggots slanting in the other direction. Remember: stitch diagrams can always be given a quarter-turn to change the stitch direction.

STITCH 7H
DIAGONAL CHAIN BORDER

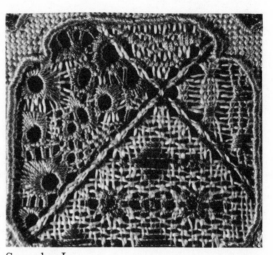

Sampler I

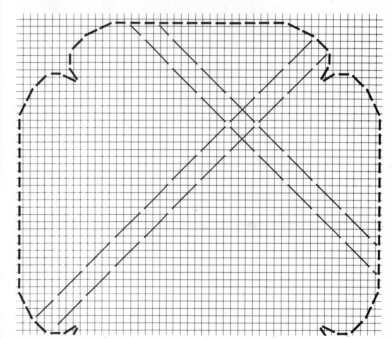

Pattern Diagram: *The journeys of diagonal chains cross each other to divide a shape.*

In this pattern from Sampler I, start at the lower left, slanting the first stitch in the direction of the row, then make a connecting stitch on the backface downward to emerge with a second slanted stitch parallel to the first. Make a connecting stitch on the backface to the left and emerge for the third slanted stitch. Continue in this manner. Cross the first journey with the second.

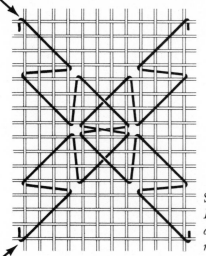

Slant single journeys of reversed faggot stitches in opposite directions. Where the routes cross each other, the stitches share holes. Use graph paper when you plan a pattern employing diagonal chains that cross one another.

Stitch Diagram: *Diagonal chains are journeys of reverse faggot stitches.*

LESSON 8

CROSS-STITCHES

A DIAGONAL CROSS FILLING

B DIAGONAL CROSS-STITCH

C DIAGONAL RAISED BAND

D OPEN TRELLIS FILLING

E CHECKER FILLING

IN this lesson, various methods are explored for employing the very versatile upright cross-stitch. In each case, the stitches travel diagonally; two journeys are required to complete one row of crossed stitches. Raised diagonal bands result when tension is employed. Shapes can easily be made without the benefit of an outline stitch by first planning them on graph paper. Cross-stitch shapes can be superimposed on other fillings; they can also pass each other by as they travel from opposite directions or cross over each other to make stars.

STITCH 8A

DIAGONAL CROSS FILLING

Sampler I

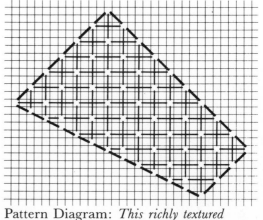

Pattern Diagram: *This richly textured filling has a strong diagonal movement.*

The crosses in this diagram, as in Sampler II, Stitch **8B**, are made over four elements in each direction. For a lighter filling, work the crosses over six elements.

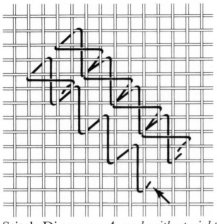

Stitch Diagram: *Ascend with straight stitches and descend by crossing them.*

First work an ascending row. Take vertical stitches over four canvas elements; for each subsequent vertical, emerge two elements to the left and two elements down. Return with a descending row of horizontal stitches that share up- and downpoints with the already worked verticals. Adjoining rows share holes as well. Each stitch hole is used four times.

STITCH **8B**

DIAGONAL
CROSS-STITCH

Sampler I

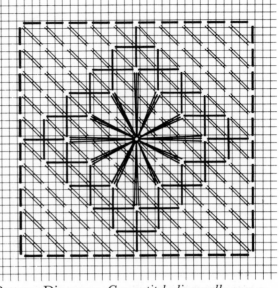

Pattern Diagram: *Cross-stitch diagonally over a filling occupying stitch holes that are already made.*

This upright cross-stitch travels in diagonal rows. Each row is made in two journeys. In this pattern diagram, a diamond shape is made from diagonally worked cross-stitches on top of a reverse faggot ground (**7E**). Use medium tension when overstitching.

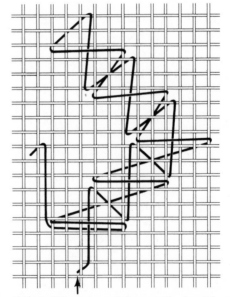

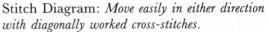

Stitch Diagram: *Move easily in either direction with diagonally worked cross-stitches.*

The cross-stitches are worked over six canvas elements for the diamond shape motif in Sampler I, and over four elements for the letters and numbers in both samplers. This stitch diagram shows how to angle to the right or left while working in two journeys.

DIAGONAL CROSS-STITCH LETTERING

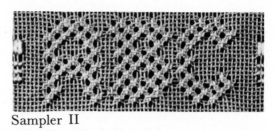

Sampler II

Pattern Diagram: *There is no need for an outline around the shapes made by diagonal cross-stitch filling.*

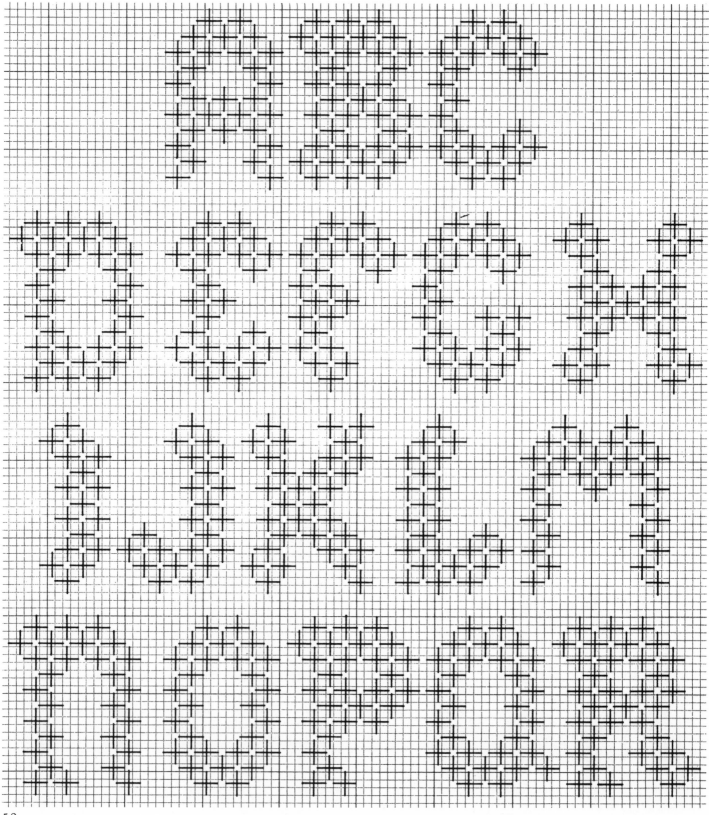

These are the letters and numbers that are fully worked in Sampler II (page 8) and that are employed for the initials and date in Sampler I (page 6). You can see how easy it is to design shapes on graph paper using diagonal cross-stitches. This is a good filling to employ when you do not plan to outline a shape. The initials and date in Sampler I are worked on a double faggot ground (Stitch 7B). The stitches are over four elements.

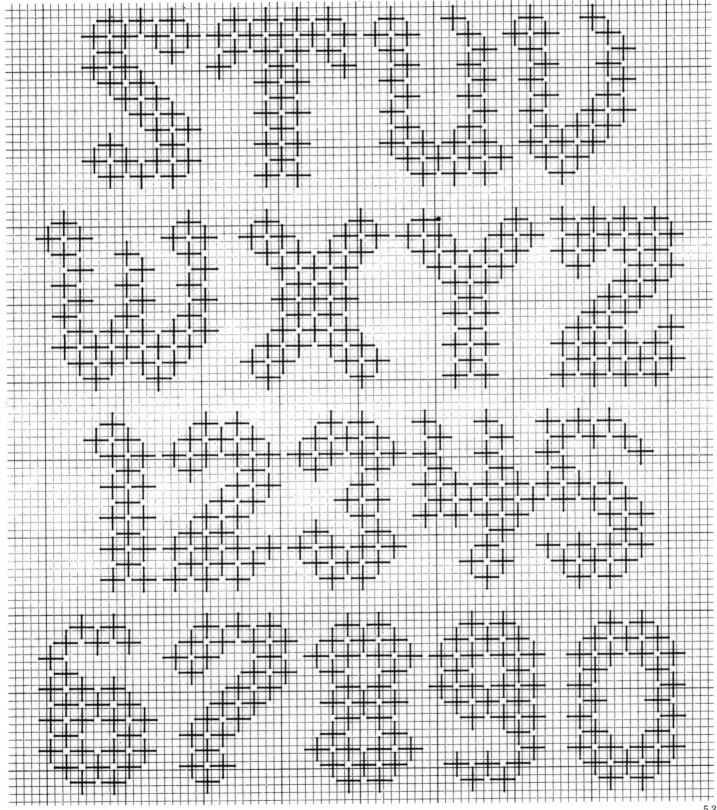

STITCH 8C

DIAGONAL RAISED BAND

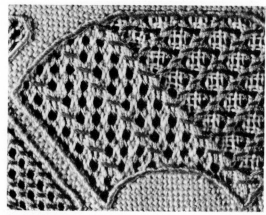

Sampler I

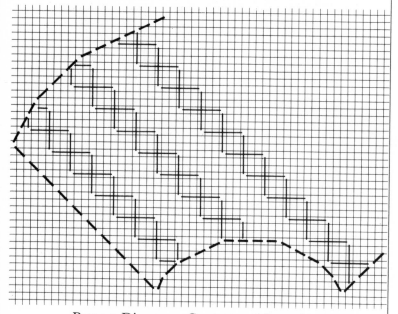

Pattern Diagram: *Create strong diagonal movement with ridges of diagonally worked cross-stitches.*

Single rows of diagonally worked cross-stitches are called diagonal raised bands because of the high ridges created by the medium or tight tension applied to these spaced rows of stitches. In Sampler I, diagonal bands alternate with fillings of Indian drawn ground (Stitch 10 I). A single or double faggot pattern could also be used to fill the spaces between the bands.

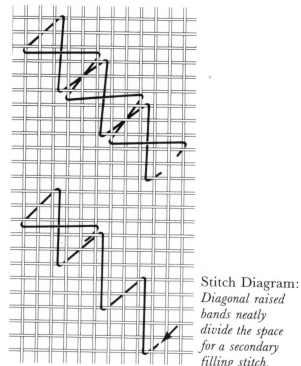

Stitch Diagram: *Diagonal raised bands neatly divide the space for a secondary filling stitch.*

Work rows of diagonal raised bands so that there are six horizontal elements left between the vertical stitches of adjacent rows (or six vertical elements between the horizontal stitches of adjacent rows). Once you establish the location of the rows by following a pattern diagram, these bands are easy to stitch. Each requires two journeys to complete.

STITCH 8D

OPEN TRELLIS FILLING

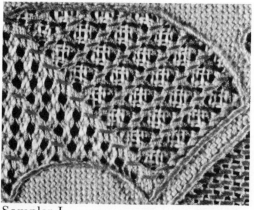

Sampler I

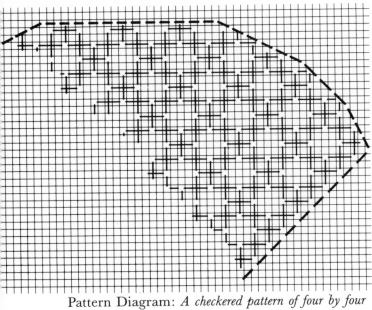

Pattern Diagram: *A checkered pattern of four by four elements appears between the crossing rows.*

This open trellis filling is achieved by two sets of diagonal raised bands worked in opposite directions. In this pattern, the cross-stitches are worked over four elements each way and a square of four elements by four elements remains vacant between the crossing rows.

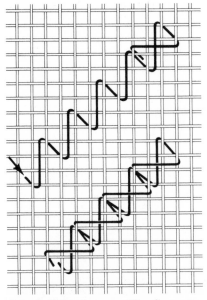

Stitch Diagram **a**: *The first set of diagonal bands for this filling slant from lower left to upper right.*

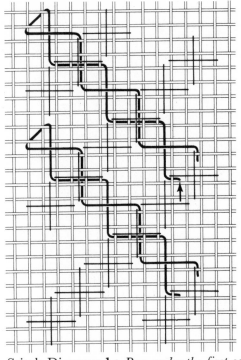

Stitch Diagram **b**: *Pass under the first set of bands as you work the second set.*

Work the first set of diagonal raised bands (**a**), leaving four vacant elements between the bands and filling the shape. Work a second matching set of raised bands, under the first, traveling in the opposite direction (**b**).

STITCH 8E

CHECKER FILLING

Sampler I

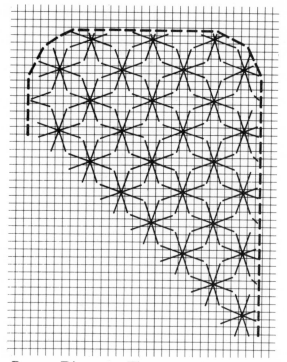

Pattern Diagram: *The pattern of dark and light squares will look like a checkerboard.*

This checker filling is worked in two stages. Slanted cross-stitches traveling in one direction completely fill the shape. Then, a second set of cross-stitches is worked in the opposite direction over the first set. A pattern of eight pointed stick stars is made in the dark positive space and pairs of crossing elements are left open in the negative space.

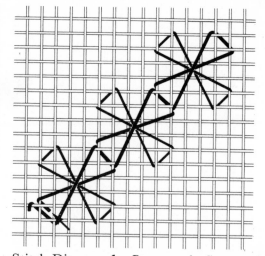

Stitch Diagram **b**: *Pass over the first set of oblique crosses as you work a second set. Only one cross-stitch of each of the first rows is shown.*

Begin the first stage of checker filling (**a**) with a journey ascending to the left. Work each stitch over six elements wide and two high on the front-face, with the connecting thread passing under two vertical and horizontal elements on the back-face. Descend in a return journey that crosses the first set of stitches and shares the same stitch holes. Leave a space of two elements wide and two high between these first sets of crossed rows. Work all the rows in the shape in this manner. Complete the pattern (**b**) with a second set of crosses that ascend to the right. Notice where the second set of crosses starts in relation to the first stage. You may find an awl or stiletto helpful to spread the up- and downpoints as a guide to placing the rows when working this pattern.

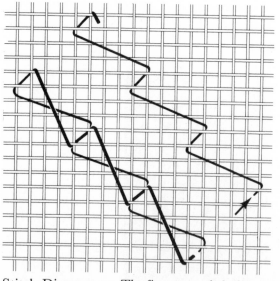

Stitch Diagram **a**: *The first stage of checker filling ascends to the left.*

LESSON 9

DOUBLE-BACK STITCHES

A SQUARE CUSHION FILLING

B DOUBLE-BACK FILLING

C FINNISH FILLING

D DIAMOND FILLING

THE patterns in this lesson are borrowed from a transparent fabric embroidery technique called shadow work. The stitch employed is a reverse herringbone called a double-back stitch. Two parallel lines of backstitches are made on the frontface in one journey by advancing on the backface with diagonally crossed working threads. The crossed threads make the transparent fabric opaque and at the same time add a padded quality to the shapes they support. Pastel embroidery threads add tints of color to a white ground. Applying this technique to a heavier, stiffer canvas requires some minor modifications. Distortion and buckling are controlled by adding some over-stitching, which also enriches the positive spaces. The padded quality of shadow work adds a valuable dimension to a vocabulary of pulled stitches.

STITCH 9A

SQUARE CUSHION FILLING

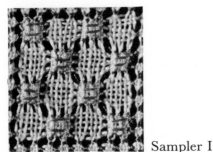
Sampler I

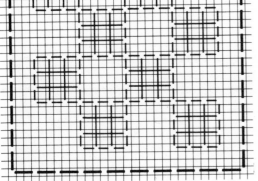
Pattern Diagram: *Raise the surface with little square cushions.*

By employing tension in working these squares of double-back stitches, little square cushions arise that are further emphasized by the addition of crosshatched satin stitches.

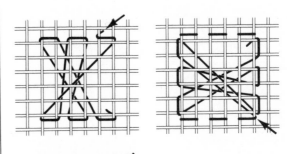

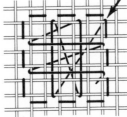

Stitch Diagrams: *Outline square shapes with parallel lines of backstitches.*

Work these units of square cushions in diagonal rows where possible. In the pattern diagram, the arrows indicate where to start rows. The working sequence of each square is soon apparent, as is the need for the crosshatched satin stitches that neatly anchor the squares. Use fine working thread for this heavily stitched pattern.

STITCH 9B
DOUBLE-BACK FILLING

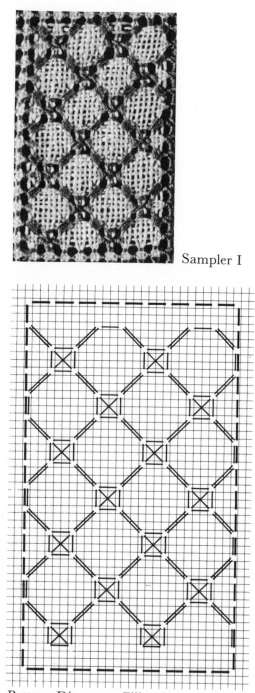

Sampler I

Pattern Diagram: *Fill a shape with double-back octagons and cross-stitched squares.*

The tension of the double-back filling raises a patterned ground of puffed up octagons. The cross-stitched squares add a secondary pattern.

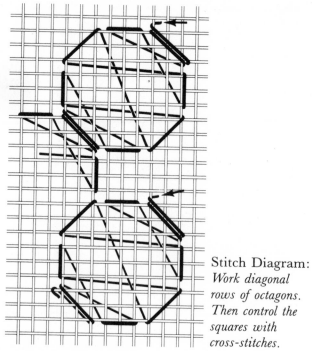

Stitch Diagram: *Work diagonal rows of octagons. Then control the squares with cross-stitches.*

Work each octagonal unit in a diagonal sequence of stitches and in diagonal rows that can descend or ascend. In this stitch diagram, the first stitch made is a compensating stitch. Except at the edges of the pattern, where compensating stitches are needed, work the diagonal stitches once for each unit. They are duplicated by adjacent units. The negative spaces form a pattern of four holes around a square of canvas. Completely fill the desired shape with double-back filling, and then control the buckling of these squares of stiff canvas by working diagonal rows of cross-stitches over them.

STITCH 9C
FINNISH FILLING

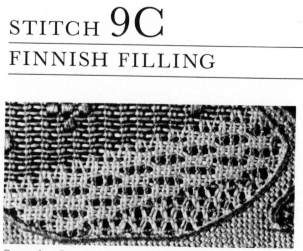

Sampler I

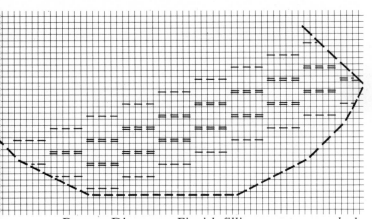

Pattern Diagram: *Finnish filling creates a gradual diagonal movement of open slits.*

Rows of staggered double-back stitch units are worked directly under one another, forcing the negative spaces into elliptical shapes.

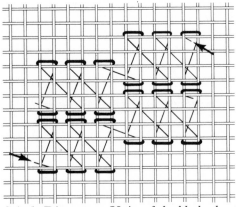

Stitch Diagram: *Units of double-back stitches drop or rise as they travel across a row.*

Work a unit of three double-back stitches, then drop two canvas elements to work the next unit. Travel in these diagonal rows of units, working the alternate rows in opposite directions.

STITCH 9D
DIAMOND FILLING

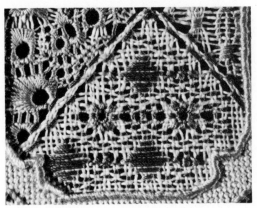

Sampler I

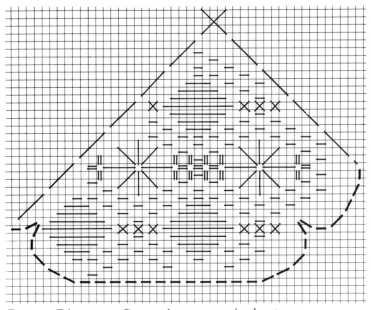

Pattern Diagram: *Create other patterns in the spaces left by diamond filling.*

The diamond filling leaves rather large areas of unfilled shapes for canvas work. In this diagram, these shapes are filled with other patterns. Two bands of bare canvas are worked with cross-stitches on either side of a large satin-stitch diamond. The center band of eyelet buttonhole and whipped satin stitches is diagramed in **11D**.

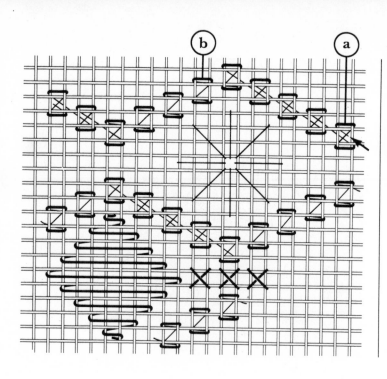

Work double-back stitches two elements high for diamond filling. Zigzag up (**a**) and down (**b**) across a row, rising or falling by one canvas element. Then reverse the zigzags to fall and rise in the opposite direction. The diamond-shaped spaces of bare canvas left between the rows can be filled with other patterns.

Stitch Diagram: *Make long herringbones ascending and short ones descending.*

LESSON 10

SIDED STITCHES

A ITALIAN CROSS FILLING

B MOSAIC FILLING

C COIL AND CROSS BORDER

D FOUR-SIDED BORDER

E DROPPED FOUR-SIDED FILLING

F DETACHED SQUARE FILLING

G THREE-SIDED FILLING

H THREE-SIDED BORDER

I INDIAN DRAWN GROUND

IN this lesson, the patterns all involve a system of wrapping the working thread around a square or triangle of elements to pull them together. Coil and cross is a mongrel of my invention and is included here because it relates slightly to the four-sided stitch. The stitches include four-sided, three-sided, and two-sided variations. Many of them can be used as borders as well as fillings. Some are dark and dense, like mosaic and Italian cross; others are light and airy, like the four-sided and dropped four-sided fillings. Explore them all; they are all very adaptable to other techniques and they all lend themselves to experimentation.

STITCH 10A
ITALIAN CROSS FILLING

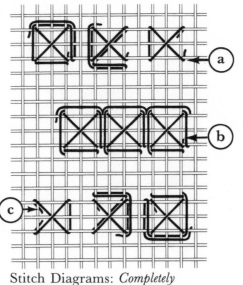

Stitch Diagrams: *Completely surround each cross-stitch on both front and backface.*

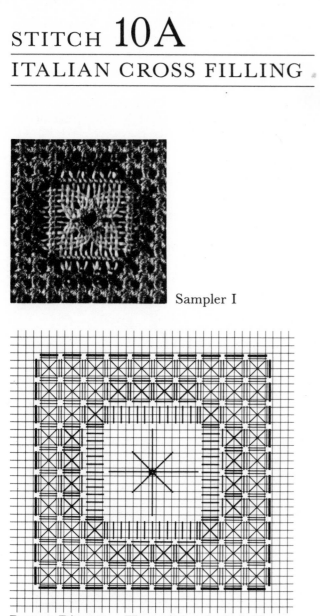

Sampler I

Pattern Diagram: *These stitch units look like a mat of fat, round beads.*

Start the first stitch of a unit heading in the direction of the row. A single unit of Italian cross-stitch is shown in three stages of development (**a**). First, the cross-stitch is completed; it is then gradually surrounded so that there are stitches both on the back- and frontface on all sides of the square, pulling it snugly into a rounded shape. Stitch Diagram **b** shows a row being worked from right to left. Stitch Diagram **c** shows the development of a unit that begins a row heading from left to right.

Using considerable tension and sufficient plies of working thread to completely cover the canvas elements, Italian cross filling makes a pattern of what look like fat, round beads in the positive space with large, round negative openings. This motif has a buttonhole eyelet in the center, diagramed in **11B**. A row of straight satin stitches frames the eyelet. Just outside of the satins, four Italian cross-stitches are worked on each side of the square in single ply. The remainder of the motif is densely worked Italian cross filling.

STITCH 10B
MOSAIC FILLING

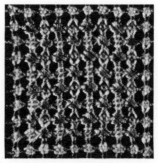

Sampler I

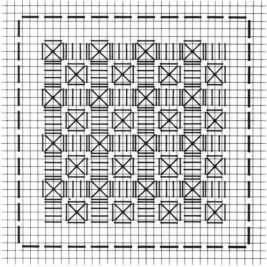

Pattern Diagram: *Connecting threads add a pattern to the negative spaces.*

This rich pattern is a combination of Italian cross filling and step stitch filling. Produce it in three separate stages of long diagonal rows. Complete each stage before beginning the next.

The first stage is to work a step stitch filling in diagonal rows to fill a planned shape. The second stage is to work one-half of every Italian cross-stitch unit, forming diagonal rows that slant from the upper right to the lower left. Stitch Diagram **a** shows an Italian cross-stitch as it begins to descend in a diagonal row. Fill every one of the unworked squares left by the step stitch filling. Then work the third stage, completing the Italian cross-stitch units, working in diagonal rows that slant from the upper left to the lower right. Stitch Diagram **b** shows a unit being completed with the connecting thread in position for the next unit. In Stitch Diagram **c** the first and second stages are completed and a diagonal row of the third stage has been worked.

Stitch Diagrams: *Italian cross-stitches fill a step stitch filling in three stages.*

STITCH 10C
COIL AND CROSS BORDER

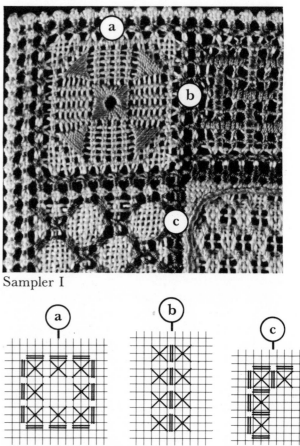

Sampler I

Pattern Diagrams: *Expand or frame a pattern with a border that enriches it.*

The coil and cross border can be worked in various arrangements of coils and crosses. It is a convenient method by which to frame fillings and to extend them in problem spaces. It is used on Sampler I in three variations: around the outer edges of the five sections of work at the top of the sampler (**a**); between the sections (**b**); and, in another color, to frame the large inside section of curved shapes (**c**).

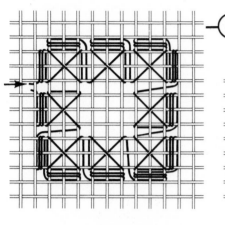
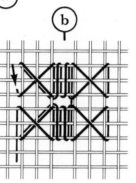
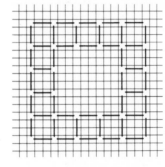

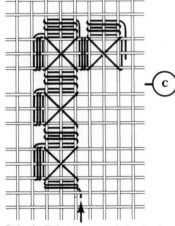

Stitch Diagrams: *Manipulate coil and cross stitches to suit any border.*

The coils may all be worked around the outer edges of the shape (**a**); they may be worked between the crosses (**b**); or they may be worked both at the outer edges and between the crosses (**c**). Notice that in some instances, the cross-stitches are crossed inconsistently. This can be avoided by sliding the needle under the first half of a cross to make the crossings match. However, in working single long rows of coil and cross, changing direction from one side to another is unnoticeable.

STITCH 10D
FOUR-SIDED BORDER

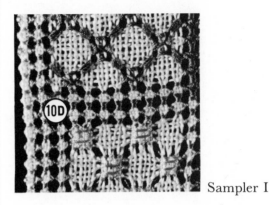

Sampler I

Pattern Diagram: *This is a light, quiet border to use with any embroidery technique.*

Use the four-sided border as a simple, light trim to contrast with richly patterned areas. It is used in Sampler I to frame the square and rectangular shapes on both sides. The four-sided border is also worked as an outer edging for both Samplers I and II. Four-sided edging is described in **12G**.

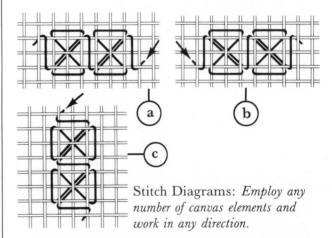

Stitch Diagrams: *Employ any number of canvas elements and work in any direction.*

The four-sided stitch works so rapidly and decoratively in so many directions, it is little wonder that it has been absorbed into so many embroidery techniques. However, the vertical stitches do slant under tension, so be consistent in the direction you travel. You can start at the right (**a**), at the left (**b**), or at the top (**c**). Notice that one of the crossings of the connecting thread on the backface is always made twice.

STITCH 10E

DROPPED FOUR-SIDED FILLING

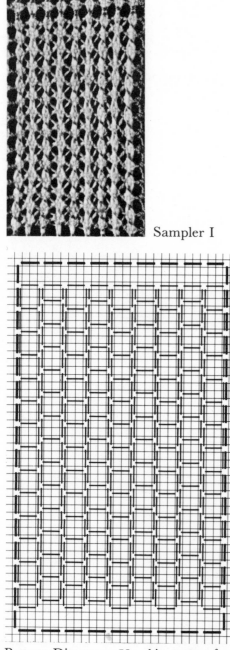

Sampler I

Pattern Diagram: *Use this pattern for a strong vertical direction with zigzag open spaces.*

By shortening the first unit at the top of alternate rows, the stitch pattern on either side of it drops. Notice that the canvas elements in the negative spaces move at angles, in sharp contrast to the strong vertical stripes of the positive space.

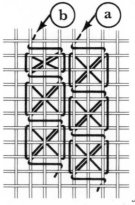

Stitch Diagram: *Shorten the first unit every other row.*

Work four-sided stitches in descending vertical rows. Start the second row (**b**) with a stitch unit made over two canvas elements in height, instead of the usual three. Proceed as for the first row (**a**). Continue to alternate rows. You can work the four-sided stitches over four elements and shorten the first stitch of alternate rows to a height of two elements to produce a regular zigzag pattern.

STITCH 10F

DETACHED SQUARE FILLING

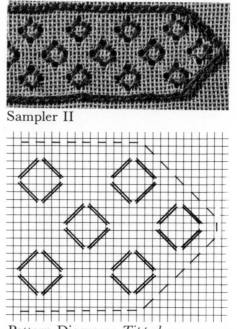

Sampler II

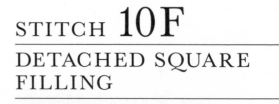

Pattern Diagram: *Tipped squares seem to float on a light, quiet ground.*

Although these tipped squares appear detached on the frontface, they are connected by upright crosses on the backface. The work must be done in two stages. Notice how the shape of the stitch fits the pointed end of the band in Sampler II.

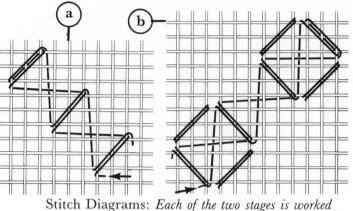 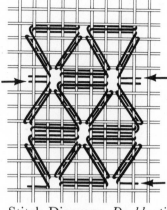

Stitch Diagrams: *Each of the two stages is worked in two journeys.*

To work the first stage, fill the area by ascending and descending in diagonal rows that slant from lower right to upper left (**a**). Notice that upright cross-stitches are made on the backface. A detached square filling is, in fact, the reverse of a diagonal cross filling. Work the second stage, which completes the squares, with diagonal rows that slant in the opposite direction (**b**).

There is a consistent, pleasing rhythm in working this pattern. It is evenly balanced in positive and negative spaces and makes a handsome filling for large areas.

Stitch Diagram: *Double-stitch rows of triangles from opposite directions.*

Travel in horizontal rows that alternate direction. Each row mirrors the preceding one. The slanted stitches appear twice on the frontface and the horizontals just once. However, when a second row is made, two horizontals appear in each position, one from each row. The three-sided stitch must be worked with the base of the triangle over an even number of elements because the slanted stitches form an equilateral triangle.

STITCH 10G
THREE-SIDED FILLING

Sampler II

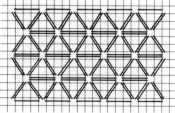

Pattern Diagram: *Large, round openings are made by stitches that pull in six directions.*

STITCH 10H
THREE-SIDED BORDER

Sampler II

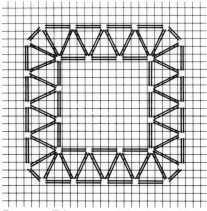

Pattern Diagram: *The three-sided border is darker and denser than the four-sided one.*

This pattern diagram shows a border of three-sided stitches turning four corners to make a frame.

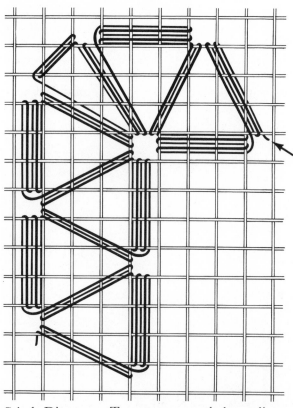

Stitch Diagram: *Turn a corner neatly by angling over two elements.*

Work each stitch twice on the frontface over four elements in width and height. Turn the corners by making the base of a three-sided stitch slant over two elements in height and width.

STITCH 10 I
INDIAN DRAWN GROUND

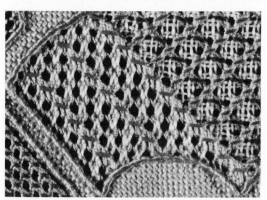

Sampler I

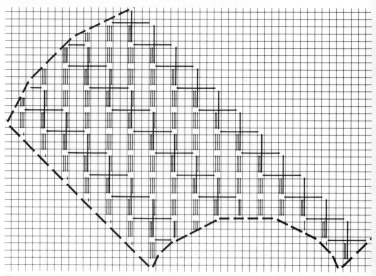

Pattern Diagram: *Combine this versatile ground with other diagonally worked patterns.*

This unique ground produces a strong pattern of solid vertical stripes. Notice that there are three vertical stitches in this pattern diagram where rows are adjacent to each other. This is because there are two from the right side of one unit and one from the left side of its neighbor (see Stitch Diagram **c**). Indian drawn ground is both quick and easy to work.

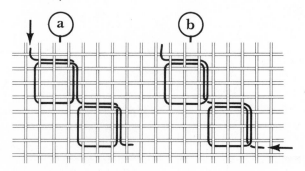

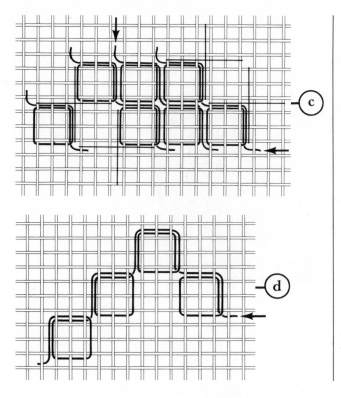

(a) and (b) In each square unit, two of the sides are doubled—one on the front- and one on the backface—as you travel in ascending or descending diagonal rows.

(c) Work rows of Indian drawn ground between the rows of diagonal raised bands for the filling in Sampler I. See Stitch **8C** for diagonal raised bands.

(d) Use Indian drawn ground as a border, changing the direction of the rows to suit the shape of the piece.

Stitch Diagrams: *Wrap twice around the side that leads the row up or down.*

LESSON 11

BUTTONHOLE STITCHES

A SPACED BUTTONHOLE

B BUTTONHOLE EYELET

C QUARTER BUTTONHOLE EYELET

D BUTTONHOLE EYELET AND WHIPPED SATIN BAND

E GREEK CROSS FILLING

F LOOP STITCH FILLING

THE buttonhole stitch heads a family of looped stitches; it is also the basic ingredient of needlemade lace and all forms of open work. Buttonhole variations are demonstrated in each section of *The Open Canvas*. In this lesson, some methods for employing the buttonhole stitch with tension are explored. I hope that they will stimulate further study and creativity. The first stitch is the most basic and most useful of the family—the spaced buttonhole stitch. Then come buttonhole eyelets, in which the festoons converge around the center hole of a unit. Buttonhole eyelets are particularly successful on canvas, with its relatively large mesh openings. The lessons conclude with two looped patterns, Greek cross and loop stitch filling, both composed of units of four buttonhole loops. Note that the term *festoon* refers to the scalloped connecting thread that falls between the two pairs of vertical stitches, or *loops*.

STITCH 11A
SPACED BUTTONHOLE

Sampler I

Pattern Diagram: *Define the perimeter of a space with spaced buttonhole stitches.*

In Sampler I, spaced buttonhole stitches create broken and solid lines that border the diamonds of **5B** and **5C.**

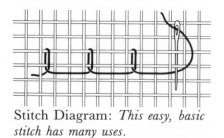

Stitch Diagram: *This easy, basic stitch has many uses.*

The spaced buttonhole stitch is also called a blanket stitch. It can be used as a border stitch, shown here; as a filling; or as a binding for an edge. When the stitches are worked closely together, they are called buttonhole stitches. See *Hemstitching* for a description of this stitch.

STITCH 11B
BUTTONHOLE EYELET

Sampler I

Pattern Diagram **a**: *This eyelet is worked over reverse faggot ground (**7E**).*

Sampler I

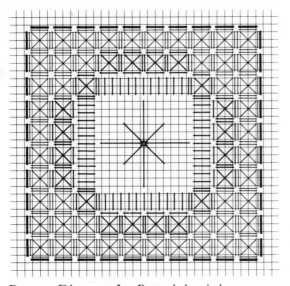

Pattern Diagram **b**: *Buttonhole stitches can converge around a center hole in many variations.*

Variations of buttonhole eyelets are worked in these motifs from Sampler I. The eyelet in Pattern Diagram **a** is worked over the reverse faggot ground of **7E**. It is stitched with one-ply twisted silk, and three stitches are made in each of the twelve locations. The buttonhole eyelet of Pattern Diagram **b** pulls the elements into four graceful petal shapes. Use strong tension and several plies.

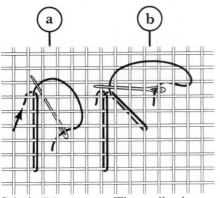

Stitch Diagrams: *The needle always emerges from the center over the working thread.*

To make buttonhole eyelets, work buttonhole stitches with the festoons converging around a center hole from which the needle emerges. In this eyelet, the needle emerges from the center hole and enters the backface six elements away. It emerges again with the thread held under the tip of the needle (**a**). This step is repeated over three or six elements (**b**), so that eight festoons converge around the center hole (**c**).

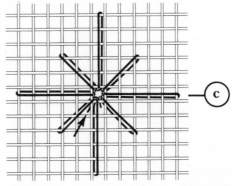

Close the unit by passing over the first festoon in the center hole and entering the backface. Work the larger, heavier buttonhole eyelet the same way, but change the number of stitches and their placement according to Pattern Diagram **a**.

STITCH 11C

QUARTER BUTTONHOLE EYELET

Sampler I

Pattern Diagram: *Create patterns from segments of buttonhole eyelets.*

Quarter buttonhole eyelets are worked in the four corners of Stitches **5B** and **5C** in Sampler I.

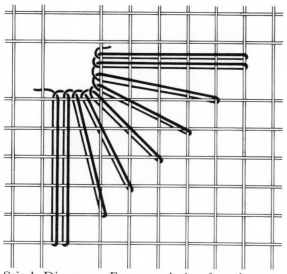

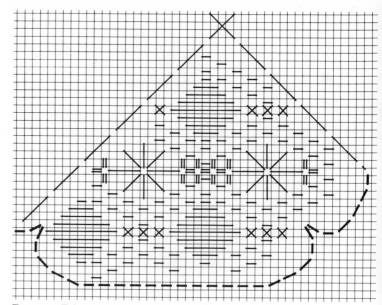

Pattern Diagram: *Tailor patterns to fit special spaces.*

Stitch Diagram: *Emerge each time from the center hole while entering the backface on the edge of the shape.*

Work a quarter of a diamond-shaped buttonhole eyelet to achieve this fan shape from Sampler I, **5B** and **5C**. Notice that there are two buttonhole stitches in the horizontal and vertical locations.

Buttonhole eyelets are combined with whipped satins in a band to fill the spaces left by the diamond filling pattern of **9D**.

STITCH 11D

BUTTONHOLE EYELET AND WHIPPED SATIN BAND

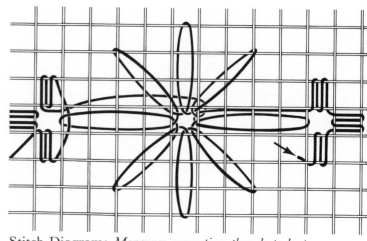

Stitch Diagram: *Maneuver connecting threads to keep them out of the openings.*

Work this pattern with a continuous working thread, traveling in either direction. After completing the last loop of the buttonhole eyelet, insert the needle into the first festoon to close the ring. Catch the connecting thread on the backface under one or more buttonhole loops before beginning the next set of overcast stitches. Occasionally, a maneuver such as this is made to prevent the connecting thread from being seen on the frontface. Follow the pattern diagram to complete the band.

Sampler I

STITCH 11E
GREEK CROSS FILLING

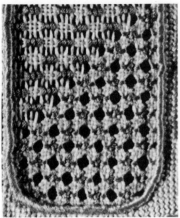

Sampler I

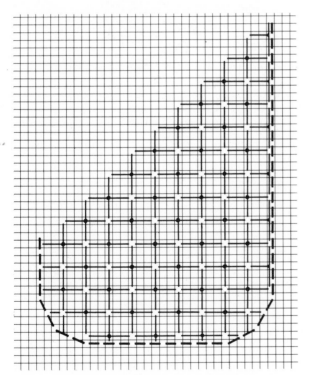

Pattern Diagram: *Large holes are made where the four arms of the four stitch units meet.*

The crosses stand very straight in this pattern, since each of the arms is a tightly pulled buttonhole stitch. The holes appear at the ends of the arms, not in the center of the cross, which is filled by the festoons.

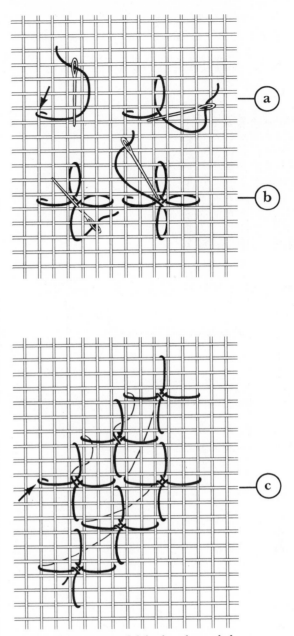

Stitch Diagrams: *Make four buttonhole loops around the center hole.*

Start a unit by emerging three elements to the left of the center hole (**a**). Moving clockwise, swing the working thread into the backface over three elements above the center hole. Emerge from the center hole with the needle over the festoon to make the first buttonhole stitch. Then work buttonhole stitches over three elements to the right and three below the center hole. Close the unit by inserting the needle over the first festoon into the center hole (**b**). Work a filling of Greek cross-stitches by traveling in diagonal rows, ascending to the right and descending to the left (**c**).

STITCH 11F

LOOP STITCH FILLING

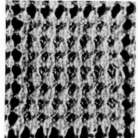

Sampler I´

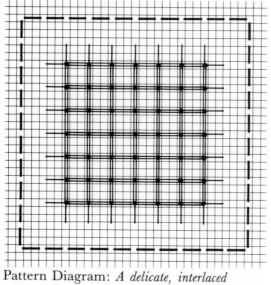

Pattern Diagram: *A delicate, interlaced pattern appears in the negative spaces.*

In the centers of the loop stitches, a lacy pattern is made by the interlaced working threads. A loop stitch is also employed in the *Hardanger* and *Filet* sections of *The Open Canvas.*

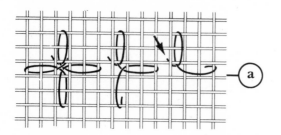

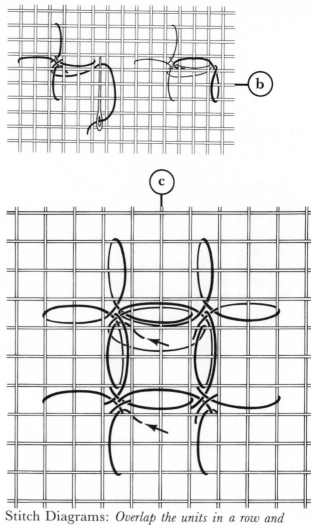

Stitch Diagrams: *Overlap the units in a row and overlap the rows.*

(**a**) The sequence of buttonhole stitches in each unit starts at the bottom and moves clockwise. Close a unit by entering the center over the connecting thread of the first and second buttonhole stitches.

(**b**) Emerge for the next unit three elements to the right and, again working clockwise, overlap the right arm of the previous unit. Complete the row.

(**c**) To start succeeding rows, emerge at the base of the unit just completed. Travel from left to right. With a little practice, you can alternate the direction of the rows.

LESSON 12

FINISHING AND EDGING

A TENT STITCH GROUND

B CHAIN STITCH OUTLINE

C WHIPPED CHAIN OUTLINE

D DOUBLE KNOT OUTLINE

E OUTLINE STEM STITCH

F COUCHED OUTLINES

G FOUR-SIDED EDGING VARIATION

THIS lesson is devoted to various finishing techniques. None of them is worked with tension except where noted. The diagonally worked tent stitch is included here as an alternative solid ground for the first pulled sampler. This may come as a welcome relief to those new or dedicated canvas workers who have been following these lessons and may now be yearning for some simple tent-stitched areas. Chain and whipped chain are classic outline stitches for pulled work patterns; they appear here along with a heavy textured outline of double knot stitches. The outline stem stitch is offered as a surface work technique; it can be used without tension to add initials and date or as an additional border employing slight tension. Three couching methods have also been included to provide additional means of outlining the shapes of pulled fillings. The technique of couching provides a way to lay down and fasten metal or silky braids and cords. The lesson ends with a simplified pulled four-sided edging, which completes both samplers and can be used to bind any canvas work.

STITCH 12A

TENT STITCH GROUND

Sampler I

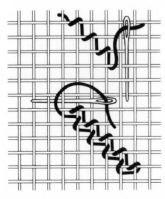

Stitch Diagram: *Make vertical stitches on the backface to descend and horizontal ones to ascend.*

A diagonally worked tent stitch ground is employed in Sampler I around the curved shapes of the central portion as a contrast to the busy open patterns. Stitch this or any other ground after completing the pulled work fillings but before embellishing them further with embroidered outlines. Work the tent stitch ground in alternately descending and ascending diagonal rows. In a descending row, hold the needle in a vertical position and make vertical stitches over two elements on the backface. In an ascending row, hold the needle in a horizontal position and make horizontal stitches over two elements on the backface. On the frontface, little slanted stitches made over one element completely cover the canvas. A basketweave results on the backface. Employ no tension—do not pull the working thread or the canvas elements. Use a waste knot technique for fastening both on and off.

STITCH 12 B
CHAIN STITCH OUTLINE

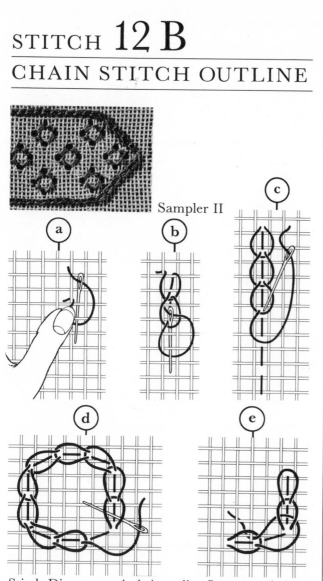

Sampler II

Stitch Diagrams: *A chain outline flows around shapes and covers awkward edges.*

Work a chain stitch outline in a consistent clockwise or counterclockwise direction around all the shapes, whether or not you plan to whip it later (see **12C**). Start a chain, emerging on the frontface. Insert the needle back into the same hole, hold a loop of working thread on the surface, and emerge again two elements away inside the loop (**a**). Then draw up the working thread (**b**). Work chain outline over backstitches (**c**) to outline shapes. In Sampler II, this method is employed at the top around the detached square filling (Stitch **10F**). In Sampler I, all the rounded shapes are outlined in a chain stitch as a prelude to creating the whipped chain (**12C**).

Close a chain outline by completing the next to the last stitch, passing the needle under the first chain (**d**), and inserting the needle back into the last emerging point (**e**).

STITCH 12 C
WHIPPED CHAIN OUTLINE

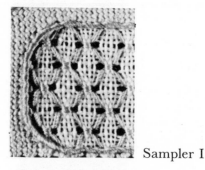

Sampler I

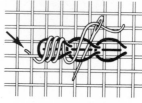

Stitch Diagram: *You can work a shiny rolled outline with whipped chain stitches.*

The whipped chain outline is worked in two stages. The first stage is to chain stitch around the shape, traveling in one direction. The second stage is to overcast each chain stitch an equal number of times, traveling in the opposite direction. Pass over each chain a sufficient number of times to cover it. The needle only passes under an element when you are fastening on or off; otherwise, the needle passes under the chain stitch threads above the elements. If you employ more than one ply, lay them in carefully for a smooth, rolled, light-reflecting appearance.

All the rounded shapes in the central portion of Sampler I are outlined in whipped chain.

STITCH 12 D
DOUBLE KNOT OUTLINE

Sampler II

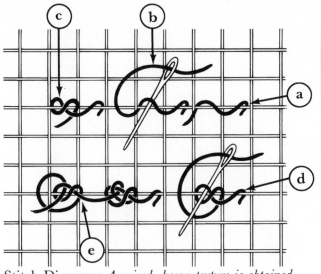

Stitch Diagram: *A raised, heavy texture is obtained with this double knot outline.*

Work from right to left, maintaining a slack tension between the double knot units. Emerge from the backface and pass over a vertical element into the backface (**a**). Emerge and pass under the working thread (**b**). Draw the thread completely through (**c**). Finish the unit with a buttonhole stitch beside the last stitch (**d**). Pass over two vertical elements before entering the backface for the next knot (**e**). On Sampler II, a double knot outline is embroidered around the festoon filling (**2C**).

STITCH 12 E
OUTLINE STEM STITCH

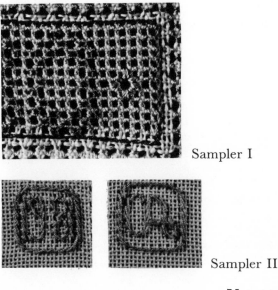

Sampler I

Sampler II

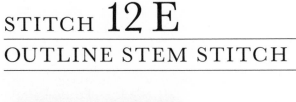

Stitch Diagram: *You can obtain smooth embroidered lines on canvas with the outline stem stitch.*

Hold the working thread above the needle for outline stem. Work from left to right with long stitches on the frontface and short ones on the backface.

Since this is in effect a reverse backstitch, you can follow the same technique for obtaining curved lines as described in **1A**. Plan your outline on graph paper with stitch lines over two elements. Translate these lines into the short stitches on the backface, which head to the left; the long, overlapping stitches on the frontface head to the right, or clockwise.

In Sampler I, there is a border of outline stem within the long rectangle at the bottom. In Sampler II, a date and initials are worked in rounded squares of outline stems at the bottom left and right.

STITCH 12 F
COUCHED OUTLINES

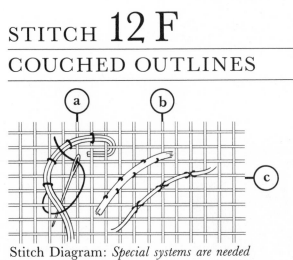

Stitch Diagram: *Special systems are needed to fasten the ends of the couched-down threads.*

Following are three techniques for couching down decorative threads (see Glossary). However, some general instructions for fastening on and off that are peculiar to couching are described here. Do not cut the thread to be couched down. It is difficult to estimate the lengths required, and these threads are usually costly or hard to find. Begin by anchoring the tail end of the decorative thread by feeding it through a large-eyed needle, chenille or crewel, and sinking it to the backface. Unthread it, and, using a sharp crewel needle and fine silk sewing thread, tack it down. (Run a silk couching thread through beeswax when couching down a metal thread to prevent the silk from being cut by the metal.) When about one inch of couching remains, cut the decorative thread, allowing a sufficient length for fastening down. Sink it once more to the backface. Complete the couching down on the frontface, and secure the tail end of the decorative thread with fine thread on the backface.

Sampler II: *Couched Japanese metal around reverse window filling (6F).*

(**a**) Couch two strands of Japanese metal at one time. Overcast the stitches ¼ inch apart, perpendicular to the metal. Angle the needle toward the metal as you insert it and away as you withdraw it. Try not to occupy the same holes in these movements.

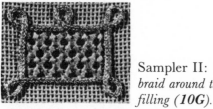

Sampler II: *Couched metal braid around three-sided filling (10G).*

(**b**) Couch metal braid with tiny overcast stitches made at regular intervals on either side. Pierce the braid to enter the backface and angle the needle to emerge close to the side of the braid. Do not exert tension, since this causes the braid to dimple.

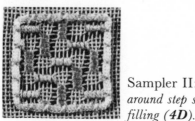

Sampler II: *Couched silk cord around step stitch filling (4D).*

(**c**) Couch a silky cord with decorative cross-stitches. Use a contrasting color for the couching thread. The photo shows couching around a geometric shape with evenly placed stitches; this stitch diagram illustrates cross-stitches worked on a curve. Pass under or into the elements with the cross-stitches.

STITCH 12 G

FOUR-SIDED EDGING VARIATION

Sampler I   Sampler II

Stitch Diagram: *Bind the canvas in two simple stages.*

This is a simple version of four-sided edging with which you can bind the raw edges of canvas work. It is employed in both pulled samplers. Other variation of four-sided edging can be found in *The Open Canvas* at the end of *Hemstitching* and the end of *Reticello and Hedebo*. Work this edging in two separate stages.

(**a**) The first stage is to backstitch over three elements around the four sides, making an extra pair of stitches in the corners at right angles. This line of backstitches is the outer edge of the completed work.

(**b**) Fold the excess canvas around the edges to the backface. Carefully match the two layers of canvas elements. Overcast three elements in height and backstitch three in width over the two layers. Cut away the excess canvas on the back.

BOOK TWO

NEEDLEWEAVING

*Either horizontal or vertical elements are
withdrawn; the remaining elements become
the warps for darned embroidery. Working
threads are also stretched across the surface as
warps and then darned, thereby producing a
raised surface.*

CONTENTS

INTRODUCTION

Needleweaving opened canvas is a versatile technique that can be employed in formally organized patterns or freely worked ones. We usually needleweave over the warps that remain after all the elements have been withdrawn from one direction within geometric or amorphous shapes. However, it is possible to employ a high-relief, sculptural technique by stretching surface warps with the working thread and shaping the needleweaving. It is also possible to needleweave in low relief by changing the order and direction of the withdrawn elements. The needleweaving sampler includes examples of the basic techniques shown in these lessons; low relief work is demonstrated in separate examples. Needleweaving will be included in almost every section of *The Open Canvas.*

A THIMBLEFUL OF HISTORY

Examples of needleweaving can be seen on ancient Egyptian and Coptic embroideries of the sixth century. In these early woven fabrics, sections of the warp were left unfilled, to be needlewoven on the loom later. The Italians traded with those ancient Arabian countries that excelled in withdrawn element embroidery on linen, and there is little doubt that the open-work linen embroidery that developed so prolifically in sixteenth-century Italy is derived from that source. In fact, needleweaving was used to produce the Venetian laces and reticello that have been famous since that time. In the *Filet* and the *Reticello and Hedebo* sections of *The Open Canvas,* needleweaving is demonstrated as it relates to these fields. You can also find more examples of needleweaving in *Hardanger.* Almost every other culture incorporated the technique of needleweaving into their embroidery.

SOME NEEDLE POINTS

It is much easier to withdraw elements from a canvas before it is stretched on a frame, particularly if you are opening a large area. However, you should open only small areas at a time in order not to loosen the tension necessary to support the embroidery. Be prepared to move the canvas off and on the frame to withdraw additional areas.

Securing withdrawn elements requires special care. Methods include darning cut ends back into the canvas, tacking them down on the backface, and cutting them at the edge of the opened space where they can be secured with acid-free glue and/or an embroidered edging. The first two methods are explored in the needleweaving sampler; the last method is shown in **7A** (padded satin border).

There are many contrasts in style between the needleweaving done in the past and contemporary work. The steady, light tension that produced straight, precise columns in the past is in contrast to the varying degrees of tension seen in today's work. None at all is employed for lacy open weaving, whereas curving or distorted effects require a firm hand.

In the past, the needleweaving within an embroidered piece was worked over a consistent number of warp elements so that the columns of ribs made a rhythmic impression like that of loom weaving. Today, the work never looks as if it's been woven on a loom; the object is to create movements that cannot be accomplished mechanically.

The long edges of needlewoven bands used to be hemstitched beforehand to prevent the warps of the unopened segments from floating into the opened spaces. This is not essential in contemporary work. Hemstitching can be added when and if it is needed, and the floating of the warps can be incorporated into the needlewoven pattern.

Canvas needleweaving has its own particular concerns. When you withdraw elements from one direction, the remaining elements are left with impressed undulations. You can easily smooth them with a light swabbing of water. If you want to deliberately loosen the remaining warps, apply more water. However, if some of the warps become too loose, you can also correct this problem. Pry up the offending element outside of the opened area, and gradually ease the excess length out into the marginal area of the canvas.

Securing working threads is always a consideration in open work. When there is no place to fasten on, start with a waste knot. Most fastenings can be accomplished by passing through the cores created by the needleweaving. The waste knots can be undone and fastened down after there is sufficient work to weave into, or even later when the work is removed from the frame. Try to use enough thread to avoid fastening off in the middle of a block. When you are working fine, taut needleweaving, insert the needle into a previous row and carry a long stitch on the backface to wherever it can be secured without being visible on the frontface.

There are no problems that cannot be solved in this flexible medium, and there is no end to its creative possibilities.

WORKBASKET SUPPLIES

CANVAS
The only special requirement of the canvas is that you must be able to unweave and withdraw selected elements from it. Mono canvas is an obvious possibility, but interlock canvas can be unwoven as well. The bars in *Reticello and Hedebo* are needlewoven over warps made by withdrawing elements from interlock canvas. Size, color, and fiber are a matter of choice. The canvas must be strong enough to take the tension of the weaving, however. Linen canvas is used for the sampler in this section, but elsewhere in *The Open Canvas,* needleweaving is worked on colored congress, tan mono, white painted mono, and white interlock canvas dyed blue.

THREADS
The earliest needleweaving was worked with threads of gold, silver, silk, wool, linen, and cotton since they were the only ones available. Today you can employ any suitable fiber for the design as long as it is strong enough to withstand the friction of the canvas and the tension of the weaving.

STRETCHERS
Use interlocking wood strips for a stretcher frame and tack down the bound canvas as tightly as possible. You will probably remove the canvas several times in the process of opening up various sections in order to retain a taut foundation while working. A canvas stretched in this way is easily taken off and put back.

Needleweaving should always be executed on a stretched canvas. No matter how free the design may be, it is still important to produce beautiful stitches, and these can only be achieved on a taut canvas.

NEEDLES AND OTHER TOOLS
Tapestry needles, with their blunt points, are used for most of the work, as they do not split the fibers of the working thread or the canvas. *Sharp crewel* or *sewing needles* can be used occasionally for fastening on or off when the needleweaving is particularly fine and tight. *Pliers* sometimes are helpful in pulling a needle through a tight spot. *Beeswax* can be used to control unruly fibers, but it does dull them. *Marking pens* of water-soluble color can be used to indicate elements to be withdrawn. These pens are fairly recent additions to the needlework notions market, and they appear to be quite harmless. Follow the manufacturers' advice carefully.

ACID-FREE GLUE
A permanent, flexible, colorless material that satisfies my conservation requirements; use it at your own discretion. A source of the glue is listed under Suppliers. It is extremely helpful in preventing canvas from unraveling and in securing the ends of working thread.

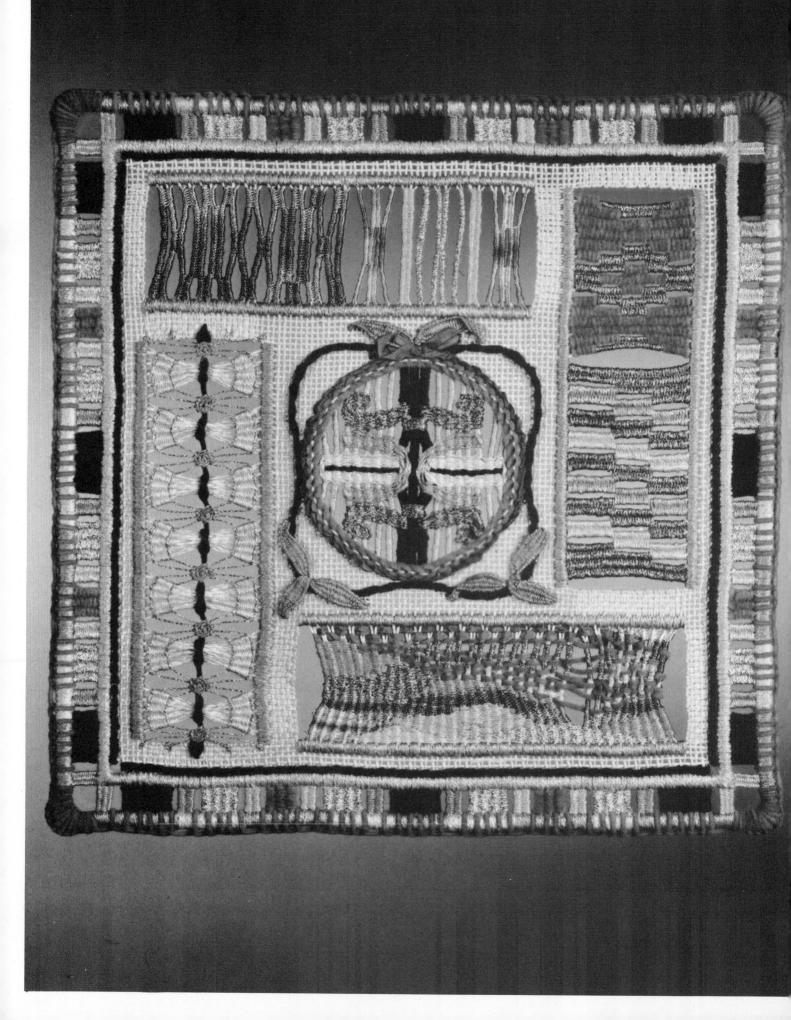

KEY TO STITCHES AND THREADS
Sampler

This needleweaving sampler is worked with linen, metal, rayon, and synthetic threads on 13/inch cream linen mono canvas. The finished size is 9¾ inches by 9¾ inches. See the accompanying key to identify the stitches and threads. The bold numbers with letters refer to the lesson and diagram where each stitch or pattern is located in *Needleweaving*. The bold italic numbers refer to the threads listed under Materials Employed.

1A Cutting and Reweaving Elements
2A Simple Bars, *2, 4, 5, 7, 8*
2B Simple Passing, *1, 2, 9*
2C Decreasing, Increasing, and Coiling, *5, 9*
3A Complex Passing, *11*
3B Crossed Coils, *8*
3C Pattern Needleweaving, *10*
4A Coral Knotted Clusters, *7*
4B Woven and Festooned Clusters, *3, 8*
4C Reverse Ribbed Wheel, *4*
5A, B Outlining with Pekinese and Stem Stitch, *2, 5, 12*
5C Rounded Shapes, *3, 7*

5D Other Shapes, *1*
5E Mirror Image Bars, *7*
5F Overlapped Weaving, *9*
5G Subtle Curves, *1* through *12*
6A Surface Needleweaving, *4*
7A Padded Satin Border, *1*
7B Blanket and Buttonhole Edging, *6*

MATERIALS EMPLOYED

CANVAS
13/inch cream linen mono, 12 inches wide by 12 inches high; edges bound

THREADS
1 Nordiska Swedish Linen, 264 lavender
2 Nordiska Swedish Linen, 332 blue
3 Nordiska Swedish Linen, 217 pink
4 Nordiska Swedish Linen, 280 green
5 Veloura, 420 sky blue
6 Veloura, 407 apple green
7 Veloura, 408 olive green
8 Lumiyarn Metal, size 1¼-inch silver
9 Lumiyarn Metal, size 1½-inch gold
10 Brazilian Rayon, Varicor Bossa Nova, 49 shaded green
11 Brazilian Rayon, Varicor Sissi, 7 lavender
12 Kanagawa Acetate Ribbon, lavender

NEEDLES
Tapestry 18, 20, 24
Crewel 8

STRETCHER STRIPS
2 pairs 12-inch

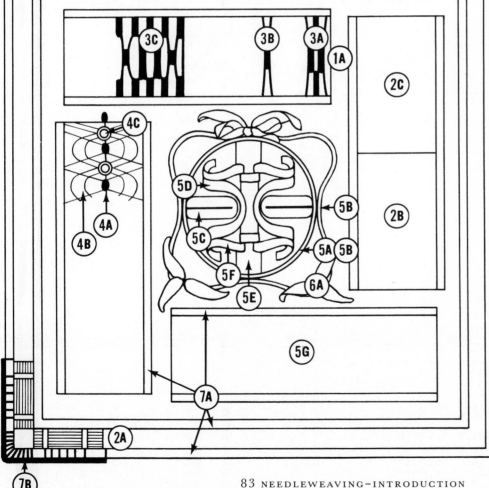

LESSON 1

CANVAS PREPARATION

MASTER PATTERN, SAMPLER

A CUTTING AND REWEAVING ELEMENTS

I N this first lesson, the ground is partially opened, and the cut elements are rewoven into the foundation canvas. Reweaving the elements back into the foundation is one way to secure the withdrawn elements. However, there are many occasions where this method interferes with the design concept, and tacking them down on the backface is a better solution. This method is described in Lesson **5**. How to needleweave two directions of warps on two or three levels is demonstrated in Lesson **8**.

MASTER PATTERN, SAMPLER

Use long basting stitches as center lines on the canvas to provide reference positions that correspond to the master pattern. The lines on the short sides of the rectangles indicate the outer edges of the withdrawn spaces. The withdrawn elements are rewoven over these edges. The solid black bands on the long sides are the padded satin stitch edges. You can open all four rectangles before stretching the canvas; they are evenly positioned on the canvas and will not cause distortion. You can also open the entire outer border, which is worked in Lesson 2. See Stitch Diagram **1A** before cutting and reweaving the elements. Open the center circle when you arrive at Lesson **5**, in which the method for tacking back withdrawn elements is taught. By that time, the four rectangles will be filled, and opening the center will not distort the canvas. The padded satin borders described in Lesson **7** can be worked at any time, but the outer edge should not be worked until Lesson **7**, when the canvas is taken off the frame for the last time. See Master Pattern on opposite page.

STITCH 1A

CUTTING AND REWEAVING ELEMENTS

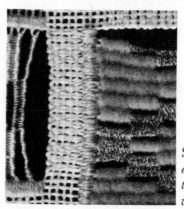

Sampler: *Create an even, dense pattern in the canvas ground using withdrawn elements.*

The rewoven elements make a dense pattern that can be left as part of the unembroidered ground, as in the sampler. Or, they can be stitched over as part of the foundation canvas.

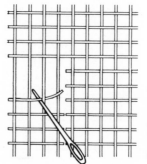

Stitch Diagram **a**: *Cut each element midway and pluck it out to the edge.*

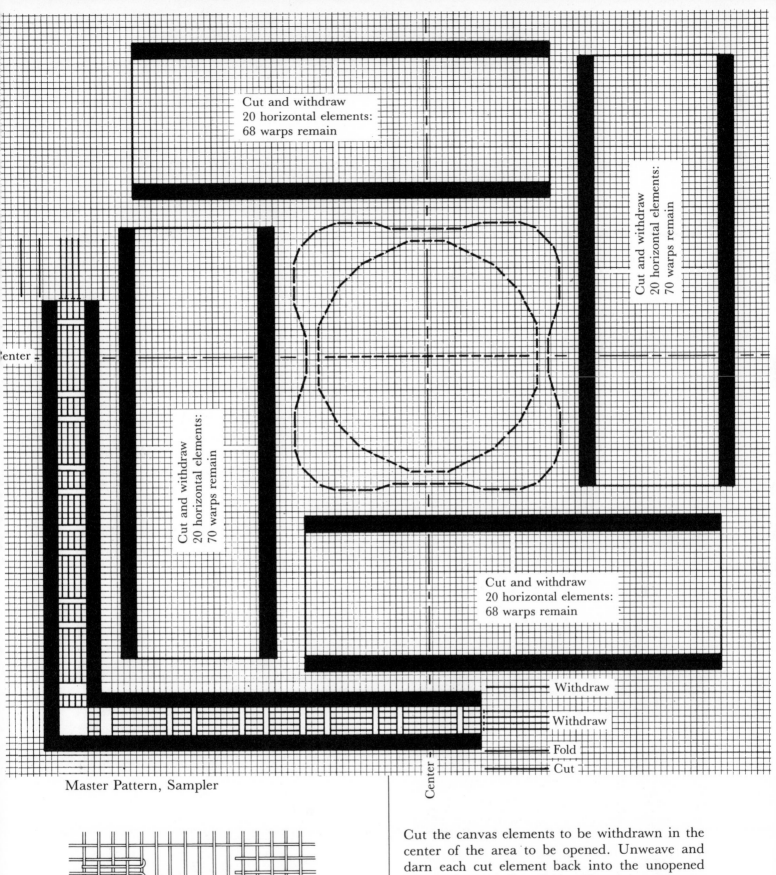

Cut and withdraw
20 horizontal elements:
68 warps remain

Cut and withdraw
20 horizontal elements:
70 warps remain

Cut and withdraw
20 horizontal elements:
70 warps remain

Cut and withdraw
20 horizontal elements:
68 warps remain

Center

Withdraw

Withdraw

Fold

Cut

Master Pattern, Sampler

Center

Stitch Diagram **b**: *Then darn it back into the canvas.*

Cut the canvas elements to be withdrawn in the center of the area to be opened. Unweave and darn each cut element back into the unopened canvas four or five times. To create an even pattern, be consistent: reweave either above or below the remaining warps in the unworked portion of the canvas, and align the cut ends on the same element on the backface. This is the method employed along the short straight side edges of the rectangles in the sampler.

Use an awl or tapestry needle for unweaving the canvas (**a**). Thread a tapestry needle with the element to reweave it into the canvas that remains (**b**). If the element is too short to thread, you can weave the needle into the canvas first and then thread it and draw it through. If the element is very stiff and unwieldy, dampen it very lightly with a sponge.

LESSON 2

BARS

A SIMPLE BARS

B SIMPLE PASSING

C DECREASING, INCREASING, AND COILING

AFTER you have secured the edges of spaces from which the elements have been withdrawn from one direction, single warp elements remain. These single warps are usually paired when they are needlewoven into patterns. They can also first be grouped at the straight edges; to see how, refer to *Hemstitching*.

In this lesson, the simple straight columns of needlewoven bars from the sampler border progress to bars that pass to the right and left, and then to bars that increase and decrease in size, providing additional methods for producing patterns in needleweaving. Coiling, or overcasting pairs of warps, is included here as well, and this technique appears as a secondary stitch pattern throughout the book.

STITCH 2A

SIMPLE BARS

A narrow border of simple needlewoven bars is shown around the four sides of the sampler. The repeat pattern is developed by alternating both the width of the bars and the color and texture of the threads. Notice that the wide central bar of the border is composed of five double warps at the top and bottom of the sampler and six double warps at the two sides (two elements are called a paired or double warp). The first and last bar on all four sides consists of three single warps. The other bars vary in the number of paired warps.

Sampler: *Alternate size, color, and texture for this simple bar border.*

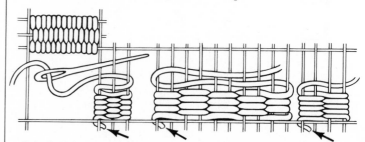

Stitch Diagram: *Pass over and under the elements; then reverse the process.*

Secure the working thread a few inches away from the first bar with a waste knot. After the bar or other adjacent work, such as the padded satin border, is completed, the end of the thread can be permanently fastened on by weaving it into the work on the backface. Emerge on the left side of the first bar, shown in the diagram as three single warps. Work the first row of weaving from left to right, passing over, under, and over the warps. Reverse the process on the second row, working from right to left: pass under, over, and under. Work the third row as the first, and continue to alternate each row. Needleweave in this way from the base upward, keeping an even, snug tension. Fasten off by passing through the hollow core on the backface, down one column and up the next. If you are working the sampler, needleweave the other bars, treating pairs of elements as single warps and alternating the width of the bars as on the master pattern.

STITCH 2B
SIMPLE PASSING

Sampler: *Move to the right or left in gradual stages.*

Simple bars can pass in gradual stages to the right or left. In this pattern, the height of the opened band is divided in thirds to make three stages of bars that move to the right.

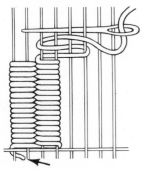

Stitch Diagram: *Weave in a new set of warps as you exclude an old set.*

Needleweave the first section of staggered bars a third of the way up. Then, omit the first pair of warps and add a new pair to form the next third. After needleweaving this section, pass to the right again, including another set of warps and omitting the second set. Needleweave to the top. At either end of the pattern, needleweave the remaining warps together as in the photograph. The first and last bars could also be worked to connect with the foundation canvas at the straight edges by needleweaving into the solid canvas.

STITCH 2C
DECREASING, INCREASING, AND COILING

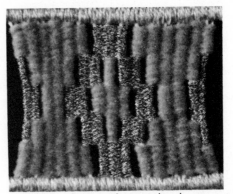

Sampler: *Stagger the weaving in even stages.*

In the sampler, a pattern is made by evenly staggering the stages of needleweaving from six double warps at the base to four and then to two at the center; the unit is completed by increasing in reverse stages to the top. A matching unit is worked skipping three double warps at the base. The intervening warps are woven in another pattern by passing in stages to the left and then to the right, working from bottom to top. The opposite side is worked in reverse. Pass the needle through the hollow core of the needleweaving to make the descending journey. Needleweaving and coiling fill the vacant warps.

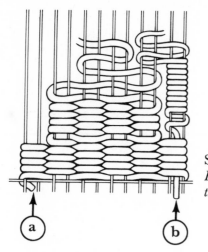

Stitch Diagram:
*Reduce or expand
the number of warps.*

You can reduce a needlewoven bar by excluding outer warps (**a**). Decrease on one side or both by as many warps as desired. Increase by including additional warps. To stagger a geometric shape evenly, divide the space the appropriate number of times with a ruler. Mark the first division lightly on a warp; then needleweave the same number of rows for each segment. Form a coil (**b**) by overcasting a pair of warps evenly and snugly. Be sure to wind all coils in the same direction; to ensure this, you can follow the twist of the working thread.

LESSON 3

COMPLEX MOVES

A COMPLEX PASSING

B CROSSED COILS

C PATTERN NEEDLEWEAVING

IN this lesson, the movement or passing from one location to another becomes more complicated. The idea is to find the most expedient route without starting a new working thread. Actually, there are no rules. To become acclimated to this kind of complex passing, travel along with the following diagrams and feel free to maneuver your way about. Make a game out of your search for the "path of least resistance."

STITCH 3A

COMPLEX PASSING

Sampler: *Plan your moves in advance.*

In this pattern, the left half of the motif is worked traveling up from the base; the right half starts at the top, reversing the entire route of the first journey. You can turn the diagram upside-down to follow this reverse journey. In the sampler, this motif is followed by a simple needlewoven bar. The coiled bar and crossed coils are shown in **3B** of this lesson.

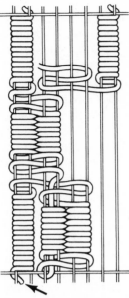

Stitch Diagram:
*Maneuver half a motif,
then reverse the process.*

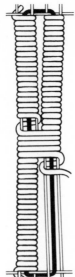

Stitch Diagram: *Add tension by using
additional supporting threads.*

Start this motif by coiling up one third of the distance from the base. Then needleweave back to the base, occupying the next two paired warps. After arriving at the base, pass the needle through the core of the left column and emerge one-third of the way up. Needleweave the first two pairs of warps another third of the way to the top, then coil the remaining distance to complete the first half of the motif. The right half starts with a coil descending from the top and reverses the first journey to the base.

When coils are overcast around paired warps, they often wiggle about because the tension of the warps is loosened. This waving motion is often used to create movement in designs. However, if the desired effect is straight, coiled bars, some control can be achieved by laying a working thread over the warps before coiling, fastening it to the foundation canvas above and below the opened areas. The coiled bars in this section of the sampler, and the crossed coils in the stitch diagram, are underlaid in this way. Work the motif in two journeys. Coil up the left pair of warps to the center, then pass over to the right pair and coil to the top. Start a second journey at the top of the left pair and coil down to the center. Coil around both pairs of warps a number of times and complete the journey, coiling down the right pair of warps.

STITCH 3B
CROSSED COILS

Sampler: *Employ coiled
bars to create patterns.*

Coiled warps, or coiling, is often used as a supplement to needleweaving. In this pattern, paired warps are coiled on either side of two crossing coils.

STITCH 3C
PATTERN NEEDLEWEAVING

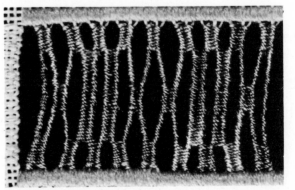

Sampler: *Organize the journeys.*

This border pattern is an example of how needle-weaving and coiling can be organized into a handsome repeat. You could use the same methods for a more contemporary, less formal pattern as well.

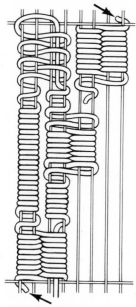

Stitch Diagram: *Work one segment at a time. Employ strategy.*

Start this pattern at the lower left and needleweave two pairs of warps a fifth of the way up. Then coil the first pair to one-fifth of the distance from the top and needleweave two pairs of warps once more to the very top. Pass the needle down through the core of the right column of needleweaving and coil the second pair of warps another fifth of the way down. Next, needleweave two pairs of warps for the central fifth of the journey, coil down the left pair of warps, and pass the needle through the core of the needleweaving at the bottom. Start again at the top by needleweaving, coil down to the central needleweaving, pass through the core of it, coil, then needleweave two pairs of warps at the lower edge. Start the next unit by needleweaving up from the base and passing to the left. After you have worked this much of the pattern, you will be able to complete the border by studying the accompanying photograph.

LESSON 4

CLUSTERS

A CORAL KNOTTED CLUSTERS

B WOVEN AND FESTOONED CLUSTERS

C REVERSE RIBBED WHEEL

I N addition to geometric, steplike arrangements of woven and coiled bars, needleweaving can be employed to group bundles of warps together into various shapes. In this lesson, a border is shown that is composed of bundles of five paired warps that are first clustered together at the center with coral knots. Each cluster is needlewoven at the top and bottom in a fan shape. Then, four festoon journeys are made across the borders, and coral knots are made at each paired warp of the clusters. After the fourth journey, or simultaneous with it, wheels are woven around the intersecting festoon and bundling threads between each cluster. This border is similar to the clustered bands seen in *Hemstitching* (Lesson 3), with the exception of the needleweaving. In subsequent lessons, additional shaping methods will be shown.

STITCH 4A

CORAL KNOTTED CLUSTERS

Sampler: *Group even bundles of warps together.*

Travel across the center of a band of withdrawn elements, collecting even groups of warps and tying them into bundles with coral knots.

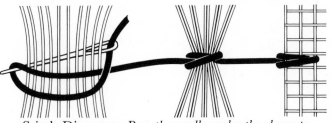

Stitch Diagram: *Pass the needle under the elements and the thread over and under the top of the needle.*

Start by making a coral knot at the center of the short side of the opened band. Use a waste knot to fasten on for the coral knot. Or, you can eliminate this coral knot and simply start with a waste knot, which can be fastened off on the backface after the band is completed. To work a coral knot: pass the needle under the canvas elements to be knotted, pass the working thread over the tip of the needle, and draw the needle through. Pull the thread taut to make a snug knot. Bundle all the clusters in the band and end with a coral knot on the far side, or fasten off on the backface. Employ a nonslippery working thread or run your thread through beeswax. Velvet thread is used in the sampler, and there are ten elements in each cluster.

STITCH 4B

WOVEN AND FESTOONED CLUSTERS

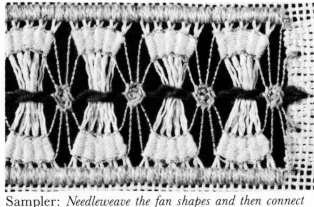

Sampler: *Needleweave the fan shapes and then connect them with festoons.*

The single elements in each cluster are now needlewoven in pairs at the top and bottom, and the weaving is worked to gently curve in a fan shape. The four festoon journeys all start at the right side and cross each other between the clusters as they scallop up and down across the border.

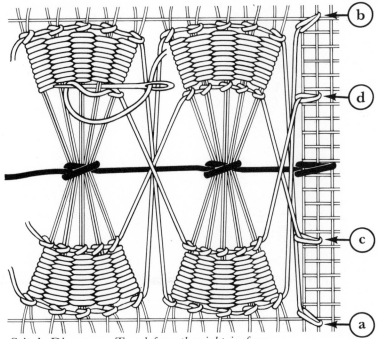

Stitch Diagram: *Travel from the right in four undulating journeys.*

Needleweave the segments individually, starting each at the bottom and needleweaving up toward the center. Turn the canvas to needleweave the upper segments. Work the festoons next. Start the first journey (**a**) at the lower right with a coral knot. Bring the thread up to the top edge and coral knot each pair of warps of the first cluster. Then bring the thread down to the bottom of the second cluster and coral knot each of these paired warps. Complete the first journey, swinging from the bottom of one cluster to the top of the next. Fasten off with a coral knot on the far side in the appropriate location on the edge. Work the remaining three serpentine journeys in alphabetical sequence with the stitch diagram. Once you have mastered the system of coral knot festoons, you can work the reverse ribbed wheel (**4C**) simultaneously with them in the last journey (**d**).

STITCH 4C
REVERSE RIBBED WHEEL

Sampler: *Employ the festoon threads as radiating warps.*

The intersecting festoon threads and the center bundling thread from the coral knotted clusters are gathered together with a coral knot to become radiating warps for a woven wheel. This reverse ribbed wheel is but one of various woven wheels; see *Hardanger* and *Hemstitching* for others. Whenever possible, wheels are woven as a continuous process with other techniques. However, we treat the procedure separately here to simplify things for the inexperienced open-work embroiderer.

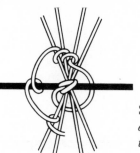

Stitch Diagram: *Pass ahead over two warps and then back under one.*

Start with a waste knot in the solid canvas, then make a coral knot that gathers all the intersecting threads snugly together into radiating warps. Pass the working thread under the clustered threads and emerge diagonally opposite on the frontface. Travel counterclockwise, passing over two warps and then retreating under one warp each time, making reversed backstitches. You can use beeswax to smooth a hairy working thread and produce a very clear woven pattern. Once you have completed several circular journeys, forming an appropriately-sized wheel, insert the needle into one of the reverse backstitches to fasten off on the backface. An alternate and economical method of moving from one wheel to the next is to overcast the bundling thread between the wheels, passing behind the woven clusters. If you are employing this method, fasten on at the right side behind the existing coral knot and work the first wheel; finish by fastening off at the far side after completing all of the wheels.

LESSON 5

SHAPES

A OPENING AND SECURING CURVED SHAPES

B OUTLINING WITH PEKINESE AND STEM STITCH

C ROUNDED SHAPES

D OTHER SHAPES

E MIRROR IMAGE BARS

F OVERLAPPED WEAVING

G SUBTLE CURVES

UNTIL this lesson, all the opened shapes have had straight edges. Now a method is demonstrated for opening a circle in the sampler in which the elements are also withdrawn from one direction. A second technique is shown at the same time for securing these withdrawn elements by tacking them down on the backface and then outlining the opened space with the decorative Pekinese and outline stem stitches. In addition to rounding opened spaces, you can needleweave in rounded shapes as well. This is demonstrated by the two flower shapes inside the center circle of the sampler. The central vertical elements are worked in coiled bars that represent stems; the "ribbons" tied around the flower stems are an example of overlapped needleweaving. Finally, freely made curves are explained. Use your imagination to create varied open spaces in pleasing shapes.

STITCH 5A

OPENING AND SECURING CURVED SHAPES

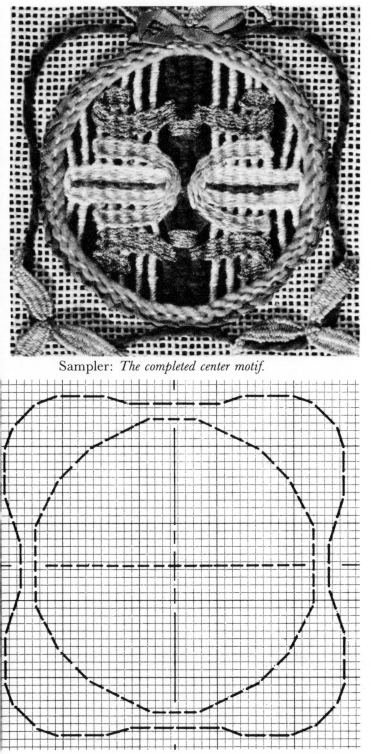

Sampler: *The completed center motif.*

Pattern Diagram: *The circle of backstitches becomes part of the Pekinese edge.*

Outline a curved shape with backstitches before withdrawing any elements. This is a very practical canvas technique because the stitches can be geometrically placed to make smooth curves. The overlapping backstitches on the backface of the canvas make a smooth, firm edge that keeps the withdrawn elements from slipping while you are tacking them down. In the sampler, these backstitches become part of the Pekinese stitch on the frontface. If you do not want the backstitches to be decorative, make them with either a matching withdrawn canvas element or a sewing thread that matches the canvas. Use the two center lines in the above graph to place the circle of backstitches. Use the *vertical* center line as a guide for cutting the elements.

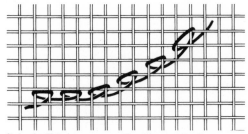

Stitch Diagram **a**: *Outline with the backstitch on the frontface.*

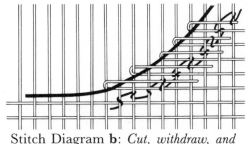

Stitch Diagram **b**: *Cut, withdraw, and tack the elements down on the backface.*

No tension should be used when you backstitch around the curved shape. Travel counterclockwise, passing back over two elements on the frontface and passing forward under four elements on the backface (**a**). After completing the backstitch outline, turn the work to the backface. Cut the elements to be withdrawn midway between the two sides of the shape. Use the *vertical* center line of the circle as a cutting line; you are withdrawing wefts within this shape. Withdraw and secure the elements in one quarter of the shape at a time to prevent confusion. Withdraw to the backstitch outline (**b**). With a sharp needle and sewing thread, tack each element down just beyond the backstitch line. Trim away the excess lengths of canvas elements.

STITCH 5B

OUTLINING WITH PEKINESE AND STEM STITCH

Sampler: *Interlace the backstitches with Pekinese stitches; then outline them with stem stitch.*

Pekinese stitches are a series of loops that never enter the foundation fabric but interlace between pairs of backstitches on the frontface. They are particularly attractive when they are worked in a heavier thread than the underlying backstitches. In the sampler, veloura is used to interlace linen stitches. The outline stem stitch, used just outside of the Pekinese stitch on the sampler, is worked with a narrow ribbon instead of thread. The outline stem is used again for the rounded square shape that frames the circle and around the perimeter of the sampler inside of the inner padded satin stitch border.

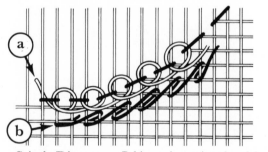

Stitch Diagram: *Pekinese is an interlaced backstitch, and outline stem is a reversed backstitch.*

To work the loops of the Pekinese border (**a**), travel in a counterclockwise direction. Come to the frontface between two canvas elements of a backstitch on the outside of the circle, as in the diagram. By starting in this precise way, you can close the ring of the circle neatly when you finish there. Slide the needle under the backstitch to the right. With the tip of the needle pointing into the curve, draw up the thread. Slide the needle under the backstitch on the left with the top of the needle pointing down and outside of the curve; draw up the thread. Continue in this manner, making a

ring on the inside of the curve and overlapping the threads on the outside. Hold your thumb on the overlapping threads as you make each new ring to maintain an even and gentle curve. To work the outline stem stitch (**b**), travel in the same direction again, holding the working thread above the needle. Essentially, you are making small backstitches over two elements on the backface as you move ahead four elements on the frontface. You can, in fact, make these backstitches on the backface, but be sure to hold the thread in a consistent position on the frontface.

STITCH 5C

ROUNDED SHAPES

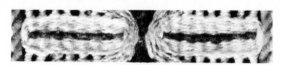

Sampler: *Add a weft element to serve as an axis.*

To needleweave in the round, add a new weft element to act as an axis. In the sampler, a veloura thread divides the circle in half, following the horizontal center line of the master pattern, and becomes the axis for two oval flower bud shapes. These flower buds are worked over eight paired warps to the left and right of a yet unworked pair of center warps.

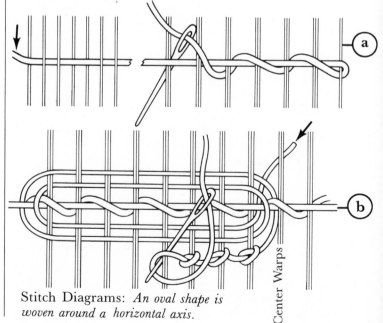

Stitch Diagrams: *An oval shape is woven around a horizontal axis.*

To create the horizontal axis of the central circle, fasten onto a single warp at its perimeter on the backface. Come to the frontface and weave over and under pairs of warps to the far side. Loop around another single canvas element in the foundation and overcast back, reversing the weave of the first journey (**a**). Fasten off on the backface. To needleweave the left oval shape (**b**), weave around the eight warps to the left of the central pair of warps in the circle, using the diameter as an axis. In the sampler, this is done four times. Complete the oval with a journey of coral knots around it. Work the oval on the other side by traveling in the opposite direction. Leave the center pair of warps empty.

STITCH 5D
OTHER SHAPES

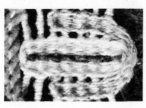

Sampler: *Use the axis as a pivot to change direction.*

Once an axis around which to needleweave is established, many shapes can be produced. In the central flower motif of the sampler, a U shape is woven over six warps above and below the bud to create petals.

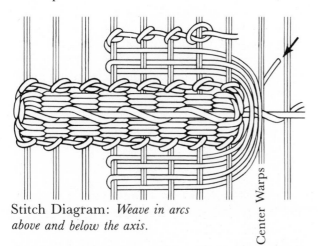

Stitch Diagram: *Weave in arcs above and below the axis.*

Center Warps

Start the U shape on one side of the center warps at the axis and needleweave in an arc traveling below and above the oval for several journeys. Complete the shape with an outline of coral knots. Reverse the procedure on the other side of the center warps.

STITCH 5E
MIRROR IMAGE BARS

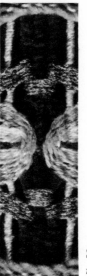

Sampler: *Reverse the pattern north and south, or east and west.*

Columns of coils are frequently used in needleweaving for additional texture. In the central circle of the sampler, three pairs of warps are coiled and woven in a pattern that reverses itself above and below the horizontal axis.

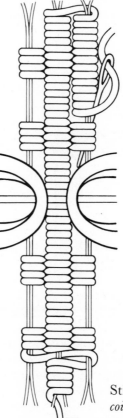

Stitch Diagram: *Complete this coiled and woven pattern in three continuous journeys.*

To work the coiled and woven center warps of the circle, start at the base of the central paired warps. Coil upwards one-fourth of the way to the center. Then needleweave the three pairs of warps four times. Coil up the center again the same number of times as before. Needleweave again over the three pairs of warps and coil to the center. Complete the rest of the journey by simply reversing these steps. Then make a downward journey on the right side, coiling all the vacant warps and passing through the woven cores. Make a final journey upward, filling the vacant warps on the left side.

several more journeys following the same procedure. End by fastening on the backface. Turn the canvas and work the other side in the same manner. The warps that are left vacant should be coiled, to hold the pattern firmly in place.

STITCH 5G
SUBTLE CURVES

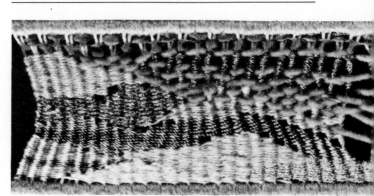

Sampler: *First sketch the curves on paper.*

Try working an opened area with freely made subtle curves of needleweaving. You can start by placing a sheet of tracing paper over the opened space and sketching some gentle, flowing lines, using a pencil. Ink over the most pleasing ones. Then tape the tracing paper under the opening and lightly transfer the patterns onto the warps with disappearing ink. Remove the pattern and develop the needleweaving further as you go along. Employ texture, color, shading, tension, and imagination. You can remove the ink marks as you approach them; eventually, you may want to eliminate the tracing process and work from a sketch alone.

STITCH 5F
OVERLAPPED WEAVING

Sampler: *Create a dimensional quality.*

By overlapping some of the needleweaving when you change the direction of a journey, you can produce raised effects. The "ribbon" shown here actually appears to turn as it changes direction.

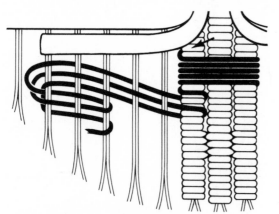

Stitch Diagram: *Each return journey lies next to the path of the preceding one.*

Begin by passing around the three pairs of needlewoven warps in the center. Weave to the left in a sweeping arc over five paired warps; reverse your direction and weave to the right in another arc over three warps. Then make the return journey, tracing the route on the stitch diagram. Make

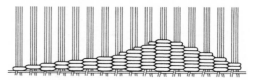

Stitch Diagram: *Increase and decrease gradually; split warps when necessary.*

In this stitch diagram, notice how a subtle curve is achieved by gradually decreasing the number of warps that are needlewoven as you ascend. Some of the paired warps are split to make the transition even more gradual.

LESSON 6

SURFACE NEEDLEWEAVING

A LAYING SURFACE WARPS AND
SHAPING A LEAF

ADD a bold third dimension to any embroidery by throwing warps on the surface—that is, creating additional warps with thread—and needleweaving them in a variety of shapes. In this lesson, a method is shown that was devised by Patti B. Russell for the Basket of Flowers tray cloth (see *Pulled Canvas* for the master pattern for it), in which the needlewoven leaves appear to be growing quite naturally. Patti also worked the leaves on the needleweaving sampler. Although leaves are a perfect subject for this technique, you can employ it wherever you want a sculptured quality. In *Filet,* there is another lesson on needleweaving warps made of threads that are stretched on the surface of the canvas.

STITCH 6A

LAYING SURFACE WARPS AND SHAPING A LEAF

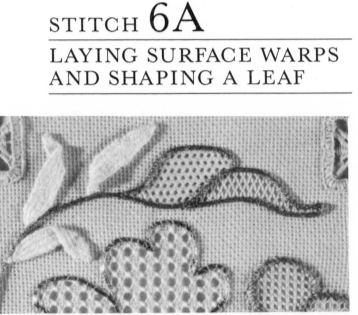

This detail comes from the Basket of Flowers tray cloth (see photo page 10).

Three of the *Open Canvas* techniques are employed in the Basket of Flowers—needleweaving (in the leaves, as shown here), hemstitching (in the border), and pulled canvas work (used in the basket, flowers, and berries).

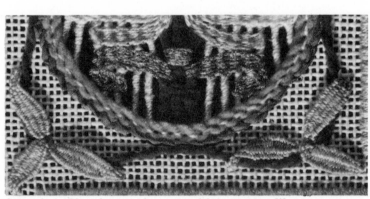

Sampler: *Place leaves wherever and however you like.*

In this technique, only the base ends of the new warps are fastened down. The far ends are temporarily held in position and are permanently secured after the needleweaving is completed. This open end gives you the freedom to twist and place the newly woven leaf or other shape into any location you like.

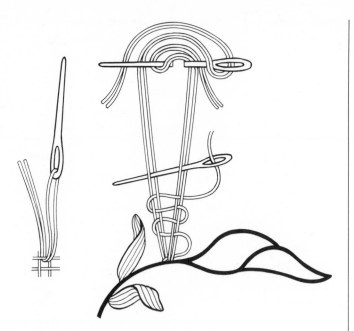

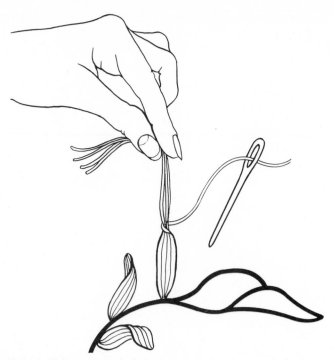

Stitch Diagram **a**: *Draw half of a doubled thread through the mesh.*

Stitch Diagram **b**: *Temporarily secure the ends around a needle. Shape by varying the tension.*

Stitch Diagram **c**: *Release the leaf and place it in a pleasing position.*

Stitch Diagram **d**: *Sink the working thread and fasten off.*

Thread a needle with single thread and even the ends. Draw just one half of the doubled thread through the mesh in position for a leaf (**a**). Cut the thread at the eye of the needle, leaving two pairs of thread of equal lengths on the frontface of the canvas. Slant the four threads in the general direction that you want the leaf to go. Secure the thread ends temporarily but very securely by wrapping them around an inserted T pin, tapestry needle (**b**), or even one of the tacks that hold your canvas to the frame. These four threads are now stretched as warps on the surface ready for needleweaving. Secure another working thread on the backface at the base of the four warps and come to the frontface. Start the needleweaving, at first very snugly; gradually loosen the tension to add breadth to the leaf. As you approach the tip, gradually tighten the tension to round it off.

Having arrived at the tip of the leaf, unwind the warp threads. Hold the four warps between fingers and thumb. Place the leaf in a pleasing position on the stem (**c**). Then sink the threaded needle into the canvas backface (**d**). Pull this thread taut and secure it behind the leaf. Feed the four warp threads through a needle and sink and secure them on the backface. To keep the leaf in the desired position, it is often necessary to secure it further by taking an extra stitch or two at intervals along its edges. When doing so, place the stitches so that they disappear into the needleweaving.

LESSON 7

EDGING

A PADDED SATIN BORDER

B BLANKET AND BUTTONHOLE EDGING

THIS lesson completes the needleweaving sampler with a padded, light-reflecting satin stitch border worked over the long edges of the opened rectangles and the four sides of the opened border. A technique is provided for binding the outer edges with the help of some acid-free glue to prevent unraveling. The outer three rows of canvas are then folded back and the satin border completed. In addition, blanket and buttonhole stitches are worked over the satin stitches, contributing added height and texture.

STITCH 7A
PADDED SATIN BORDER

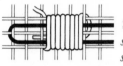

Sampler: *This border contrasts nicely with the needleweaving textures.*

Use a padded satin border to create a smooth, light-reflecting frame for the needlewoven textures. In the sampler, three satin stitches are carefully placed on top of long horizontal threads between each of the vertical canvas elements.

Stitch Diagram: *Padding supplies coverage and bulk for the straight stitches on the canvas.*

Lay two or more matching lengths of working thread along the canvas elements to be covered with satin stitches. Use extra padding threads wherever elements have been withdrawn to maintain an even surface. Cover this padding with satin stitches. Work more satins than fit comfortably; they should belly out on each side between the vertical elements to cover them nicely. Feed the stitches in carefully, poking them with the tip of the needle to line them up side by side. Trim the excess canvas at the corners.

PADDED SATIN EDGE

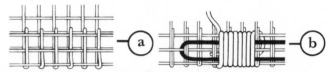

Stitch Diagrams: *The padded satin border can also be used as an outer edging.*

When using the padded satin border as an outer edging, first make a neat, finished, flexible edging with the help of some acid-free glue. Remove the completed work from the frame and apply a narrow line of glue along the sixth canvas element from the border on all four sides. Use a toothpick or awl as an applicator. The glue dries very quickly. This will allow you to cut away the excess canvas without fear of unraveling. Now, fold back three rows of canvas to the backface (**a**) and work the satin stitch edge (**b**).

STITCH 7B
BLANKET AND BUTTONHOLE EDGING

Sampler: *This stitch enriches a padded satin edge.*

A second edging of blanket and buttonhole stitches can be superimposed over the padded satin edge. Blanket stitches are, in fact, spaced buttonhole stitches. A more interesting border is achieved by varying the spacing.

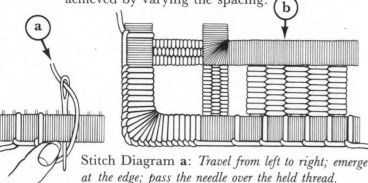

Stitch Diagram **a**: *Travel from left to right; emerge at the edge; pass the needle over the held thread.*

Stitch Diagram **b**: *Space the buttonhole stitches widely on the long sides and ease them in closely around the corners.*

To work a buttonhole edge, travel from left to right with the needle emerging at the looped base, or festoon, of the stitch. Start a row by emerging on the frontface at the edge. Hold the working thread with the thumb of one hand and insert the needle into the backface at the top of the stitch with the working hand (**a**). Emerge and pass the needle over the held thread and draw it through to make the first stitch. Continue, holding the thread for each stitch, passing over it on emerging and creating a series of festoons at the edge. To work a blanket and buttonhole edge as in the sampler (**b**), position the buttonhole stitches between each pair of warps on top of the padded satin edging, except where the pairs of warps make the narrowest bars. Gently round the corners by working close buttonhole stitches. Ease them in to lie neatly side by side.

LESSON 8

FREELY WORKED NEEDLEWEAVING

A WITHDRAWING ALTERNATE ELEMENTS FROM ONE DIRECTION

B WITHDRAWING ALTERNATE ELEMENTS FROM TWO DIRECTIONS

DON'T look for examples of this lesson in the needleweaving sampler; they aren't there. These techniques are included in *Needleweaving* to enable you to experiment with withdrawn element work. They primarily involve canvas preparation, although some examples of needlewoven work using these prepared canvases are shown; you can

either try to copy this work or create your own, using the techniques you have learned in this section of *The Open Canvas.*

The idea of withdrawing specific elements in order to produce various levels of warps on which to work was first brought to my attention by Edith John's book, *Experimental Embroidery.* The examples I have chosen to illustrate provide you with either two or three levels of elements on which to work. The first (**8A**) involves withdrawing every other element from only one direction, producing—as if by magic—three levels of warps on which to needleweave. The second (**8B**) involves withdrawing alternate elements from both the horizontal and vertical directions, producing two levels of warps. This section also includes a variation in which you deliberately change the alternation once in each direction, producing two interlocking layers.

This may all sound extremely intimidating, but you should try working it out on some spare canvas. Although the directions seem somewhat complicated, they are remarkably easy to accomplish. And these withdrawn element variations can be the foundation of some truly lovely and unusual needlewoven designs.

TECHNIQUE 8A

WITHDRAWING ALTERNATE ELEMENTS FROM ONE DIRECTION

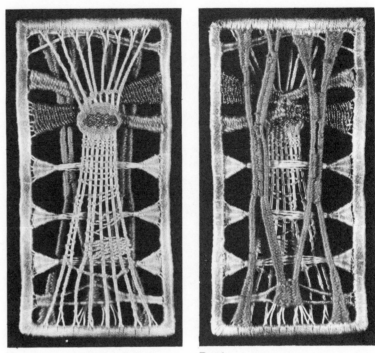

Front   Back

An example of three levels of needleweaving on a prepared canvas.

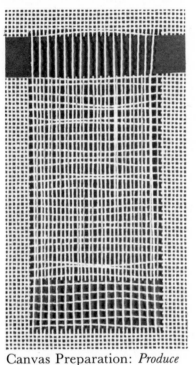

Canvas Preparation: *Produce three levels of warps.*

To produce three levels of warps, cut and withdraw only alternate horizontal elements. In this unworked canvas, each alternate horizontal element was first cut in the center. Then each half was withdrawn to the long edge and cut again. A line of acid-free glue was laid along both long cut sides of the opened space. The withdrawn elements could also have been woven back into the sides or tacked down there on the backface.

When you change the structure of the foundation canvas from a single layer of warps to three levels of warps, be prepared to take advantage of them. It is important to plan the order of work so that you can get to the middle level with some degree of ease. This piece was worked on 12/inch white mono canvas with pearl cotton and metal thread. Fasten the canvas on a stretcher after the elements are withdrawn. The top layer was worked first, and in the brightest colors. Some white canvas was left uncovered to add light value. The third level was worked next, most of it from the backface. It was worked in the darkest color, to keep it in the background. This exposed the middle layer, making it easy to work, partly from the frontface and partly from the backface. The piece was then removed from the stretcher to work the padded satin edging that is demonstrated in Lesson 7. The finished size of this piece is 3 inches by 6½ inches.

TECHNIQUE 8B

WITHDRAWING ALTERNATE ELEMENTS FROM TWO DIRECTIONS

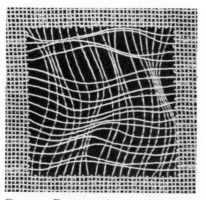

Canvas Preparation **a**: *Alternate elements are withdrawn evenly from two directions.*

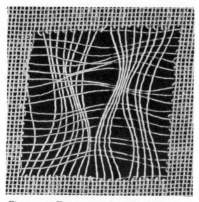

Canvas Preparation **b**: *Two center vertical elements are withdrawn; otherwise, same as* **a**.

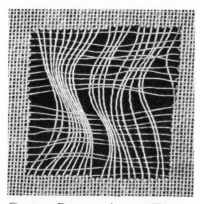

Canvas Preparation **c**: *Two center verticals and two center horizontals are withdrawn; otherwise, same as* **a**.

These three methods of withdrawing elements were first demonstrated in Edith John's *Experimental Embroidery.* I prepared these canvases five years ago, and since then, the warps have become misshapen in a most delightful manner. Their gentle waving motion immediately suggests patterns for needleweaving. A light misting and a little neglect would probably produce similar results. In the first example (**a**), alternate elements were withdrawn evenly from both directions. This resulted in two levels of warps running in opposite directions. Both are worked as warps, although one is actually made up of weft elements. In the second canvas (**b**), the two center vertical elements were withdrawn; then, working out from the center, alternate single vertical elements were withdrawn. In the horizontal direction, every other element was withdrawn. This resulted in half of the horizontal elements staying on the upper level and half dropping to the lower level. In the third example (**c**), the two center vertical *and* horizontal elements were withdrawn; then, moving out from these central axes, alternate elements were withdrawn in both directions. This resulted in an interlocking pattern.

An example of layered needleweaving.

The ground for this piece was prepared as shown in the third photograph (**c**), by withdrawing the two central vertical *and* horizontal elements, and then continuing to withdraw every other element in both directions. It was worked with 6-cord crochet cotton, silk, and metal threads on 13/inch cream linen mono canvas. The finished size is 4 inches by 4 inches.

BOOK THREE

HEMSTITCHING

Elements are withdrawn from one direction, cut, and secured. The long sides of opened bands are then stabilized by grouping the remaining warps with a variety of simple stitches. Wider spaces, and the completely open spaces that result when intersecting bands are withdrawn, are filled with additional openwork embroidery.

CONTENTS

INTRODUCTION

These lessons demonstrate a collection of hemstitching techniques on the bands and borders of two samplers. Sampler I serves as an introduction to some basic methods. Sampler II provides a larger, more comprehensive survey.

Hemstitching involves the grouping of warps in opened bands. This can be accomplished in one or two stages: primary or secondary groupings. In primary grouping, the warps are collected only once; in secondary grouping, you regroup the primary warps once more. Lesson 2 deals with primary groups, which can either be used alone or set the stage for the secondary groups of Lessons 3, 4, and 5. Systems are developed in Lesson 6 for filling the open squares that are the inevitable result of opened bands crossing each other. Since *Hemstitching* deals mainly with bands that serve as borders, the open squares are shown as corners. These corners are filled with needlewoven patterns worked over radiating warps. The methods differ from those covered in *Needleweaving*, where the warps are vertical or horizontal. Lesson 7 consists of two methods for throwing independent circular warps over completely open squares. In Lesson 8, elements are withdrawn to establish a four-sided edge for Sampler II.

A THIMBLEFUL OF HISTORY

Hemstitching is an appropriate term to describe the bands and borders that have been used to embellish the ends of cloth for centuries. Examples of embroidered open bands have been found in ancient Egyptian tombs, but because of the fragility of the loosely woven opened linen fabric, little remains. The earliest work employed mainly gold and silver thread. By the end of the sixteenth century, when the making of linen thread was perfected, the skill and delicacy of withdrawn element work developed rapidly. These early forms were classified as *punto tirato,* and included both deflected-element work (see *Pulled Canvas*), where the elements were drawn together, and work in which elements were withdrawn from one direction only. In 1880 a taste for "drawn work" was revived, and it continued to

be popular until after the turn of the century. Ladies' magazines and embroidery books of this period offered elaborate patterns and instructions for hemstitched bands and borders for garments and home furnishings. These fine, complicated patterns are still a source of pleasure and inspiration.

The Teneriffe squares of Lesson 7 are named for the island of Tenerife in the Canary Islands (the embroidery retains an older spelling of the name). It is said that the current method of employing a circle of pins on a firm pincushion to form a web of stretched threads originated there in the seventeenth century. Teneriffe lace evolved from the embroidery employed in the opened squares of intersecting bands of hemstitching. The treatment of these opened squares became particularly elaborate in sixteenth-century Spain. This ultimately resulted in a kind of openwork embroidery that was made *without* a fabric ground. A web of embroidery threads became the warps for stitches; the result was an open, lacy circle of *punto in aria,* or true, lace—embroidery with no foundation whatsoever. Because of its shape, this "free" embroidery became known as *sol,* for sun, or *rueda,* for wheel. These techniques were brought to South America, where, particularly in Peru, spectacularly beautiful work was produced. These elaborate Teneriffe circles are now an inspiration for the corners of hemstitched borders.

From the turn of the century until recently, hemstitching was used to stitch hems on fine linens. Several parallel elements were withdrawn at a short distance from the final edge of the fabric. The remaining edge of fabric was double-folded back to meet the withdrawn band. A line of stitches was worked, bundling small, even groups of remaining elements while attaching them to the folded edge. Small open spaces were thus left between the clusters. The hemstitching was done on the backface so that the corners could be neatly mitered. This decorative finish has now been replaced by machine hemstitching.

SOME NEEDLE POINTS

Today, the use of hemstitching is purely decorative and serves no practical function. The narrow bands of Lesson **2**, however, are composed of variations of the hemstitches employed in turning hems on fine linens. In the subsequent lessons, where wider bands are opened, these same stitches from Lesson **2** are employed to stabilize the edges on the long sides of the opened bands to prevent the remaining wefts of the unopened canvas from floating into the opened band. Employ sufficient tension in working each stitch unit to draw the warps together within the group. All of the methods shown in these lessons can be used in bands and shapes in any position on the canvas, to embellish garments and home furnishings.

WORKBASKET SUPPLIES

As with other forms of open work, drawn work has traditionally been done in white, ecru, and pale pastels. However, color has entered the world of textiles and fibers as a result of advancements in dyeing processes, and our tastes have kept pace with science. There are no limitations on the use of color other than those of artistic consideration, particularly if you are willing to dye or paint your own canvases and dye your own working threads. Otherwise, you are limited to what is commercially available.

CANVAS
Use only mono canvas, as its elements can easily be withdrawn from one direction by unweaving. The even weave of canvas is a great asset in bundling even groups of warps. Use fine meshes for delicate lace effects and coarser ones for bold,

dramatic work. Canvas is available at this writing in white and tan cotton, cream linen, and apricot toile. There is also a small range of colored congress canvas.

THREADS
Use strong twisted threads for the major work. These include linen, DMC embroidery and cutwork thread (coton à broder), 6-cord crochet cotton (cordonnet), Cebelia crochet cotton, silk twist, and any special thread for lace making. Textured threads for embellishment can include Veloura, Bella Donna Rayon, or any threads used for surface work.

STRETCHERS
Use interlocking stretcher strips, and tack the work down as taut as possible. This method makes it convenient to remove the canvas from the frame at various stages of work to open additional areas. By not opening the entire canvas at one time, you retain more tension on the stretched canvas.

NEEDLES AND OTHER TOOLS
You will need tapestry needles in sizes to suit the weights of the thread. Beeswax can be used to strengthen or control unruly threads.

ACID-FREE GLUE
This is a fairly new product that should meet the approval of textile conservationists. Since it contains no acid, there should be no side effects to its use; it dries in a pliable condition, is colorless, and it does the job of securing canvas elements or working threads. I have found it to be extremely useful and suggest using it for open canvas work. See Suppliers for sources.

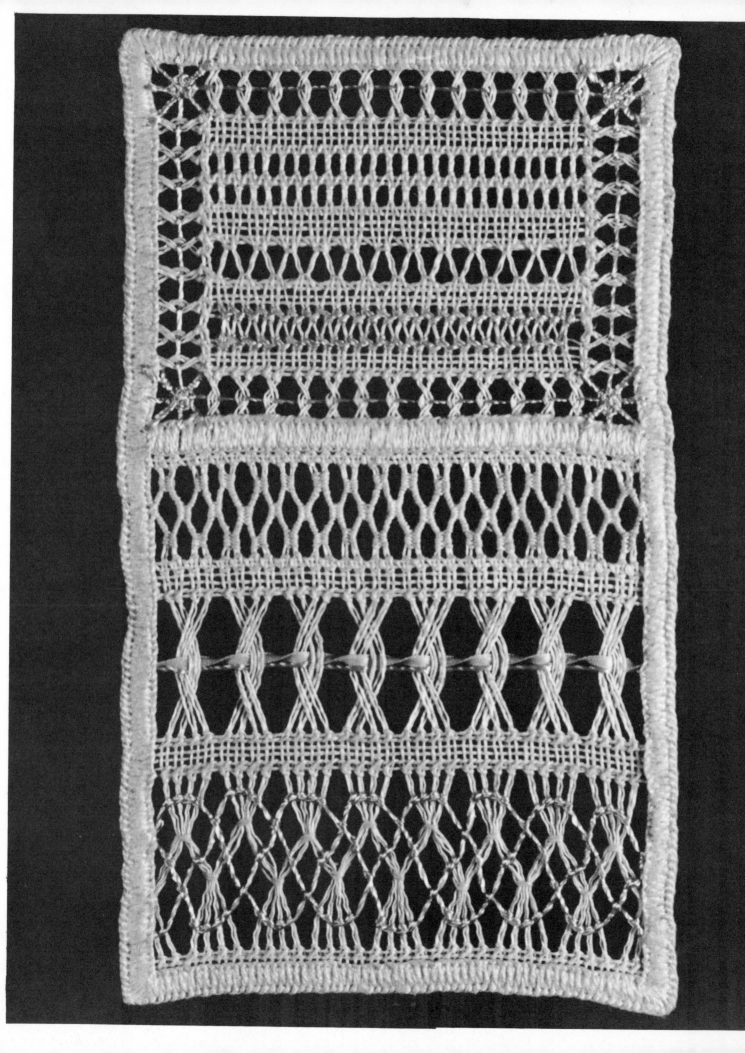

KEY TO STITCHES AND THREADS
Sampler I

Sampler I is worked with linen and rayon thread on 13/inch cream linen mono canvas. The finished size is 5¼ inches by 9½ inches. See the accompanying key to identify the stitches and threads. The bold numbers with letters refer to the lesson and diagram where each stitch or pattern is located in *Hemstitching*. The bold italic numbers refer to the threads listed under Materials Employed.

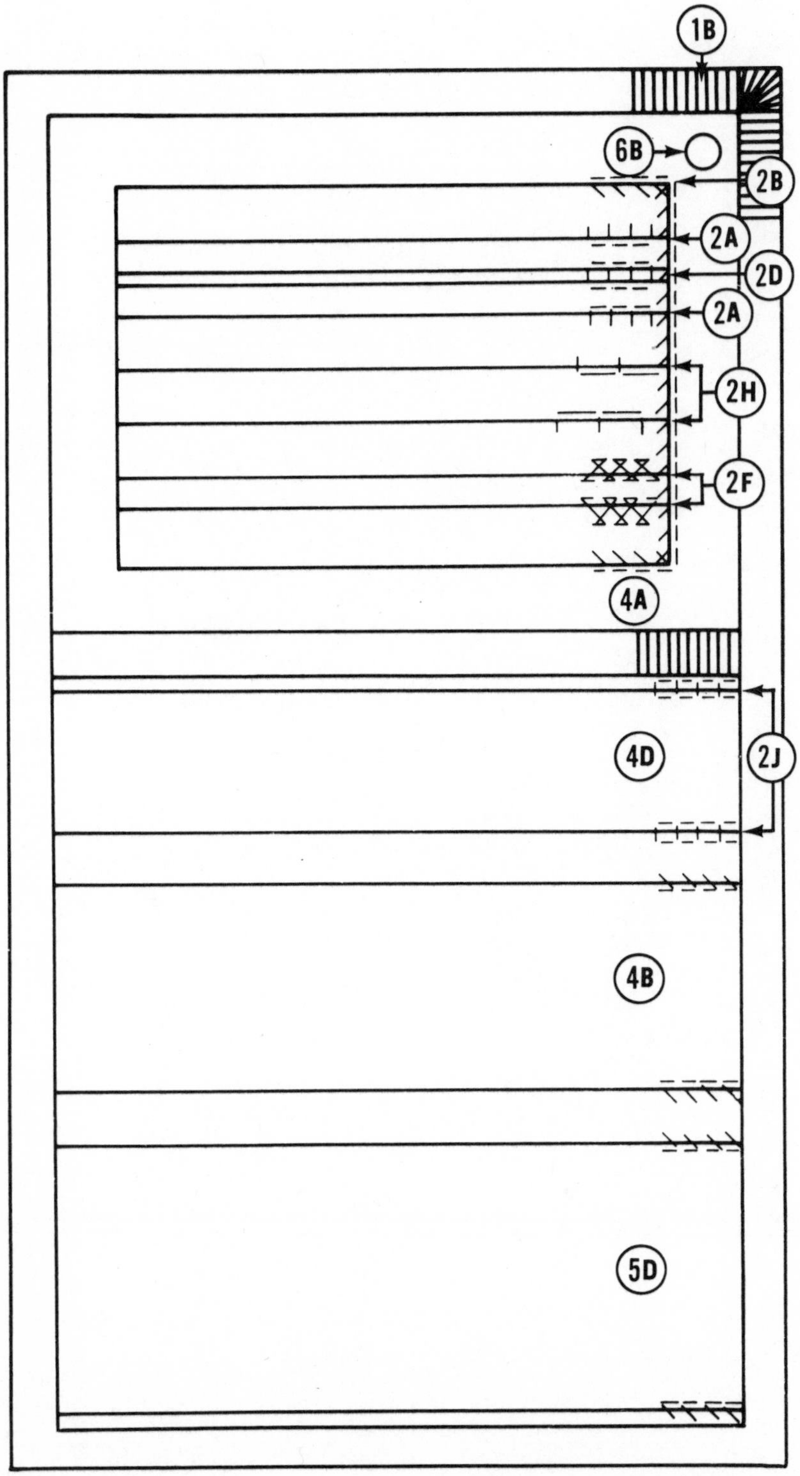

1B Double Buttonhole Edge, *2*
2A Simple Straight, *1*
2B Simple Slanted, *1*
2D Double, *1*
2F Herringbone, *3*
2H Serpentine, *1*
2J Four-Sided, *1*
4A Two Warps Inverted Once, *3*
4B Four Warps Inverted Once, *3, 4*
4D Interwoven Serpentine Bars, *1*
5D Concealed Serpentine Knotting, *1, 3*
6B Continuous Spider, *3*

MATERIALS EMPLOYED

CANVAS
13/inch cream linen mono; 9 inches wide by 13 inches high; edges bound

THREADS
1 Nordiska Swedish linen, 328 light yellow
2 Square Sale Irish linen, size 10/2 maize
3 Bella Donna rayon, 806 peach
4 Silk ribbon, ⅛-inch wide, light yellow

NEEDLES
Tapestry 18, 20

STRETCHER STRIPS
1 pair 9-inch, 1 pair 13-inch

Sampler I

KEY TO STITCHES AND THREADS
Sampler II

Sampler II is worked with embroidery and cutwork cotton, crochet cotton, and Veloura nylon on 18/inch apricot toile mono canvas. The finished size is 10½ inches by 10½ inches. See the accompanying key to identify the stitches and threads. The bold numbers with letters refer to the lesson and diagram where each stitch or pattern is located in *Hemstitching*. The bold italic numbers refer to the threads listed under Materials Employed.

1C Padded Buttonhole Edge, *1*
2A Simple Straight, *2*
2B Simple Slanted, *2*
2C Ladder, *2*
2D Double, *2*
2E Stem, *2, 5*
2F Herringbone, *2*
2G Interlaced, *2*
2H Serpentine, *2*
2I Serpentine Bars, *2*
3A Coral Knot Clusters, *4*
3B Coral Festoons, *4*
3C Ribbed Wheels on Clusters, *2, 3*
3D Coral Festoon Variation, *4*
3E Woven Wheel on Cluster, *2, 3*
4A Two Warps Inverted Once, *4, 5*
4C Two Warps Inverted Twice, *4, 5*
5A Double Coral Knot, *4*
5B Netting with Wheels, *4, 2*

5C Serpentine Knotting, *4, 5*
6A Simple Spider, *2*
6C Pinwheel, *4*
6D Fan, *2, 3, 4*
6E Butterfly, *1, 2, 3, 4*
7A Needlewoven Bars, *4*
7B Single Web with Center Wheel and Circle of Little Wheels, *4, 2*
7C Knotted Spiral, *4, 2*
7E Interlaced Double Web, *4, 2*
7F Woven Flower, *4, 2*
8A Four-sided Edge, *2*

MATERIALS EMPLOYED

CANVAS
18/inch apricot toile mono; 14 inches by 14 inches; edges bound

THREADS
1 DMC Embroidery and Cutwork, size 16, 353 peach
2 DMC Embroidery and Cutwork, size 16, 3326 pink
3 DMC Embroidery and Cutwork, size 16, 741 orange
4 DMC Cordonnet Crochet cotton—6-cord, size 10, white
5 Veloura 406 dusty rose

NEEDLES
Tapestry 18, 20, 24
Crewel 8

STRETCHER STRIPS
2 pairs 14-inch

ACID-FREE GLUE
Jade #403 PVA adhesive

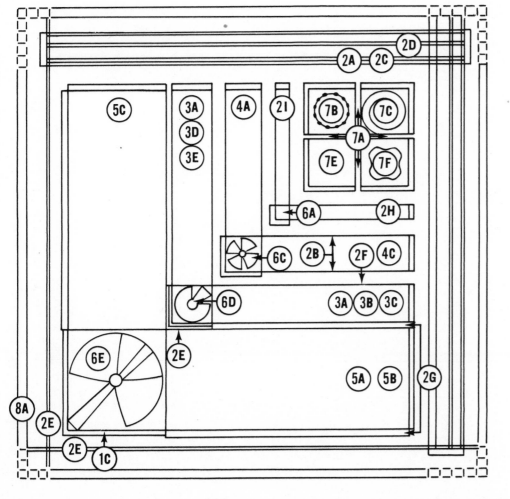

ampler II

LESSON 1

CANVAS PREPARATION

MASTER PATTERN, SAMPLER I

MASTER PATTERN, SAMPLER II

A CUTTING, WITHDRAWING, AND REWEAVING ELEMENTS

B BUTTONHOLE EDGES, SINGLE AND DOUBLE

C BUTTONHOLE EDGE, PADDED

THIS first lesson in canvas preparation sets the stage for the hemstitching in the lessons that follow. A plan is important for this work, since you must allow sufficient space for the various stitches. With an accurate plan, you will be able to provide ample numbers of warps to work rich patterns within the bands and borders. A master pattern is included for each of the two samplers, along with instructions for transferring them onto canvas. Each sampler offers a different method of securing the edges of the cut and withdrawn elements. These methods are supplied especially for open canvas work, where a simple buttonhole edge is not always sufficiently secure or dense enough for a canvas's large mesh openings and comparatively coarse elements. Sampler I demonstrates a double buttonhole edge, and Sampler II a padded buttonhole edge. All of the work, including preparation, can be done with the canvas on the stretcher frame. But if you find this awkward, prepare the canvas off the stretcher, and return it to work the hemstitching.

MASTER PATTERN, SAMPLER I

Use long basting stitches to locate the center lines on the canvas, providing matching reference positions with the master pattern. The heavy bands of lines around the sampler and the dividing band of heavy lines indicate a double buttonhole edging. Since the canvas is fairly coarse in Sampler I, the elements are cut and secured in limited areas at a time. Cut and withdraw the elements in the top section first (see **1A**, Canvas Diagram **a**). Then reweave the cut ends, as in **1A**, Canvas Diagram **b**. You will be left with an open square in each corner. Now, withdraw the narrow bands within the top square section to within two vertical elements from the opened side borders. Weave these

elements a short distance down the remaining narrow side strips of canvas; you will work over them as you hemstitch around the square border following Stitch Diagram **2B**. Work the wide band of double buttonhole stitches that divides the two sections of the sampler (Stitch Diagram **1B**), and the narrow bands of hemstitching shown in **2A**, **2B**, **2D**, **2F**, and **2H**. Open the wide bands and hemstitch the long edges (**2B** and **2J**). Then work the square border shown in **4A** and **6B**. Complete bands **4B**, **4D**, and **5D**. Bind the outer edges with the double buttonhole edge shown in **1B**, and cut away the excess canvas.

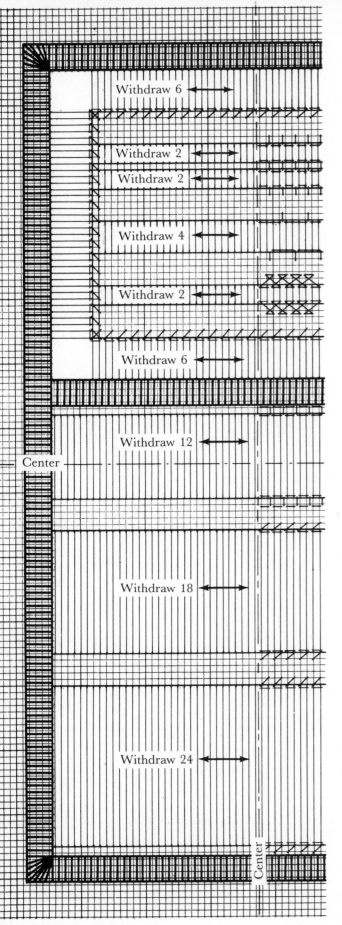

Withdraw 6

Withdraw 2

Withdraw 2

Withdraw 4

Withdraw 2

Withdraw 6

Withdraw 12

Center

Withdraw 18

Withdraw 24

Center

Master Pattern, Sampler I

MASTER PATTERN, SAMPLER II

Use long basting stitches to locate the center lines on the canvas and provide matching reference positions with the master pattern. Once you have withdrawn the narrow bands, remove the basting. Notice that the two narrow bands of stem stitches shown at **2E** are withdrawn to the outer edges of the sampler. All the other bands are bound at their short ends with buttonhole stitches. Cut, withdraw, and secure all the bands as described in **1A** and **1C**. Do not cut and withdraw elements from the four open squares for Teneriffe lace until you reach Lesson **7**. Prepare these squares just prior to working them to prevent canvas distortion. The use of acid-free glue is recommended at the cut ends of the opened bands before buttonholing them. This step is not essential, but it will provide extra strength so the edges won't unravel. You can do this neatly on the backface using an awl or toothpick as an applicator. Simply lay a line of glue along the cut edge. Start the hemstitching by working all the narrow bands and primary groupings of Lesson **2** first. Work the rest of the sampler following the lessons in sequence.

TECHNIQUE 1A
CUTTING AND WITH-DRAWING ELEMENTS

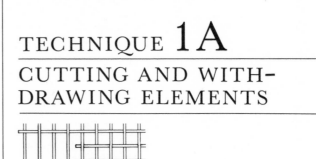

Canvas Diagram **a**: *Cut the horizontal element midway and pluck it out as desired.*

In the center of the band to be opened, cut the canvas elements to be withdrawn. With an awl or tapestry needle, pluck the element out on both sides of the cut to provide the desired space or number of warps in the opened band. You can secure the cut ends in various ways. Weave them back into the canvas (**b**), as in Sampler I. You can also cut the elements at the far ends of the band and secure the edges with buttonhole stitches, as shown in **1C**. Or, you can cut the elements and reinforce the edge with a line of acid-free glue on the backface before buttonholing, as suggested for the opened bands of Sampler II.

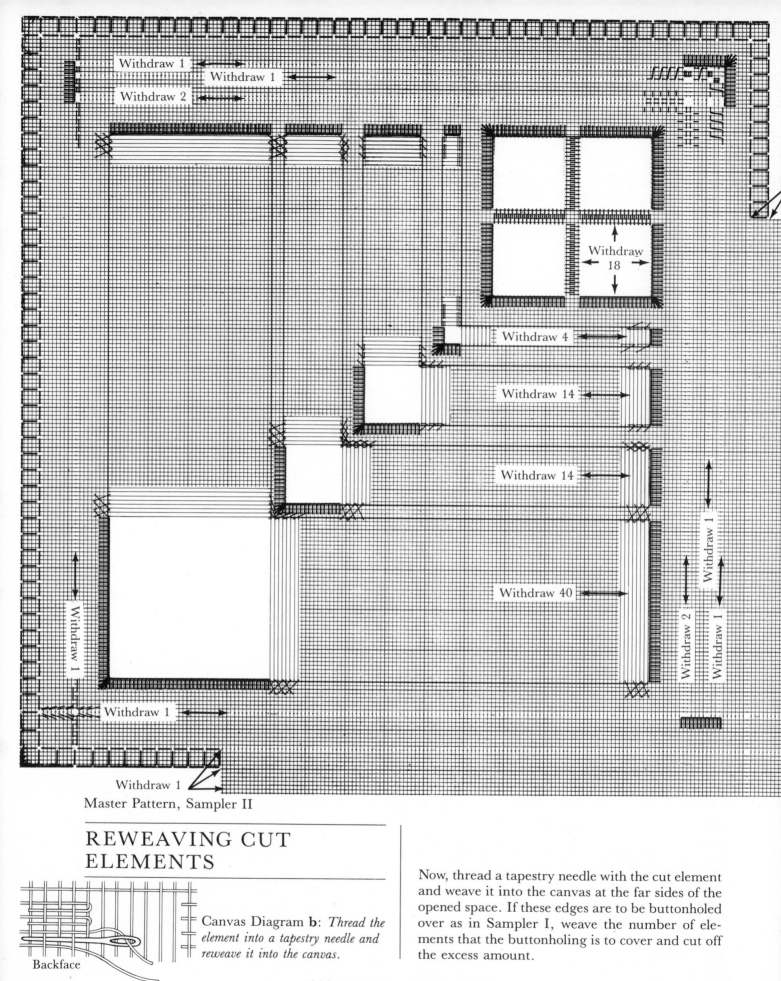

Withdraw 1
Withdraw 1
Withdraw 2

Withdraw 18

Withdraw 4

Withdraw 14

Withdraw 14

Withdraw 40

Withdraw 2
Withdraw 1
Withdraw 1

Withdraw 1

Withdraw 1

Withdraw 1
Master Pattern, Sampler II

REWEAVING CUT ELEMENTS

Backface

Canvas Diagram **b**: *Thread the element into a tapestry needle and reweave it into the canvas.*

Now, thread a tapestry needle with the cut element and weave it into the canvas at the far sides of the opened space. If these edges are to be buttonholed over as in Sampler I, weave the number of elements that the buttonholing is to cover and cut off the excess amount.

STITCH 1B

BUTTONHOLE EDGES, SINGLE AND DOUBLE

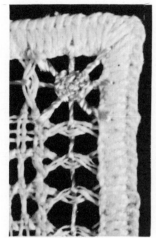

Sampler I   Sampler II

Buttonhole edges are used to secure the cut elements and bind the canvas.

Work a double buttonhole edge over four canvas elements to bind a canvas. It is shown here as it appears in Sampler I, where it divides the canvas in two segments, as well as binding the edges. A single buttonhole edge is shown binding the cut elements of a band in Sampler II. Stitch Diagram **1C** will illustrate how to accomplish this, using an underlay of padding.

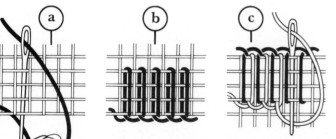

Stitch Diagrams: *Interlock a single buttonhole edge with a second one.*

Work a buttonhole edge from left to right, with the needle emerging at the looped base (festoon) of the stitch. Start the row by emerging on the frontface at the edge (**a**). Hold the working thread with the thumb of one hand and insert the needle into the backface at the top of the stitch with the working hand. Emerge, passing the needle over the held thread and drawing it through to make the first stitch. Continue, holding the thread for each

stitch, passing over it on emerging, and creating a series of festoons at the edge. The buttonhole stitches around Sampler I are first worked with the festoons on the inside edge of the opened band. Place each stitch between two canvas elements (**b**), to allow room for the second journey, which is worked next with the festoons on the other side (**c**). Work this second journey after completing the first one, or after completing all of the other work, prior to cutting away the excess canvas.

STITCH 1C

BUTTONHOLE EDGE, PADDED

Sampler II: *Lay horizontal threads to mask the vertical canvas elements.*

A buttonhole edge on canvas usually requires an underlay, or padding, of a matching working thread to prevent the vertical canvas elements from peeking through between the straight stitches.

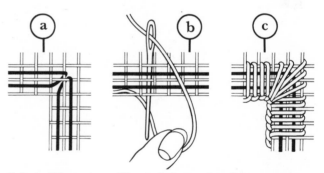

Stitch Diagrams: *The underlay makes for a smoother background than the canvas.*

Lay long threads along the length of the edge to be buttonholed, catching them under elements to secure them when necessary (**a**). Then buttonhole over them (**b**). To improve the appearance of a buttonhole edge, you can work two stitches between each pair of vertical canvas elements to cover them. However, when you turn a corner, use single stitches in each space to prevent overcrowding (**c**).

LESSON 2

NARROW BANDS OR PRIMARY GROUPINGS

A SIMPLE STRAIGHT

B SIMPLE SLANTED

C LADDER

D DOUBLE

E STEM

F HERRINGBONE

G INTERLACED

H SERPENTINE

I SERPENTINE BARS

J FOUR-SIDED

THE narrow bands of hemstitching in Lesson 1 are all worked at the long edges of bands and borders from which one to four elements have been withdrawn (see the master patterns for both samplers). However, some of them can be used on the wider bands and borders shown in the lessons that follow. This will serve to stabilize the edges. Simple straight and slanted hemstitches are most frequently employed for this purpose, but double, herringbone, interlace, and four-sided hemstitches are also used. You can see examples of these regroupings in both samplers.

STITCH 2A

SIMPLE STRAIGHT

Sampler II: *This is similar to the antique hemstitch.*

The simple straight hemstitch is similar in construction to an antique hemstitch, which is traditionally employed to hem the folded edges of handkerchiefs and fine linens. However, antique hemstitch is worked on the backface; the needle passes diagonally into the fold and only a horizontal stitch shows on the frontface. This type of hem is also suitable for canvas, but the corners must be carefully trimmed to avoid bulkiness.

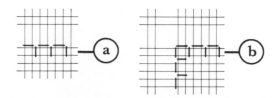

Pattern Diagram **a**: *Withdraw two elements, then group two elements.*

Pattern Diagram **b**: *Turning a corner.*

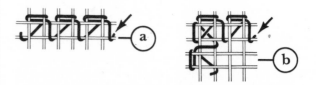

Stitch Diagram **a**: *The warps of the opened band are grouped and the unopened canvas is stabilized.*

Stitch Diagram **b**: *Turn a corner with a slanted stitch on the backface.*

Work this simple straight hemstitch from right to left. Turn the work to travel in the opposite direction. The backstitch at the top of the unit draws the groups of warps together in the opened band. Although the vertical stitch of a unit is straight in the stitch diagram (**a**), it becomes slanted when you employ some tension. Group two, three, or four vertical warps and incorporate two, three, or four horizontal elements of the unopened canvas for a unit. You can easily turn corners by taking a slanted stitch on the backface of the first stitch unit going in the opposite direction (**b**).

STITCH 2B
SIMPLE SLANTED

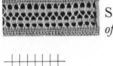

Sampler II: *A simple pattern of grouped warps appears.*

Pattern Diagram **a**: *The reverse of straight hemstitch.*

Pattern Diagram **b**: *Turning a corner.*

You can barely distinguish this slanted form of hemstitch from the straight one. Use whichever you find most comfortable. Vary the stitch count if you like for both the number of warps that you group with the backstitch at the top and the number of horizontal canvas elements that you incorporate in the stitch.

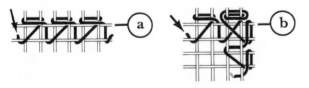

Stitch Diagram **a**: *Travel from the left with a slanted stitch on the frontface.*

Stitch Diagram **b**: *Complete the last stitch, turn the canvas, and work the first stitch on top of the last stitch.*

Work the simple slanted hemstitch from left to right. Turn the work to travel in the opposite direction. Start with a slanted stitch on the frontface; encircle a group of warps and make a straight stitch on the backface (**a**). To turn a corner, complete the last stitch of a row. Then turn the work and make the first stitch of the new direction on top of this last stitch, producing a crossed stitch at the corner (**b**).

STITCH 2C
LADDER

Sampler II: *Ladder with straight hemstitches.*

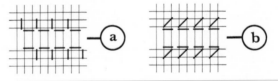

Pattern Diagram **a**: *Straight hemstitch ladders.*

Pattern Diagram **b**: *Slanted hemstitch ladders.*

Work a simple straight or slanted hemstitch on both sides of a narrow band of withdrawn elements to stabilize them, making neat straight lines of warps resembling the rungs of a ladder.

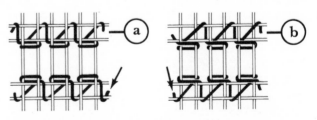

Stitch Diagram **a**: *For straight ladder hemstitch, work each side from right to left.*

Stitch Diagram **b**: *For a slanted stitch, work each side from the left.*

Complete the hemstitching at one long edge of the band; then turn the work and bundle the same groups along the opposite side. This turn will enable you to work in a consistent direction.

STITCH 2D

DOUBLE

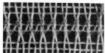 *Sampler II: Group paired warps on each side of a solid band.*

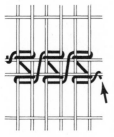 Pattern Diagram: *Stabilize two edges with a single journey of double hemstitching.*

The double hemstitch is also called Italian hemstitch because it is so often seen on Italian openwork embroidery. It is worked over a solid band of canvas between two bands of withdrawn elements. The edges of the open bands on either side can be worked in straight hemstitch, grouping parallel pairs of warps.

Stitch Diagram: *Connect the rows with a diagonal stitch on the back and a straight one on the front.*

Start a row from the lower right and backstitch over the two lower warps. Then carry the working thread on the backface diagonally across the woven band and emerge to make a backstitch directly above the first one over the two upper warps. Begin the next unit with a backstitch over the next two lower warps by making a connecting vertical stitch on the frontface.

STITCH 2E

STEM

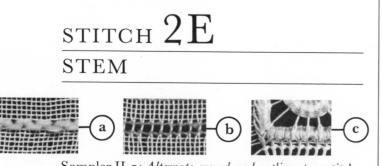

Sampler II **a**: *Alternate crewel and outline stem stitches.*

Sampler II **b**: *Outline and crewel slant in opposite directions.*

Sampler II **c**: *Work stem between two open bands.*

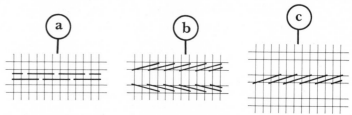

Pattern Diagram **a**: *Crewel and outline.*

Pattern Diagram **b**: *Outline on the top edge; crewel on the lower one.*

Pattern Diagram **c**: *Outline stem.*

There are two types of stem stitches: *outline stem*, which produces a smooth line, and *crewel stem*, which produces a textured one. Crewel and outline stem were used in three different ways on Sampler II, illustrated by these Pattern Diagrams.

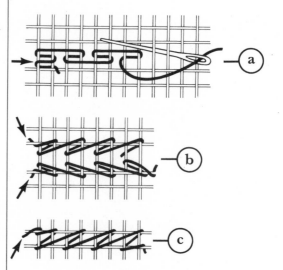

Stitch Diagram **a**: *Two lines of stitches result from a single journey that alternate outline and crewel.*

Stitch Diagram **b**: *Invade the canvas by one element with outline (top) and crewel (bottom).*

Stitch Diagram **c**: *Outline stem was used in Sampler II to group elements when no other hemstitch would fit.*

To work both outline and crewel, advance on the frontface over four elements and retreat on the backface over two. When traveling left to right, hold the thread below the needle for outline, and above the needle for crewel. Reverse these instructions when traveling in the opposite direction.

STITCH 2F
HERRINGBONE

Sampler I

Sampler II

Sampler I: *Produce a zigzag band by matching the rows.*

Sampler II: *Reverse this row on the second side of the band to produce straight warps.*

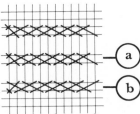

— **a**

— **b**

Pattern Diagram: *Produce either zigzag or matching groups. An identical second row produces a zigzag open band between them (**a**). A reversed row produces matching groups with straight warps between them (**b**).*

When you employ herringbone on two sides of an opened band, you must be careful about how you work the second side. If you work identical rows on either side, you produce a serpentine pattern in the warps. Reverse the procedure of the second row to produce matching groups of warps on both sides.

Stitch Diagram: *These matching rows create a zigzag pattern.*

Work from left to right. Advance with slanted stitches over three elements of the solid canvas on the frontface and retreat with horizontal stitches over two elements of the opened band on the backface. Notice that the rows in the stitch diagram start with a compensating (shortened) stitch. If you reverse the bottom row (see Pattern Diagram **b**), straight warps result.

STITCH 2G
INTERLACED

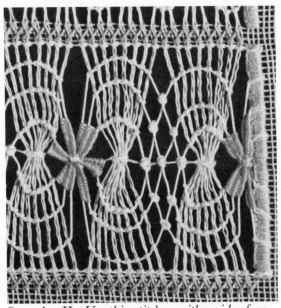

Sampler II: *Use this stitch on either side of an opened band or to connect two opened bands.*

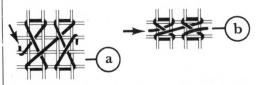

— **a**   — **b**

Pattern Diagram **a**: *Interlaced between opened bands.*

Pattern Diagram **b**: *Interlaced over two canvas rows along one edge of an opened band.*

In this hemstitch band from Sampler II, interlacing groups the warps in pairs as it edges the bottom of the opened band. At the upper edge, it groups pairs of warps between the two opened bands.

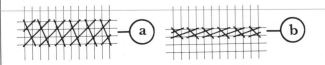

— **a**   — **b**

Stitch Diagram **a**: *Start (and finish) with a compensating stitch.*

Stitch Diagram **b**: *After the compensation, move ahead four, back two, across two, back two, and repeat.*

To work interlacing between opened bands (Sampler II and Stitch Diagram **a**), start with an abbreviated or compensating stitch on the front-face. Group two warps from the lower edge of the upper opened band on the backface. Then take a slanted connecting stitch on the frontface to group a matching pair of warps from the upper edge of the lower opened band. Start the next unit with a long diagonal stitch on the frontface over four warps, which will put you in position for grouping the next pair of warps. This stitch can also be done over two elements high (**b**).

STITCH 2H

SERPENTINE

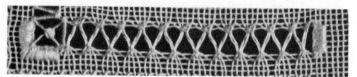

Sampler II: *Produce a zigzag pattern.*

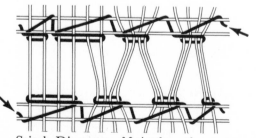

Pattern Diagram: *Start one side of the band by grouping two warps and the other by grouping four.*

A serpentine or zigzag pattern is produced when the hemstitching on the sides of the withdrawn band pulls alternate warps in the opened band in opposite directions. Each stitch must include an even number of warps; half will be pulled in one direction and half in the other. To finish a band evenly, the number of warps in the band should be a multiple of the number of warps used in each stitch. Withdraw at least four elements for the pattern to show well.

Stitch Diagram: *Notice how the warps are collected differently on each side.*

To follow this diagram, you group four warps with a simple slanted hemstitch along one side of an opened band from which four elements have been withdrawn. Start one side of the band with a group of two warps and the other side with a group of four. The first stitches in the diagram are shown without tension for the sake of clarity.

STITCH 2I

SERPENTINE BARS

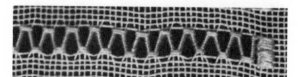

Sampler II: *Overcast a zigzag pattern.*

Pattern Diagram: *This indicates how the warps are grouped; most of the overcast stitches are omitted for clarity's sake.*

Achieve another serpentine pattern, as shown in Sampler II, by staggering the groups of four warps on either side of an opened band. Start the zigzag movement by employing only two warps. The work proceeds quite differently in all other respects from the previous serpentine pattern (**2H**).

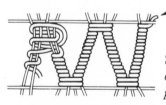

Stitch Diagram: *Snugly overcast the warps to produce bars.*

Work this band in a single journey. Start by snugly overcasting the first two warps from one side of the opened band. Just as you reach the opposite edge, pick up two more warps and incorporate them by overcasting the four warps twice. Then overcast only the two new warps to the other edge. Again pick up two new warps and overcast all four. Repeat this back and forth movement from one side of the band to the other. The solid canvas is not entered, as it is in serpentine (**2H**).

STITCH 2J
FOUR-SIDED

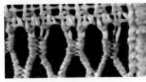

Sampler I: *Use this multipurpose stitch to group warps in the opened band.*

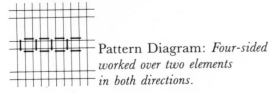

Pattern Diagram: *Four-sided worked over two elements in both directions.*

The four-sided stitch is another universal stitch found in almost every type of embroidery. Use it to group warps on either side of an opened band, or to group two sets of warps between two opened bands in a single journey. It can be worked over two, three, or four elements in either direction.

Stitch Diagram: *Group pairs of warps in the opened band and pairs of warps and of wefts in the solid canvas.*

Four-sided stitches are done at the base of an opened band; turn the canvas to work the other side. Group two warps and enter the solid canvas over two elements. The vertical stitches slant under tension, so be consistent in the direction you travel. Start with a vertical stitch on the frontface; then cross on the backface to group two elements at the base of the unit on the frontface. Cross again on the backface to emerge and group two elements in the opened band, and finally cross a third time to emerge in position to start the next unit with a vertical stitch. Each unit thus has three stitches on the frontface and three on the backface.

LESSON 3

CLUSTERS

A CORAL KNOT CLUSTERS

B CORAL FESTOONS

C RIBBED WHEELS ON CLUSTERS

D CORAL FESTOON VARIATION

E WOVEN WHEELS ON CLUSTERS

THIS lesson involves the working of wider bands. Fourteen elements have already been withdrawn from the length of each of the wide bands in Sampler II. A completely opened square has resulted at the intersection of the bands. The cut edges of the square and the cut straight ends have been secured and buttonholed. The long edges have been hemstitched to group the warps in pairs. Now you can further group the warps into bundles, called clusters, and embellish them with festoons and wheels. Each arm of the band is worked in a different pattern; both are started from a right side at the short ends, and the working threads fastened off on the far side of the open square. These threads, which stretch across the open square, become warps for the woven corner motifs that are dealt with in Lesson 6. Lesson 3 begins with the coral knot that bundles the clusters; this stitch plays a leading role in the technique of hemstitching.

STITCH 3A
CORAL KNOT CLUSTERS

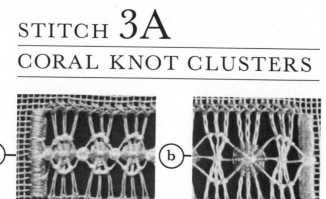

Sampler II: *Bundle together secondary groups of paired warps.*

Use these coral knots to bundle paired warps into secondary groups called clusters. Travel across the middle of an opened band, from right to left, working a coral knot around evenly grouped elements. Turn the canvas if necessary. Bands that are less than one inch in width may not need this further embellishment. Shown here are the two bands from Sampler II that are the subject of this lesson.

Stitch Diagram **a**: *Pass the needle under the warps and into the loop of thread.*

Stitch Diagram **b**

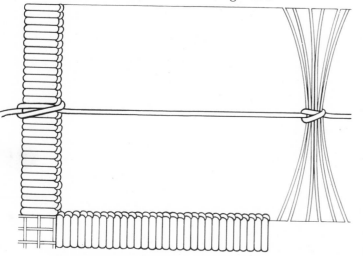

In this stitch diagram and in the bands of Sampler II, the first coral knot is worked over the buttonhole edge. Although you may prefer to work the first coral knot around the first cluster, anchoring the first knot in the manner shown gives stability to the edge. To start, fasten on under the buttonhole edge and emerge on the right side. Pass the needle under the edge, or the warps, and bring the loop of working thread over and under the tip of

the needle. Hold the knot in position with the thumb of one hand and draw the needle through with the other; draw the thread taut with a tug to make a snug knot (**a**). After bundling each cluster in the band in this way, end with a coral knot over the buttonholed edge at the far side. If you are working a band that ends at a corner, as do these bands from Sampler II, stretch the working thread straight across the opened corner and make the final coral knot at the buttonhole edge on the far side (**b**). This stretched, or thrown, thread becomes a warp for further embellishment.

STITCH 3B
CORAL FESTOONS

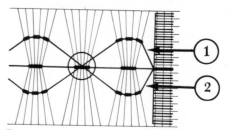

Pattern Diagram: *Journeys **1** and **2** are coded to match the far corner in Lesson **6D**.*

After the clusters are bundled together with coral knots, they can be further embellished in various ways (see **3A**, photograph **a**). In this diagram, two journeys of coral knotted festoons travel from the buttonhole edge. Each festoon journey rises and falls over every other cluster, one reversing the path of the other. Ribbed wheels (**3C**) are woven where the two journeys cross. Note the gentle arcs made by the knotted festoons.

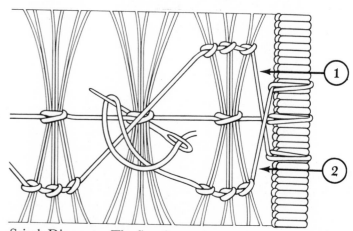

Stitch Diagram: *The first festoon journey bypasses every other cluster; the second one makes a coral knot there.*

Fasten on with a coral knot on the buttonhole edge at the right side of the band (as in Stitch Diagram), or on the backface of the buttonhole edge under the *first* coral knot (as in Pattern Diagram). Pass the working thread over the center clustering thread and make a series of coral knots around each group of warps at the top of the first cluster. Then descend, bypassing the second cluster, and coral knot across the third cluster. Continue to work these festoons across the length of the band and fasten off with a coral knot a third of the way up (or down) on the far side. Reverse the festoons on the second journey, working another additional coral knot over the intervening clusters instead of bypassing them.

STITCH 3C

RIBBED WHEELS ON CLUSTERS

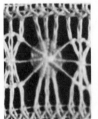

Sampler II: *Use these wheels to embellish the knotted centers of clusters.*

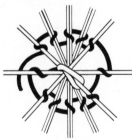

Stitch Diagram: *Backstitch around the radiating warps.*

Work ribbed wheels at the centers of clusters where a coral knot bundles the grouped warps together. In this border from Sampler II, the festoon threads supply four extra warps on *alternate clusters.* Start a wheel by fastening on at the backface. Backstitch around the wheel in a counterclockwise direction, passing the working thread back over one radius on the frontface and forward under two on the backface. Travel around the cluster about five times and fasten off on the backface.

STITCH 3D

CORAL FESTOON VARIATION

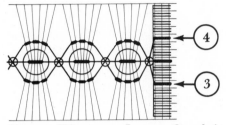

Pattern Diagram: *Journeys 3 and 4 are coded to match 6D.*

This variation of the coral festoon has journeys that intersect in the opened spaces between the clusters (see **3A**, photograph **b**). After the clusters are bundled together with coral knots, make two journeys of festoons that cross each other between each cluster. As the second journey crosses the first, a knot is made and a little wheel is woven; then the festoon resumes its course. Each cluster is further embellished at its coral knotted center with another type of woven wheel (**3E**). Later, in Lesson **5**, this simple juncture of festoon threads is expanded into a net pattern.

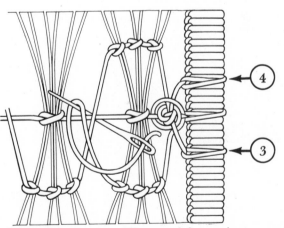

Stitch Diagram **a**: *The second festoon journey makes a coral knot at the intersection, then a wheel.*

Stitch Diagram **b**: *Work the wheel by passing under and over the radiating warps.*

Fasten on with a coral knot at the bottom half of the buttonhole edge on the right side of the band (**3**). Pass the working thread over the center clustering thread and make a series of coral knots around each group of warps at the top of the first cluster. Then descend and coral knot across the lower half of the second cluster. Continue to work these festoons across the band and fasten off on the far side with a coral knot a third of the way up (or down). Reverse the festoons on the second journey (**4**), *but* work an additional coral knot between each cluster over the bundling thread where the two festoon journeys cross. *Then,* with the same working thread, work a small wheel (**b**) before continuing the journey. Fasten off one-third of the way down (or up) at the buttonhole edge on the far side of the opened square.

STITCH 3E
WOVEN WHEELS ON CLUSTERS

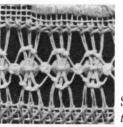

Sampler II: *Pass over and under the same warps.*

Stitch Diagram: *Work all the woven wheels across the opened band in a continuous journey.*

Weave all the wheels of the band in a single journey, traveling from right to left. If you are alternating the colors as in Sampler II, make one journey for each color. Fasten on the backface of the first cluster. Weave clockwise, passing over horizontal and vertical warps and under diagonals for three revolutions. Enter the backface of a preceding round to lock the wheel; then overcast to the next cluster.

LESSON 4

INTERLACE

A TWO WARPS INVERTED ONCE

B FOUR WARPS INVERTED ONCE

C TWO WARPS INVERTED TWICE

D INTERWOVEN SERPENTINE BARS

IN addition to the clusters of the previous lesson, primary groups of warps can be regrouped by interlacing them. In this lesson, bands from Samplers I and II demonstrate several ways to invert warps and also a method for needleweaving them. One more method of serpentine knotting remains to be covered in Lesson **5**. The inverting of warps requires strong tension on the working thread, so be sure to select one that can withstand pressure without breaking, such as linen, crochet cotton, or rayon.

The work can proceed from either direction. The diagrams shown here start at a secured straight edge, but they could as easily begin at an opened square, as shown in the square border of Sampler I. In the first three stitches in this chapter, the basic stitch is the same; only the number of warps changes. There are countless variations that you can also pursue. Allow wider opened bands for greater manipulation of warps.

STITCH 4A

TWO WARPS INVERTED ONCE

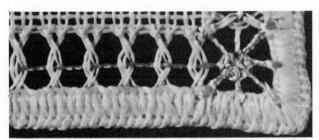

Sampler I: *Interlace the inverted bands and work the spiders in the four corners with a single journey.*

Sampler II: *Overcast the interlacing thread and the two rows of coral knots at top and bottom.*

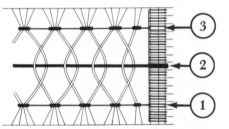

Pattern Diagram, Sampler II: *Here, 1, 2, and 3 are coded to match the pinwheel corner in 6C.*

In Sampler I, an interlaced band of inverted warps is shown in which a square border and all four corner spiders (see **6B**) are worked in a single journey. To accomplish this, fasten on the working thread at the right side of the lower right open corner. Throw the thread across this corner and start the first inversion at the first pair of warps. When you arrive at the lower left corner, turn to Stitch **6B** for the corner spider.

In the Sampler II band, the working thread has been overcast with a textured thread. Also, a row of coral knots has been worked at the top and bottom of the band, regrouping the warps once again. This coral knotting thread is also overcast with a textured thread.

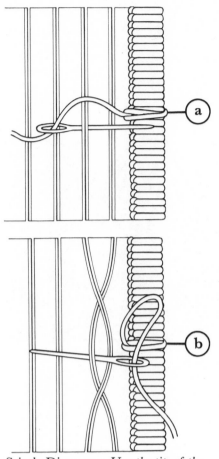

Stitch Diagram: *Use the tip of the needle as a pivot and rotate the shank.*

Begin (**a**) with the thread securely fastened. Point the needle in the direction opposite to the journey and pass the tip of it under the pair of warps that is to be bent to the right (the second pair), and over the pair to be bent to the left (the first pair). Use the tip of the needle as a pivot and rotate the shank to point the needle in the opposite direction (**b**). Hold the bent warps with one hand as you draw the needle through. A slight tug on the working thread will maintain a straight, taut lacing thread. Interlace the remaining warps in the same way. In Sampler I, narrower bands of the same interlaced and inverted warps make a square border. The interlacing threads stretch across the opened squares at the corners and become warps for spider motifs.

STITCH 4B
FOUR WARPS INVERTED ONCE

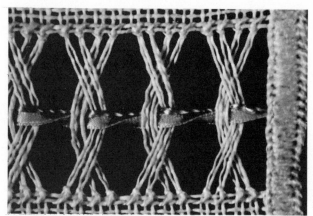

Sampler I: *Warps can be bent in either direction depending on which way you point the needle.*

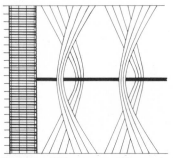

Pattern Diagram: *Two pairs of warps are inverted over two others.*

This pattern differs from the previous one in two respects. The number of interlaced warps has been doubled; and the direction of the inversion has been changed. The adventurous needleworker can experiment with changing direction within a single band for some interesting effects. The working thread shown here is rayon; a silk twisted ribbon is fed through the same spaces.

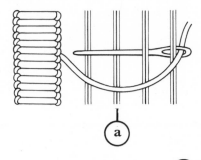

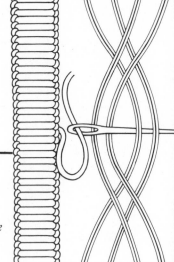

Stitch Diagrams: *Pass the needle under and over the paired warps; then rotate the shank end.*

Start this band at the left side. Point the needle to the left and pass it under the group that will bend to the left and lie on top, and over the group that will bend to the right and lie underneath (**a**). Use the tip of the needle as a pivot and rotate the shank to point the needle in the opposite direction (**b**). Hold the bent warps with one hand and draw the needle through. Exert a slight tug to maintain a straight, taut working thread.

STITCH 4C
TWO WARPS INVERTED TWICE

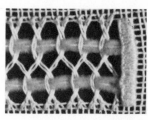

Sampler II: *Interlace along two different paths.*

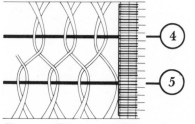

Pattern Diagram: *Offset the pattern in the second journey (**4** and **5** are coded to match the corner in **6C**).*

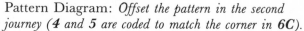

This band from Sampler II is made of two journeys of inverted warps. The second journey incorporates one warp from each of two neighboring pairs from the first journey by omitting the first pair of warps at the right edge. In the photograph, a second thread follows the path of the thread for additional texture. Turn to **6C** to see a diagram for the pinwheel corner.

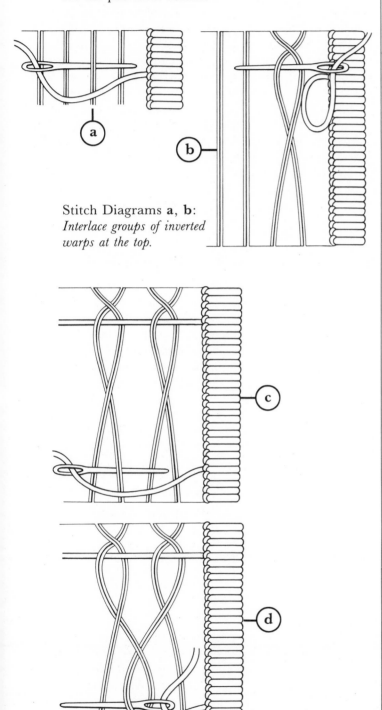

Stitch Diagrams **a**, **b**: *Interlace groups of inverted warps at the top.*

Stitch Diagrams **c**, **d**: *Start the second journey by inverting the second and third groups.*

Start this band a third of the distance from the top edge on the right side. Work the first journey as in **4A**, inverting consecutive pairs of warps (**a** and **b**). Work the second journey a third of the way up from the bottom edge, but offset the pattern by inverting the second and third pairs (**c** and **d**). Employ a strong, fine thread for the main work. You can then overcast it and feed decorative threads through the open spaces.

STITCH 4D

INTERWOVEN SERPENTINE BARS

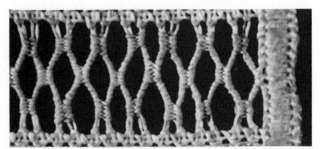

Sampler I: *Combine needleweaving with hemstitching for this stitch.*

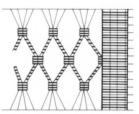

Pattern Diagram: *Group and regroup the secondary warps in two undulating journeys.*

Warps are regrouped in this hemstitched band by making two journeys of needleweaving in serpentine rows that interlace consecutive pairs of warps. It serves to illustrate some of the ways you can combine open canvas techniques. A needlewoven pattern such as this is very sturdy and therefore practical for items that receive hard wear, such as handbags or upholstery. The linen thread used in Sampler I was run through beeswax first to smooth the fibers for a neater finish.

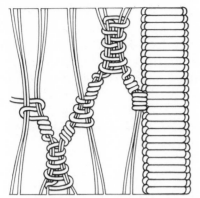

Stitch Diagram: *Coil up and down in zigzag fashion, use needleweaving to pass from one group to another.*

Start the first journey at the middle of the right edge by overcasting the first two warps to the buttonhole loops. This compensates for the joins of the pattern, made across the center of the band.

Coil the first pair of warps a set number of times for all coils (four in the sampler), pick up an adjacent pair and needleweave the two of them for a distance equal to the coiling. Now, carry the working thread down by passing into the backface, inserting the needle into the core of the needleweaving. Then coil downward the same number of stitches you coiled up, pick up an adjacent pair of warps, and needleweave it to the coiled pair. Reverse the work of the top half of the pattern to work the bottom half of the next unit. Complete the band in this manner, zigzagging from the top half to bottom half. Start the second journey at the left side to complete the pattern. Omit the needleweaving across the center of the pattern; this has been accomplished in the first journey. Pass the working thread through the needleweaving and continue to coil either in an upward or downward direction.

LESSON 5

NETTING

A DOUBLE CORAL KNOT

B NETTING WITH WHEELS

C SERPENTINE KNOTTING

D CONCEALED SERPENTINE KNOTTING

THE hemstitched bands in this lesson are wider and more ornate than those in previous lessons. Warps are manipulated more and the knotted festoon journeys resemble a lacy netting. In the first band illustrated, **5B**, a technique for traveling in six festoon journeys is shown along with a method for weaving small wheels at the junctions where five working threads cross. In **5C** and **5D**, another system is employed for regrouping primary warps. A serpentine pattern moves across the center section of each open band. Different methods of knotting are explored as well as two plans for involving the serpentine bands in the netting of the festoon journeys. The bands of **5B** and **5C** are fastened off on the far sides of open corners, which are the subject of the next lesson.

STITCH 5A

DOUBLE CORAL KNOT

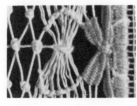

Sampler II: *Work a second coral knot over the first one.*

For more emphasis and extra tension, work a second coral knot over the first one when you bundle groups of primary warps into clusters.

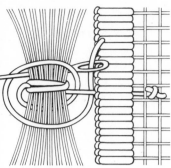

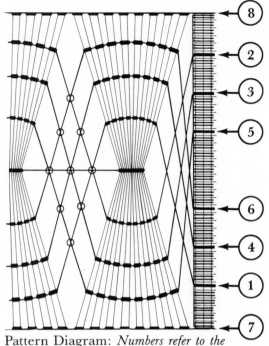

Stitch Diagram: *Start a free-standing cluster with a waste knot.*

Notice in this stitch diagram, and in the netted band that follows, the first and last coral knots have no connecting threads between them and the buttonholed edges. To accomplish this, use a waste knot to fasten on to the solid canvas at the right side of the band while you make the first double coral knot. After the band is completed, remove the waste knot and fasten off behind the first cluster, passing under the double coral knot. Work the first coral knot as described at **3A**. Then work a second one over it: pass the needle and thread to the right side of the cluster, then pass the needle under the warps; finally, pass the loop thread over and under the tip of the needle. Hold the thread so that it lies neatly around the first coral knot as you draw the needle and thread through.

STITCH 5B
NETTING WITH WHEELS

Pattern Diagram: *Numbers refer to the sequence of festoon journeys. They are coded to the butterfly corner shown in* **6E**.

You need to withdraw many elements to have sufficient space to work an elaborate band such as this one. Forty elements are withdrawn from the wide perpendicular bands of Sampler II. In addition to the thread that moves across the center of this band, bundling eight paired warps into clusters, six journeys of coral knotted festoons travel the length of the band, creating a netting. Between alternate clusters, little wheels are worked at each intersection of the festoon threads. The unknotted festoon threads later become warps for needlewoven flowers. If you are following Sampler II, work the flowers after studying and working the corners in Lesson **6**, when you should have ample skill to complete them (see one version of a flower in **7F**). To work the festoons, follow the sequence of numbers indicated on this diagram. They are started at regular, evenly spaced intervals at the buttonholed edge. Pattern Diagram **6E** illustrates where each festoon journey fastens off on the far side. Notice that there is a straight row of coral knots across the top and bottom of the band. These two rows are added in order to supply two additional pairs of warps for corner **6E**.

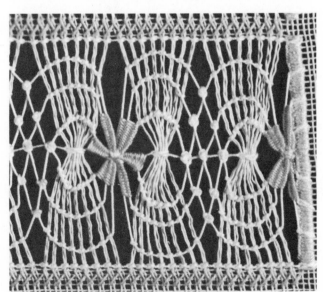

Sampler II: *Alternate needle lace with needleweaving between the festooned clusters.*

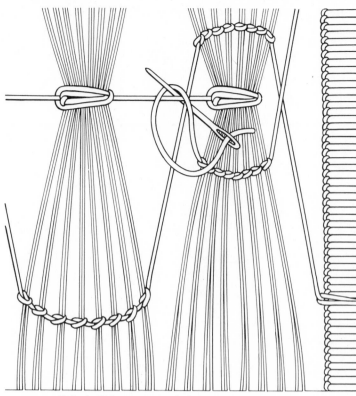

Stitch Diagram **a**: *Work small wheels over intersecting festoons between alternate clusters.*

Stitch Diagram **b**: *Knot the intersecting working threads, then pass under and over them in two revolutions to work the small wheels.*

Secure the thread for the first journey one-eighth of the distance up from the lower edge. Ascend to one-fourth of the distance up from the center and work a series of coral knots across the first cluster. Descend to the first level of the second cluster and coral knot across. Alternate from lower cluster to upper cluster along this route to the far side of the band. Secure the thread for the second journey one-eighth of the distance down from the top edge and descend to coral knot across the first cluster one-fourth of the distance down from the center. This time, when you ascend on your way to the top of the second cluster, you intersect the festoon thread from the first journey (**a**). Make a coral knot at the junction and a small wheel (**b**). Continue with the second journey as in the pattern diagram, working small wheels between every

other cluster at the same location. Work the remaining journeys in this way, following the paths established in the pattern diagram; you can trace entire journeys by examining the photograph of the band. Work the small wheels in each journey whenever you intersect another festoon thread. A diamond pattern emerges in the netting between the alternate clusters.

STITCH 5C
SERPENTINE KNOTTING

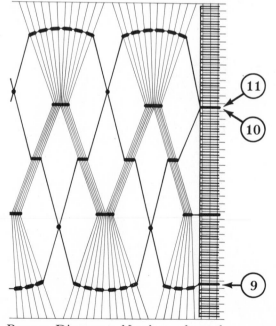

Sampler II: *Bundle and rebundle across the band, then work the netting in three journeys.*

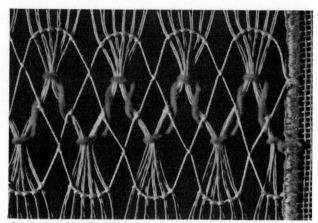

Pattern Diagram: *Numbers refer to the sequence of the festoon journeys. They are coded to the butterfly corner shown in **6E**.*

Serpentine knotting is another technique for re-grouping primary warps. First, bundles of six primary warps are divided and regrouped to make a serpentine pattern across the midsection of the band. Three festoon journeys ascend and descend over the divided bundles, making coral knots across the clusters at top and bottom and turning the band into a netting. If you are working Sampler II, turn the canvas to follow this pattern. As you work the festoon journeys, work a coral knot around each of the divided bundles. Also, on the second and third festoon journeys, work a coral knot as you intersect another festoon thread. See the photo to trace the complete journeys. If you are working the sampler, fasten off on the far side as in Pattern Diagram **6E** (the butterfly corner). Turn the canvas back to its original position to follow **6E**.

bundle shown on Sampler II are compensating ones, composed of three pairs of warps. All of the other bundles are composed of six pairs of warps—three acquired from a previous bundle and three newly acquired. Encircle the three pairs with a knot (**a**). Then pass the thread on the frontface another third of the way up, and encircle six pairs in a knot (**b**). Pass the thread down on the frontface and encircle six pairs in a knot (**c**). Complete the serpentine knotting across the band in this way. Notice in the sampler that the textured serpentine knotting thread does not fasten off on the far side. Pass it to the backface of the last compensating bundle and secure it with fine sewing thread. Employ a nonslippery working thread for serpentine knotting. If necessary, you can run the thread through beeswax or make a second knot over the first one.

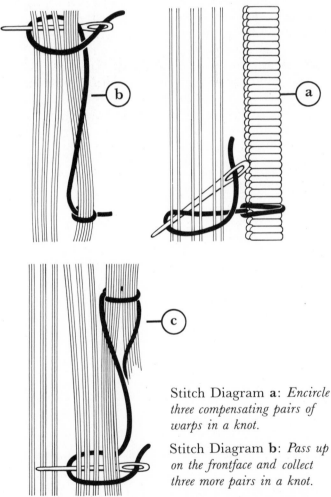

STITCH 5D

CONCEALED SERPENTINE KNOTTING

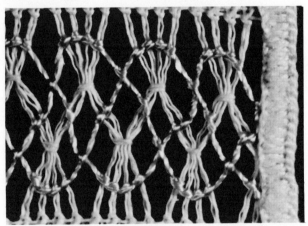

Sampler I: *Hide the connecting thread on the backface.*

Stitch Diagram **a**: *Encircle three compensating pairs of warps in a knot.*

Stitch Diagram **b**: *Pass up on the frontface and collect three more pairs in a knot.*

Stitch Diagram **c**: *Pass down on the frontface and collect six pairs in a knot.*

Start the serpentine knotting a third of the way up the band. Fasten on with a coral knot or on the backface of the buttonhole edge. The first and last

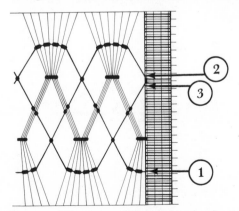

Pattern Diagram: *Work serpentine knots, then three journeys of festooned netting. The sequence is coded to **6E**.*

In this band from Sampler I, bundles of four paired warps are divided and regrouped across the center third portion of the band with serpentine knotting. The connecting threads between the knots are concealed on the backface by special maneuvering. Next, three journeys of festoons ascend and descend over the band. With each journey, coral knots are worked across the clusters, at the junction with another festoon, and at the middle of each segment of a divided cluster. You can trace the complete pattern of the festoons in the photograph.

Start at the bottom of the serpentine knot segment by fastening the first two primary pairs of warps to the buttonholed edge with a coral knot. The first and last compensating bundles of the band are composed of two paired warps. All the other bundles are composed of four paired warps—two from a previous bundle, plus two new ones. These serpentine bundles are knotted twice in each location in order to secure the connecting threads on the backface.

To work the first knot over four pairs of warps (**a**), pass the working thread upward and behind the first two warps (see pattern diagram for the location of the first bundle). Hold a loop of thread on the right side, pass the needle under the four warps, pointing to the right with the thread on top of the warps and above the needle; pull the needle through the loop and draw the thread taut. Pass the needle and thread behind the four pairs of warps to the left side (the needle points to the left). Holding a loop of thread, pass the needle under the four warps again, pointing to the left (**b**). Pass the working thread behind the point of the needle, pull the needle through the loop, and draw the thread taut. The lower bundling is similar (see **c** and **d**). Notice that the position of the thread is exactly the reverse of **a** and **b**. Complete the knotting; then work the festoons as in the pattern diagram and photograph.

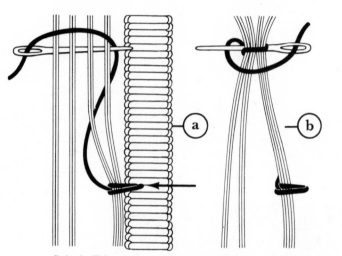

Stitch Diagram **a**: *Pass the thread up behind the two pairs of warps. Knot with the thread above the needle.*

Stitch Diagram **b**: *Knot again, with the point of the needle to the left and the thread below the needle.*

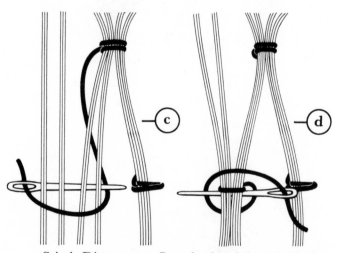

Stitch Diagram **c**: *Pass the thread down behind two paired warps. Knot with the thread below the needle.*

Stitch Diagram **d**: *Knot again, with the needle pointing to the left and the thread above the needle.*

LESSON 6

CORNERS

A SIMPLE SPIDER

B CONTINUOUS SPIDER

C PINWHEEL

D FAN

E BUTTERFLY

F BASKET OF FLOWERS CORNER MOTIF

THE completely open square spaces that result when elements are withdrawn from intersecting perpendicular bands are the subject of this lesson. Four systems are provided for filling these openings, which occur in working a square hemstitched border. These techniques can also be applied to hemstitching opened canvas in other locations. Corners are examined progressively, from the simplest to the most complex, in which working threads are fastened off in unexpected places.

The simplest solution is to fill the corner after completing the hemstitched bands. This method is illustrated in **6A**, in which two bands of simple serpentine hemstitch are ended with coiled bars; an independent spider with a woven center wheel is then added. (To work large, elaborate, independent corners, such as the Teneriffe patterns shown in Lesson **7**, several of the end warps of the opened bands need to be buttonholed first to match the bound corners of the withdrawn edges.) A second method is explored in **6B**. One band is completed, a corner is worked, and the second band proceeds in a continuous process. The third method is shown in **6C** and **6D**, in which extra warps are added to those from the bands to needleweave the patterns. In **6E**, an even more unusual plan has been devised for adding more warps when they are needed to work a needlewoven corner pattern. If you are creative, you can add extra warps almost anywhere to create your own unique needlewoven corner patterns.

STITCH 6A
SIMPLE SPIDER

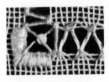

Sampler II: *An easy solution to a small open corner.*

Pattern Diagram: *Crossed spokes become warps for a woven wheel at the center.*

After two narrow perpendicular bands are completed, a small opened square in the corner is filled with a spider, as in Sampler II. The spider is independent of the two bands; all it shares with them are the corner holes where the spokes are fastened. A larger opened square would need buttonholed edges on all four sides.

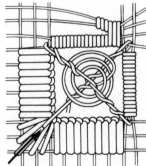

Stitch Diagram: *Throw a spoke into a corner and overcast back four times.*

After fastening on under the buttonhole edge, emerge from the lower left corner of the open square. Throw a diagonal spoke by entering the backface at the upper right corner. Emerge and wind the working thread around the spoke twice, following the twisting direction of the working thread. From the center of this first spoke throw the thread to the lower right corner. Emerge and wind twice; then throw the thread to the upper left corner. Emerge and wind twice to center. You are now ready to make the wheel. Working clockwise, pass the needle over the first spoke, and under the next. Continue to weave at least two revolutions. Insert the needle into a previous row to the backface, then complete the first spoke with two winds and fasten off behind the starting point at the lower left corner.

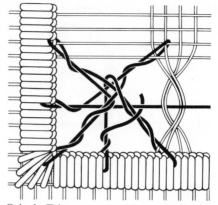

Stitch Diagram **a**: *Throw spokes into the corners and overcast back, ending with the spoke that heads into the next direction.*

STITCH 6B
CONTINUOUS SPIDER

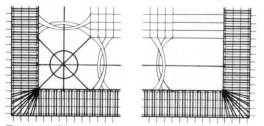

Sampler I: *Work the corners as you pass from one band to the next.*

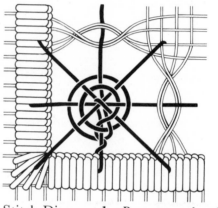

Stitch Diagram **b**: *Pass over and under the radiating spokes for two revolutions.*

Pattern Diagrams: *Throw the interlacing thread across the open corner, where it becomes the first pair of a series of radiating spokes.*

This is the corner spider that is worked in Sampler I along with the interlaced inverted warps shown in **4A**. This same spider can be worked along with various hemstitched bands, including simple coral knotted clusters.

Note that in this band from Sampler I, the corner where you fasten on is not worked until the other three corners and all four sides are completed. Start a corner spider by throwing the working thread across the opened space to the far side, entering the backface at the buttonhole edge. Follow Stitch Diagram **a** as you emerge and wind to the center. Throw a spoke into the upper right corner, emerge, and wind to the center again. Throw a spoke into the lower left corner, emerge and wind to center. Continue following the stitch diagram, ending by emerging after the last straight spoke. Next, follow Stitch Diagram **b**, weaving a small wheel around the center for two revolutions. Then, insert the needle into the backface between the revolutions and emerge in position to start the next band of the square border. Work the next three corners in the same way. The last corner should already have one warp—the stretched working thread that you fastened on when you started the band.

STITCH 6C

PINWHEEL

Sampler II: *Needleweave four segments of radiating warps.*

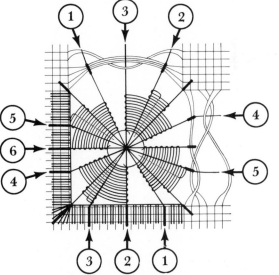

Pattern Diagram: *Numbers 1, 2, and 3 are coded to match the band worked in 4A; 4 and 5 are coded to match the band in 4C.*

The corner needlewoven pinwheel design on Sampler II was created by first adding more warps to those that are thrown across the open square from the perpendicular bands. This pattern diagram illustrates how the spokes become the radiating warps that are then woven in four segments. Each segment is started at the center wheel, occupying four warps; when it is completed, it occupies only two. Notice that after the last needleweave, the thread enters the backface between two interlocking weaves; it is carried on the backface with a long stitch to the center, from which you can either continue with another segment of the pinwheel or fasten off.

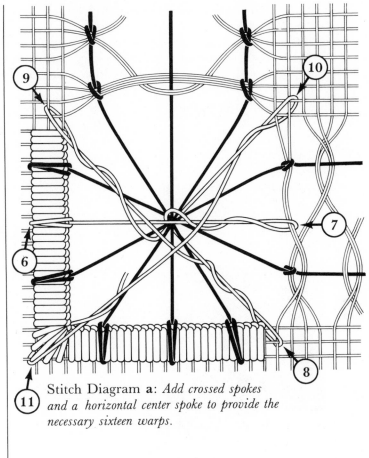

Stitch Diagram **a**: *Add crossed spokes and a horizontal center spoke to provide the necessary sixteen warps.*

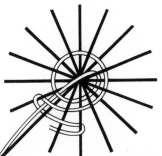

Stitch Diagram **b**: *Pass over and under the crossed spokes to draw them together; needleweave the first blade.*

Start this needlewoven pinwheel by throwing the additional six spokes necessary to supply the sixteen radiating warps for its construction. There are already six warps from the band worked in **4A** and four from the band in **4C**. Fasten on at the buttonhole edge, marked **6**, and pass over the center axis and loop around **7**. Wind back to center and pass under the center axis to cast a corner spoke to **8** and wind back to center. Cast a corner spoke to **9** and wind back to center. Pass under the axis and cast a corner spoke to **10**; wind back to center. Cast a corner spoke to **11** and wind back to center. You now have the sixteen warps you need. Pass into the backface and emerge to form the wheel, passing over and under each warp. Employ tension to draw all the warps together. Then needleweave the lower left blade of the pinwheel. Near the end of the blade, needleweave over only the two central warps. Complete all blades in this manner.

STITCH 6D

FAN

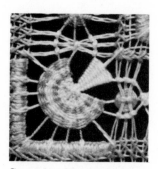

Sampler II: *Divide the warps unevenly; needleweave a fan shape and a handle.*

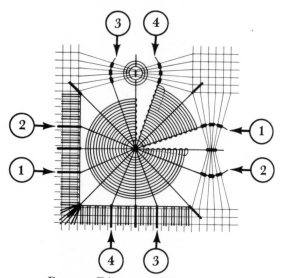

Pattern Diagram: *The numbers 1 and 2 are coded to match the band in 3B; 3 and 4 match the code in 3D.*

To work this needlewoven fan, crossed corner spokes are added to the thrown clustering threads in the opened square. You are then ready to needleweave the fan shape. You can change colors

during the weaving for added interest, as in the sampler. Pass over and under the warps, moving back and forth and omitting the three warps in the upper right corner of the square. When you have completed the head of the fan, fasten on a new thread at the center and needleweave the three warps of the handle. All fastening off and on is accomplished on the backface at the center of the wheel. To return to the center, insert the needle between two weaves and carry a long thread on the backface to the axis.

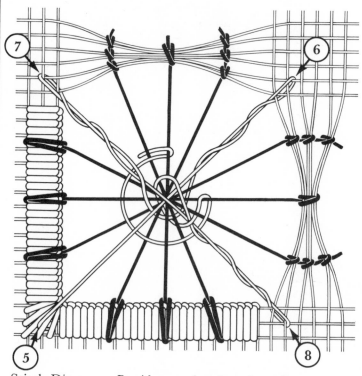

Stitch Diagram: *Provide crossed spokes, then collect all but the three for the handle and needleweave them.*

Throw spokes that cross from corner to corner to complete the sixteen warps needed to work this fan shape. Fasten on at the lower left corner and throw a spoke into the upper right corner first. Overcast to center, pass under the axis, and come to the frontface diagonally opposite the warp just made. Throw a spoke into the upper left corner, overcast back, pass over the axis and throw a spoke into the lower right corner. Overcast to center and enter the backface diagonally opposite the last spoke made. Emerge again to the left of the last spoke. You now have sixteen warps. Draw them all neatly together with a little tension; needleweave the head of the fan first, then the handle.

STITCH 6E

BUTTERFLY

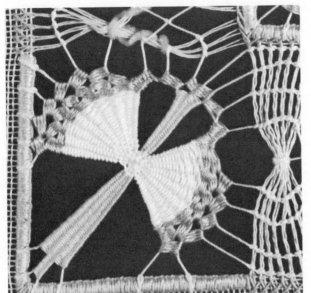

Sampler II: *Throw working threads across a corner, or wherever they help in needleweaving the design.*

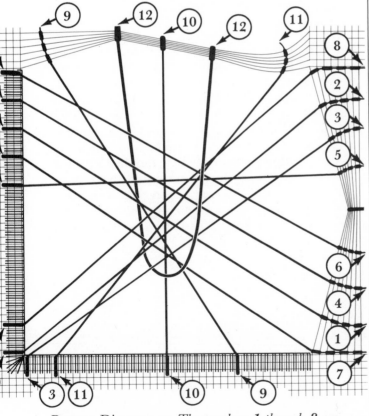

Pattern Diagram **a**: *The numbers 1 through 8 are coded to match the band in 5B; 9, 10, and 11 match the code in 5C.*

Fasten off at an open corner wherever the hemstitching threads can assist in needleweaving a particular pattern. You can also add warps that do not stretch across the corner. In this pattern diagram for the butterfly in Sampler II, you can see how the festoon threads from the two wide bands worked in **5B** and **5C** are fastened off. The numbers on this pattern diagram are consistent with the festoon journeys of those diagrams. At **12** on this diagram, notice that a warp has been added from one of the coral knots of band **5C**; it scoops up the thrown threads in a noose and returns to another coral knot, also marked **12**. The accompanying stitch diagram illustrates this further.

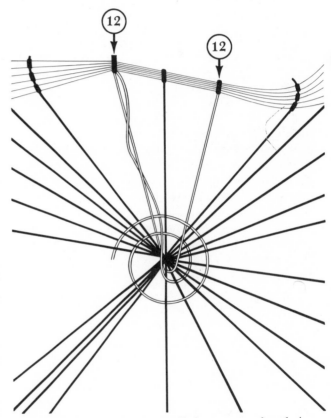

Stitch Diagram: *Scoop up all the crossing threads in a noose and weave a small circle.*

Fasten on at one of the two coral knots, marked **12** in these diagrams. Pass the working thread over all the crossing festoon threads, then under them, scooping them all together (with some tension) into a noose and returning to the second coral knot (also **12**). Catch the working thread behind or around this knot and wind to center. Pass over the axis into the backface, emerge again and weave a small wheel around the radiating warps.

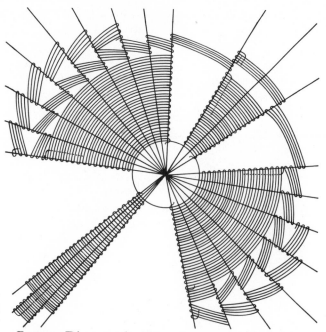

Pattern Diagram **b**: *Weave a segment at a time.*

This pattern diagram illustrates the needleweaving that is worked after the warps are gathered in a noose (Pattern Diagram **a**) and a small wheel is woven at the center (Stitch Diagram). With a very long working thread, weave each wing, using nine warps for the left wing and eight for the right. Then, in another color and/or texture, weave the long body over three warps at the top and four graduating to two at the tail. Achieve lacy edges by weaving two warps together at a time in the direction of the slant. To move around the edge, use a long overcast to add a new warp. Then drop the first and needleweave the new pair together. This edging is made in two journeys.

MOTIF **6F**
BASKET OF FLOWERS CORNER MOTIF

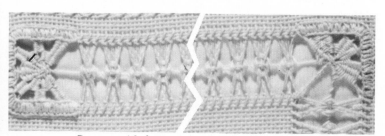

See page 10 for entire photo.

The pattern and stitches for this basket of flowers appear in *Pulled Canvas;* the foliage is in *Needleweaving.* The hemstitched borders are shown here. The very narrow border closest to the outer edge is stem stitch (**2Eb**), worked on a band from which one element has been withdrawn. The narrow border next to it is worked in serpentine bars (**2I**); four elements have been withdrawn. A pattern diagram follows for the wider corner bands of hemstitching. The little butterfly sitting on a strawberry is worked in long spaced buttonhole stitches and coral knots.

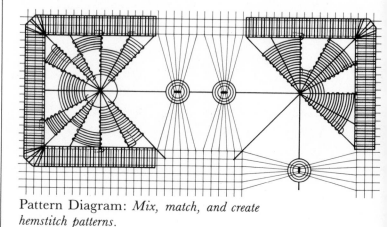

Pattern Diagram: *Mix, match, and create hemstitch patterns.*

Once you have mastered the techniques of adding more spokes and collecting them into small wheels, you can create needlewoven patterns to fill any open space. To work a corner band such as this, withdraw fourteen elements from each direction for the length of opened space you require. This pattern diagram is a shortened version of the Basket of Flowers border. The bundled clusters are worked first, as in **3D**, omitting the festoon journeys. Small wheels are woven, and then diagonal spokes are thrown in the opened spaces and overcast to the center. The pattern on the right is needlewoven like the pinwheel (**6C**). The pattern on the left progresses by passing from one group of warps to another.

LESSON 7

TENERIFFE LACE SQUARES

A NEEDLEWOVEN BARS

B SINGLE WEB WITH CENTER WHEEL AND CIRCLE OF LITTLE WHEELS

C KNOTTED SPIRAL

D DOUBLE WEB

E INTERLACED DOUBLE WEB

F WOVEN FLOWER

FOUR completely opened squares for Teneriffe lace are shown in this lesson. Although the elements are completely withdrawn from both directions, they are included in this volume because the concept of the open square is derived from hemstitched borders. When using these Teneriffe squares at intersections of opened bands, you may want to provide extra support for them by leaving some warps in the opened bands for buttonholing or needleweaving. Both procedures are described here. The second and third patterns, **7B** and **7C**, employ webs of single warps radiating from a center wheel. The construction of a web with double warps is illustrated in **7D** which becomes the first stage of the squares shown in **7E** and **7F**. An infinite number of patterns can be developed once you have constructed these webs.

STITCH 7A

NEEDLEWOVEN BARS

A large cross of four long vertical elements crossing four long horizontal elements remains after eighteen elements are cut and withdrawn from the four corners of the large square. You can see the location of this Teneriffe section of Sampler II on the master pattern. The outer padded buttonhole edge is described in **1C**.

Sampler II: *Divide a large opened square into four smaller squares with a large needlewoven cross.*

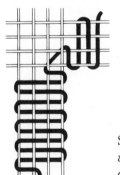

Stitch Diagram: *Start at the base, weave to center, turn the work, and weave a perpendicular bar.*

Needleweave the large cross that provides the support for the Teneriffe lace. Start the process at the base of a bar and needleweave pairs of warps to the center mesh square. Then, turn the work and needleweave a bar at a right angle to the one just completed, working from the center out to the edge. Follow the same procedure for the remaining two bars. Whenever possible, needleweave away from yourself; this enables you to use the needle as a shuttle, so that you can compress the stitches and align the warps. To start a bar, emerge on the frontface between pairs of warps. Pass over one pair of warps, then under all four elements, emerging on the other side. Fill the remainder of the bar by inserting the needle from the frontface between the pairs of warps, emerging alternately on the left and right sides of the bar. Complete the last bar by passing over the two warps closest to the next bar to be worked. Emerge between the pairs of warps on the next bar and continue; start each new bar in this fashion.

STITCH 7B

SINGLE WEB WITH CENTER WHEEL AND CIRCLE OF LITTLE WHEELS

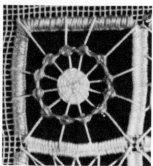

Sampler II: *Surround a center wheel with smaller ones worked at each spoke.*

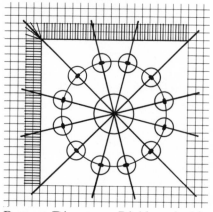

Pattern Diagram: *Divide each side of the square in thirds. Center the little wheels on the warps.*

Divide each side of the square into three segments by throwing the working thread across it in the order shown by the stitch diagram and to the locations shown in this pattern diagram. Draw the thrown threads into taut, radiating warps with a center wheel. Then describe a circle with a series of coral knots worked in the middle of each warp, and in a second journey, weave a little wheel over each knot.

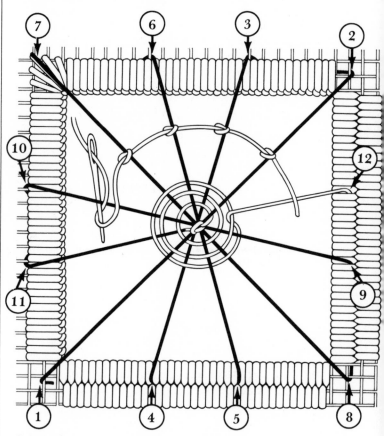

Stitch Diagram **a**: *Collect the warps with a wheel; then work a circle of coral knots.*

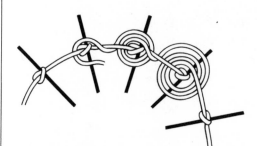

Stitch Diagram **b**: *Weave a little wheel around each coral knot.*

Start this single warped web by emerging at **1** in the lower left corner (**a**). Throw the working thread diagonally across the square and enter the backface at **2**. Pass the connecting thread on the backface to the left and emerge at **3**. You can catch connecting threads on the backface to prevent them from showing on the frontface. Continue to work counterclockwise around the square. Do not throw the last warp into **12** until you complete the center wheel. After emerging at **11**, fasten a coral knot at the center and collect the radiating warps by passing under and over them counterclockwise. When the wheel is large enough, insert the needle into a preceding row and throw the last warp at **12**. If you are changing color, as in Sampler II, fasten off; if not, wind back to the center of the twelfth warp and start the circle of coral knots. When you change color you can fasten on the new thread with a waste knot at the side to start the first coral knot. After you complete the circle of coral knots, weave each of the wheels (**b**). Pass over the warp above the knot, pass under the connecting thread, and over the warp below the knot. Encircle each coral knot twice before passing to the next one.

STITCH 7C

KNOTTED SPIRAL

Sampler II: *Turn a center wheel into a spiral.*

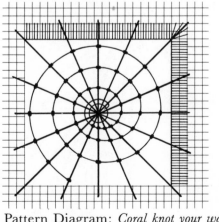

Pattern Diagram: *Coral knot your way around the warps.*

Divide each side of the square into four segments by throwing the working thread across it in the order shown by the stitch diagram and in the locations shown by the pattern diagram. Draw the thrown threads into taut radiating warps with a center wheel. Then, in a continuous operation, turn the wheel into a spiral by working a coral knot over each warp.

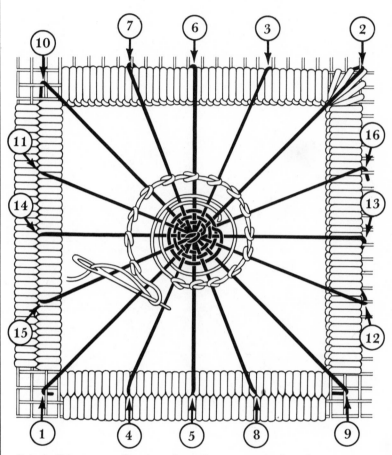

Stitch Diagram: *Continue from the center wheel to the spiral, revolving in the same direction.*

The method for stretching this single web is the same as for the previous web (**7B**). Start at **1** and follow the same system, completing warp **16** *after* weaving the center wheel. If you are employing the same working thread for the spiral, wind back after completing warp **16**. Or, weave a round or two of a new color, as in Sampler II. Then work the coral knots over each warp, circling the web in the same direction as the center wheel. Turn the work as you progress.

STITCH 7D

DOUBLE WEB

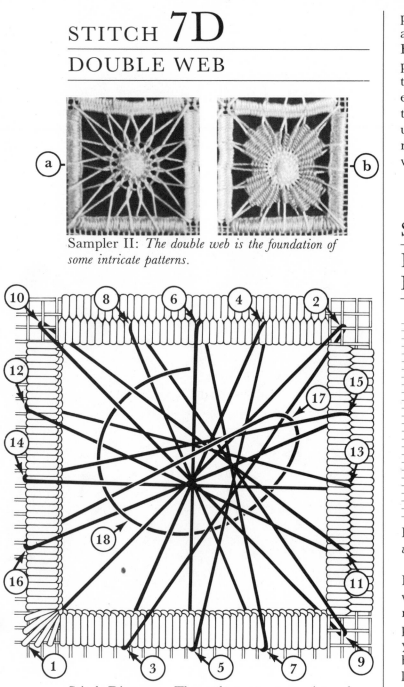

Sampler II: *The double web is the foundation of some intricate patterns.*

Stitch Diagram: *Throw the warps at even intervals back and forth around the square.*

The method for producing the double web shown in this diagram is employed in the following two patterns, **7E** and **7F**. The technique is similar to that of Teneriffe lace, where the thrown threads loop around pins at the perimeter of a circle. In these two patterns, the thrown threads loop around the bound edges of the squares. The sixteen double warps are caught in the center by a woven wheel. Start the web at **1** in the lower left corner. Notice that this is the only single stretched thread; it becomes a double warp after you com-

plete the wheel. Throw the thread diagonally across the square and enter the backface at **2**. Emerge and throw the thread to **3**. Continue to pass counterclockwise around the square; enter the square each time from the frontface. After you emerge from **16**, the last thrown thread, pass over the center and enter the backface at **17**; pass under the center and emerge at **18**. This last maneuver collects all of the warps. Now proceed to weave a center wheel.

STITCH 7E

INTERLACED DOUBLE WEB

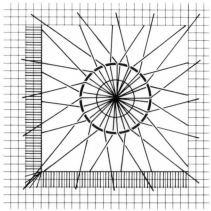

Pattern Diagram: *Interlace inverted warps around a double web.*

First establish the double web with woven center wheel described in Stitch Diagram **7D**. Then regroup the radiating warps by inverting adjacent pairs. When you interlace the inverted warps as you pass around the web, you produce the sunburst pattern (**7Da**) so typical of Teneriffe, or *sol,* lace.

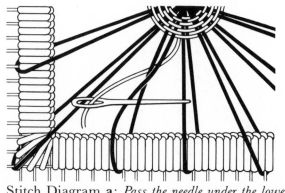

Stitch Diagram **a**: *Pass the needle under the lower warp and rest the tip on an upper one.*

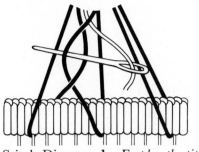

Stitch Diagram **b**: *Employ the tip of the needle as a pivot as you rotate the shank.*

Use very little tension as you throw the warps to produce this double web. You will be employing tension when interlacing them and will require a little play in the warps. Weave the center wheel, treating each of the paired warps as single ones. The interlaced inverted warps in this pattern are copies of those in the band shown in **4A**. Fasten on the interlacing thread behind the wheel and work in a clockwise direction, inverting a top warp of one ray with a lower warp of the ray to the left of it. To accomplish this, pass the tip of the needle under the lower warp and rest the tip on an upper one (**a**). Employ the tip of the needle as a pivot and rotate the shank to point the needle in the opposite direction (**b**). Hold the bent warps with one hand as you draw the needle through. Exert a slight tug on the working thread to maintain a taut lacing. Interlace the remaining warps in the same way.

STITCH 7F
WOVEN FLOWER

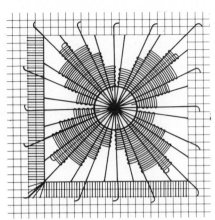

Pattern Diagram: *Include eight warps in a segment; reduce to six, then four, then two.*

To work the needlewoven flower shape as in this Teneriffe square from Sampler II (**7Db**), you first establish a double web as described in **7D**. When you work the center wheel, pass over and under every single warp to separate the thirty-two shown in this diagram. This many warps enable you to produce many needlewoven patterns. Start each of these four needlewoven segments by including eight warps; then omit the two end warps and needleweave six warps. Continue to decrease by omitting the end warps until only two remain. Fasten off by inserting the needle between the last two weaves and carrying a long thread to the center. Catch the working thread there and work the other three segments in the same way.

LESSON 8

FOUR-SIDED EDGE

A FOUR-SIDED EDGE

FOUR-SIDED edge is a traditional method for turning back the raw edges of square embroidered linens. It is shown here as an edge for Sampler II, where it is worked between withdrawn elements to complete the sampler and conclude the hemstitching lessons.

STITCH 8A
FOUR-SIDED EDGE

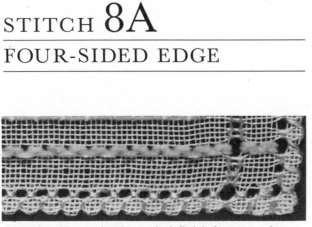

Sampler II: *A simply worked finish for a sampler.*

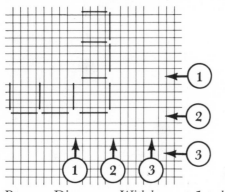

Pattern Diagram: *Withdraw at **1** to locate the top of the stitch and at **2** for the base. The cutting edge (**3**) will align with **1** when the edge is folded.*

Withdraw single elements from three positions along each of the four sides of the canvas (see the master pattern, Sampler II). Withdraw the first element (**1**) to locate the top of the four-sided stitch. Then, four elements away toward the outer edge, withdraw the second element (**2**) to locate the base of the stitch and the final folded edge. Four elements beyond this, withdraw a third element (**3**) that will align with the first one when the edge is folded to the backface. If you are working a four-sided stitch over three by three or two by two elements, withdraw the elements a corresponding distance apart.

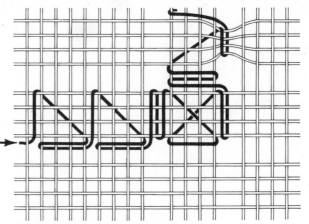

Stitch Diagram **a**: *Work the first journey in an open four-sided stitch.*

Stitch Diagram **b**: *Then fold back a matching set of elements and work a second journey.*

Travel left to right. Work extra overcasts at the sides of the corners where an element has been withdrawn (**a**). Use medium tension to draw the elements together; the straight stitch becomes slanted. After completing the first journey, remove the canvas from the frame. Turn back the hem and finger-press along the base of the stitches, being careful to align the canvas elements of both layers. Now begin a second journey where you started the first, reversing the procedure. This will close the squares (**b**). Work the other three sides of the canvas in this way. At the corners, be careful to align the elements; clip away some of the excess canvas. You can secure the cut ends with acid-free glue.

THE OPEN CANVAS
IN COLOR

*Originally, open work was stitched with white threads;
color contributes a contemporary excitement. The work
shown here employs techniques from* The Open Canvas.

*This Basket of Flowers tray cloth contains needleweaving,
hemstitching, and pulled canvas work.*

Pulled Canvas *Sampler I*

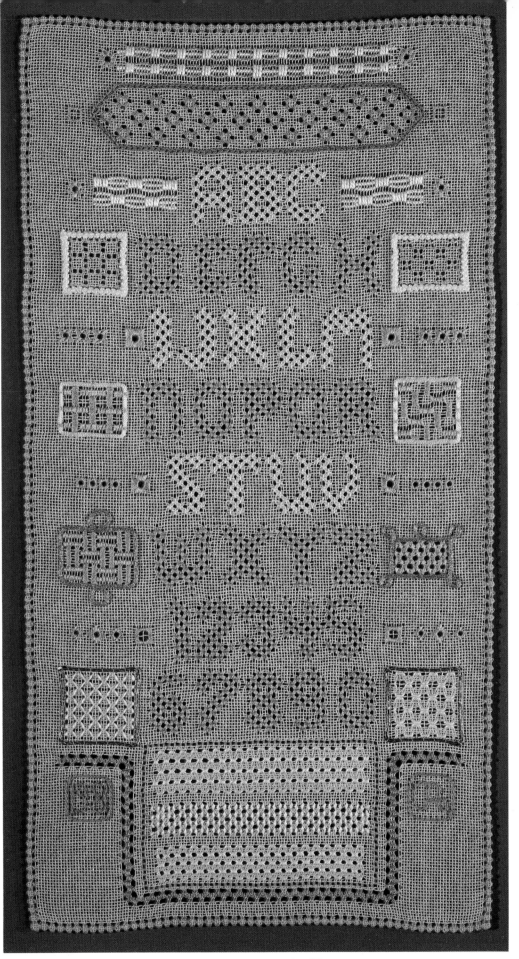

Pulled Canvas *Sampler II*

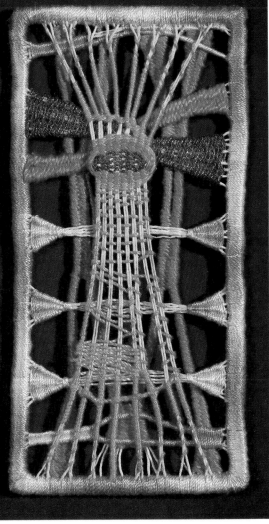

Three levels of needleweaving are freely worked on carefully selected warps.

An opened circle of freely-worked needleweaving from the darned cardigan shown later in this section.

The selected warps are interwoven in this example of freely-worked needleweaving.

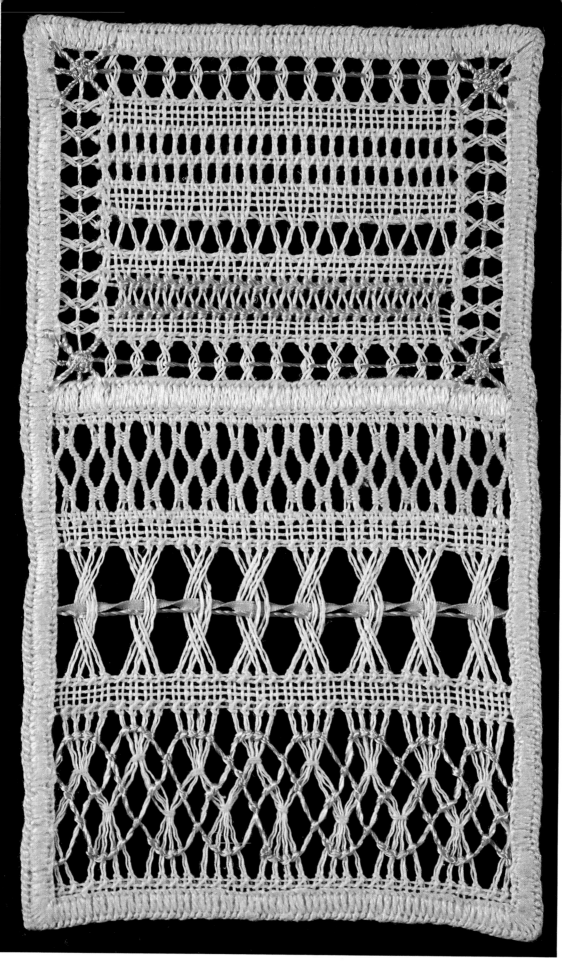

Hemstitching *Sampler I*

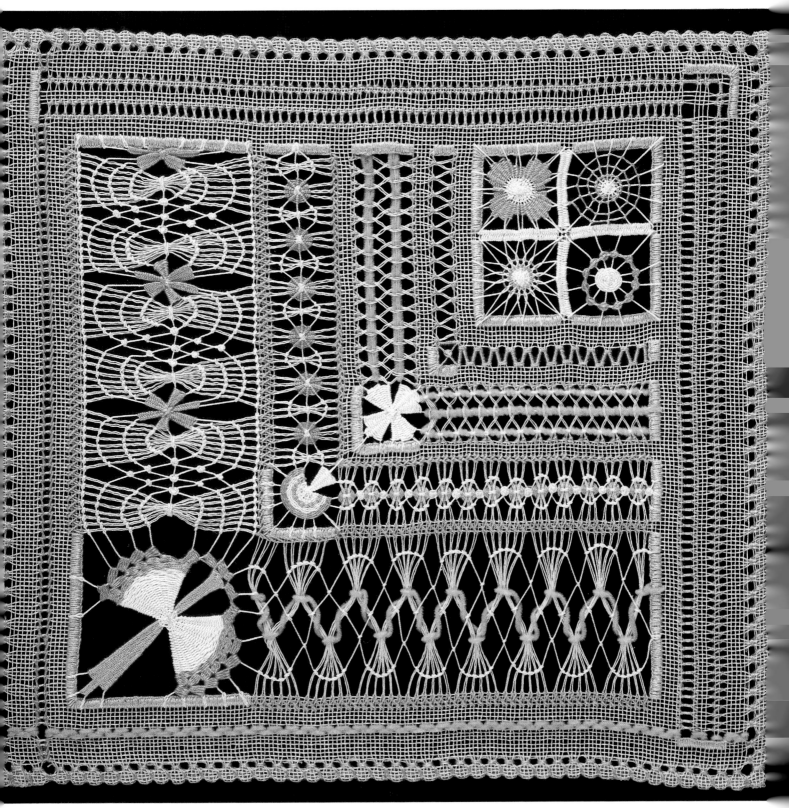

Hemstitching *Sampler II*

Filet *Sampler I*

Filet *Sampler II*

*Each opened octagon and circle on the
darned cardigan is filled with a different pattern.
These are all worked in filet.*

*This Tree of Flowers tray cloth is also
worked entirely in filet.*

Hardanger *Neck Ruff*

*These shapes from the darned cardigan
are filled with Hardanger. Mix and match your
own fillings in any way you choose.*

Hardanger *Sampler*

Reticello and Hedebo *Sampler*

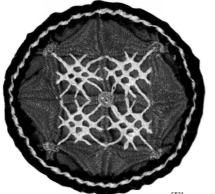

These opened shapes demonstrate a variety of techniques from The Open Canvas. The circles have outlines of Pekinese stitch from Needleweaving. The octagons have buttonhole outlines from Filet. The double diamonds shown on the first page of this section have backstitched outlines and are filled with pulled canvas and blackwork patterns.

The darned cardigan has a background of black darning stitches on tan canvas.

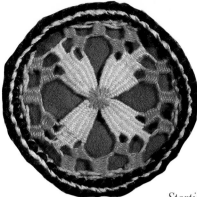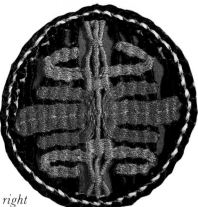

Starting on the opposite page and reading from left to right are a circle using reticello and Hedebo; an octagon using Hardanger and filet; a circle using hemstitching; a circle using Hardanger and filet; an octagon using filet and reticello; and a circle using needleweaving. An embroidery hoop was used to work each of the opened shapes.

The binding of the darned cardigan is knitted; the buttons are crocheted.

*This quilted kimono has an attached canvas band
filled with blackwork and pulled canvas.*

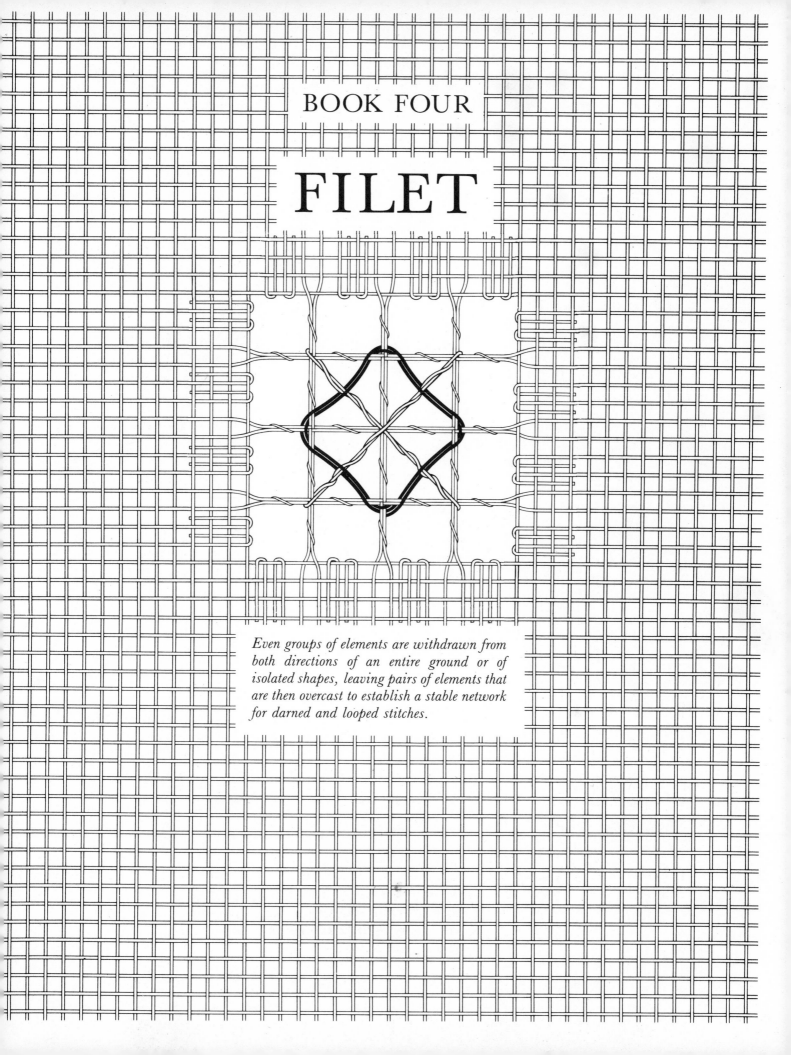

BOOK FOUR

FILET

Even groups of elements are withdrawn from both directions of an entire ground or of isolated shapes, leaving pairs of elements that are then overcast to establish a stable network for darned and looped stitches.

CONTENTS

INTRODUCTION

Filet, pronounced *filay,* is a French term for either a net ground or the pattern on it, depending on the lace authority consulted. However, when the word filet is used in this volume, it applies to the ground only. It may also refer to a single pair of elements. Two samplers are provided to explore this rich field of withdrawn element embroidery. Sampler I serves as a thorough introduction to the many stitch techniques that you can employ on a filet ground. Sampler II serves to illustrate how you can introduce filet into a canvas work composed of other techniques. It is not necessary to work these particular samplers to understand filet; however, they do demonstrate each stitch of the lessons. Study them as you practice each stitch. The first lesson on canvas preparation deals with the withdrawal of the elements. Then, in each subsequent lesson, a family of related work is explored, and the samplers are gradually completed. On page 154, there is a photograph of a Tree of Flowers design by Patti Baker Russell, who drew the diagrams for *The Open Canvas.* After completing *Filet,* the artist was inspired to create her own flowers using the stitches she had drawn.

A THIMBLEFUL OF HISTORY

Lacis, filet guipure, filet Richelieu, filet lace, darned netting, netted lace, and *guipure d'art* are some of the names associated with this ancient lace form. The first nets were probably used for fishing or trapping. The earliest recorded filet used for needleweaving has been seen on Egyptian tomb paintings, where the robes of the royal figures are darned networks of gold, silver, and colored silks; examples of this work have also been found on mummy wrappings. Darned netting apparently continued to be employed through the middle ages and into the sixteenth century, when it became highly fashionable in Italy, France, and England.

This hand-knotted netting, made much as it is today, was called the *réseau,* and was used unornamented for bed coverings, curtains, and valances. When it was decorated with patterns it was called *lacis* or darned netting. The fillings that were considered correct and tasteful up to the middle of this century were the cloth, ladder, darned outlines, and loopstitch of Lessons **2** through **5.** Needleweaving was considered a debased Victorian innovation by recognized lace authorities and collectors when it first appeared.

Various pattern books for ladies of the leisure class were printed in the sixteenth century. The earliest, *Il Burato,* appeared in Italy in 1527. It is interesting to note here that these patterns were for darned lace on a woven lenogauze, a stiff material used for sieves. However, the most popular volumes, particularly amongst the women of the French court, were by a Venetian named Federic Vinciolo. The first editions were published in Paris in 1587. In one book, *Point Coupé,* rich geometric patterns were printed white on black for reticello, as seen in the *Reticello and Hedebo* section of *The Open Canvas.* The second book was *Lacis,* in which patterns were shown in squares with counted stitches, much like the Tree of Flowers pattern on page 154. The designs were of flowers, animals, birds, and fashionable goddesses. Catherine de' Medici, then the queen of France, is said to have given Vinciolo the exclusive right to manufacture the large starched ruffs that she made so fashionable.

Catherine learned embroidery and lace making as a girl attending convent school in Florence. Later, during her unsatisfactory marriage to Henry II, needlework became her chief source of pleasure. Her daughter-in-law, Mary Stuart, whose life was even more miserable, acquired her knowledge of embroidery and *lacis* while a young bride at Catherine's court, previous to 1560. Mary also found solace in needlework. When Catherine died, almost a thousand squares of netted lace were found among her possessions. Queen Mary disposed of her large store of netting in her will.

At this time in history, small netted squares were worked that were later joined together to make large hangings and bed valances. These squares were also combined with other needlework, including reticello. By the nineteenth century, darned netting was being made in Venetian lace factories. The net was stretched on large frames, and about a half-dozen girls darned large curtains and bedspreads. Fine linen thread was used in the small squares and for clothing, coarser thread in the larger squares and for home furnishings. After the turn of the century, with the immense popularity of crochet, a corruption of darned netting became the familiar crocheted filet.

There are many lace makers today using the old *lacis* techniques in a contemporary manner. And, as shown in *Filet,* the fillings can be adapted for use on grounds of withdrawn canvas elements as well as on hand-knotted networks.

IMPORTANT NOTE

In drawing the stitch diagrams for *Filet,* it was necessary to employ two techniques. In over half of the drawings, the two paired elements that make up a filet are drawn with two lines, as if they were already overcast together (see **1B**). However, in order to illustrate a number of the stitches more clearly, the elements were sometimes drawn separately, as if they were *not* overcast (as in **1E**). In most cases, this was done to show how stitches could be "locked" in place by passing the working thread between the two elements.

WORKBASKET SUPPLIES

CANVAS

Mono canvas is the only variety that allows you to withdraw alternate pairs of elements without any difficulty. Use the best quality, as the canvas filet network becomes an integral part of the work—as important visually as the embroidery threads. The size of the mesh depends on the design and the degree of your patience. Large mesh, like the 10/inch of the two samplers, can be worked with fine threads and is easily turned into a network. On the other hand, 24/inch congress canvas is more delicate, but it requires more patience as well.

THREADS

Use a working thread that matches the color of the canvas for overcasting the network. This part of the stitching is done as subtly as possible, with no contrast of any kind. Embroidery floss is a good choice. For filling the network, use twisted or lightly twisted threads that are easy to manage, such as any of the DMC cottons, silk twist,

smooth linen, and fine twisted metals. Patti Russell used J & P Coats Dual Duty cotton threads on her Tree of Flowers design, which proves that threads need not be expensive or difficult to find. Colored threads are exciting and interesting; white, ecru, and pale pastels are quiet and dignified. The weight of the thread is very noticeable in this work. Cloth, ladder, loopstitch, and needleweaving should be worked in a thread that is finer than the canvas elements. Darning, as shown in Lesson **4**, is usually employed for emphasis, and thread should be the same weight as or heavier than the canvas elements. Combining weights of threads adds interest and texture to filet.

STRETCHERS

As in the other sections of *The Open Canvas,* stretcher strips are recommended because they can be turned over easily, and securing threads can be gotten out of the way while the work is in progress.

NEEDLES AND OTHER TOOLS

You will need tapestry needles in appropriate sizes; crewel and sharps for securing elements or difficult working threads; and a chenille needle if you are sinking a heavy couched thread or stitching with chenille in Sampler II. An awl is a useful pointed tool for tracing the movement of working threads when studying stitch diagrams and for locating and enlarging eyelet holes.

SOME NEEDLE POINTS

If you have attempted knotting a network and found the technique not to your liking, try this withdrawn element method to obtain a netted foundation. The technique is similar to that of a Russian drawn ground, where three elements were withdrawn alternately in each direction from fine white linen and the remaining elements overcast. In the drawn work of prerevolutionary Russian embroidery, charming pictorial scenes were worked employing the same stitches shown in Lessons **1** through **5**. However, withdrawing canvas elements is much less tedious than withdrawing the hundreds of fine linen threads needed for a Russian drawn ground, and also easier than constructing an entire netting by a series of knots. The canvas elements can be woven back into the canvas ground, a method employed in Sampler II for finishing the outer edges.

There are many advantages to working on a

canvas network besides its ease of production. The overcast pairs of elements provide convenient locations for securing working threads on the backface. The already stiffened body of the canvas elements comfortably supports the darned and looped stitches.

It should be noted here that isolated shapes can be opened without employing the embroidered borders shown in Sampler II. Use the same withdrawing and tacking techniques, and with a sharp needle and a thread that matches the canvas, tack the withdrawn elements to the canvas invisibly on the backface.

In Lesson 2, cloth stitch is explored; it was used exclusively in the earliest *lacis*. Although it is a very simply worked double darning, the plotting of its movement can be challenging. You must chart a course ahead of the work in order to proceed with a minimum of starting, stopping, and twisting. All of this is explained by the diagrams in Lesson 2. The names of *filet Richelieu* and *guipure d'art* were given to the darned netting of a later period, when the remaining stitches were added to the repertoire of netted lace stitches. You will find many of the techniques very similar to other forms of open work, but on the canvas network they must be employed in a slightly different way.

KEY TO STITCHES AND THREADS
Sampler I

Sampler I is an entire ground of canvas filet worked with linen, cotton, and silk thread on 10/inch tan mono canvas. The finished size is 9 inches by 13 inches. See the accompanying key to identify the stitches and threads. The bold numbers with letters refer to the lesson and diagram where each stitch or pattern is located in *Filet*. The bold italic numbers refer to the threads listed under Materials Employed.

1B Overcasting the Network, *1*
2A Squares, *4*
2B Twisting, *4*
2C Simple Flowers, *4*
2D Cross, *4*
2E Large Shape, *4*
3A Ladder Filling, *5*
3B Ladder in Two Directions, *5*
4A Darned Outline, *6*
4B Overcast Darned Outline, *2*
4C Stalks and Tendrils, *7*

4D Darned Outline or Underlay, *2*
4E Darned Border, *7*
4F Darned Corners, *6*
5B Loopstitch Ground, *2*
5C Loopstitch Border, *2*
6A Pyramid, *5*
6B Maltese Points, *8*
6C Leaf with Stem, *5*
6D Leaves with Two Veins, *5*
6E Crossed Leaves, *2*
7A Four-Pointed Star, *3*

7B Six- or Eight-Pointed Star, *3*
7C Super Star, *7*
8Ba Woven Wheel, *5*
8Bb Darned Wheel, *5*
8Ca Ribbed Wheel, *5*
8Cb Reverse Ribbed Wheel, *5*
8Da Ribbed Diamond, *5*
8Db Reverse Ribbed Diamond, *5*
8E Reverse Ribbed Pyramid, *5*
8F Darned Rim, *5*
8G Darned Corners with Spokes, *5*
9A Loop and Ladder, *2* on *5*
9B Small Circles and Loopstitch, *3, 8*
9C Large Circles, *7*
9D Ladder and Spoke, *5, 8*
9E Basketweave, *3*
9F Crossed Loopstitch, *8* on *3*
9G Checker, *3*
10A Buttonhole Filling, *8*
10B Buttonhole Star, *8*
10C Double Buttonhole Edge, *1*
10D Looped Picot, *2*
12A Bullion Knots, *2*

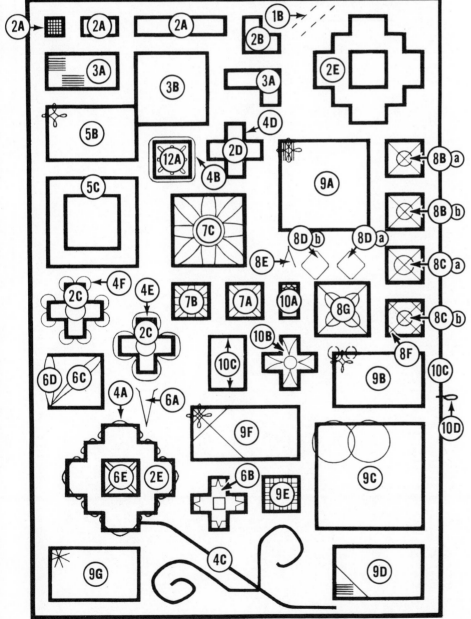

MATERIALS EMPLOYED

CANVAS
10/inch tan mono
12 inches wide by 16 inches high; edges bound

THREADS
1 DMC 6-strand embroidery floss, 613 tan
2 DMC Pearl Cotton, size 8, 957 pink
3 DMC Soft Embroidery and Tapestry Cotton (matte finish), 2818 pink
4 Külort lingarn Swedish linen, size 16/2, 319 beige
5 Külort lingarn Swedish linen, size 16/2, 202 yellow
6 Square-Sale Scottish linen, size 10/2, pink
7 Square-Sale Scottish linen, size 10/2, maize
8 Embroidery silk twist, pink

NEEDLES
Tapestry 18, 20
Millinery

STRETCHER STRIPS
1 pair 12-inch   1 pair 16-inch

Sampler I

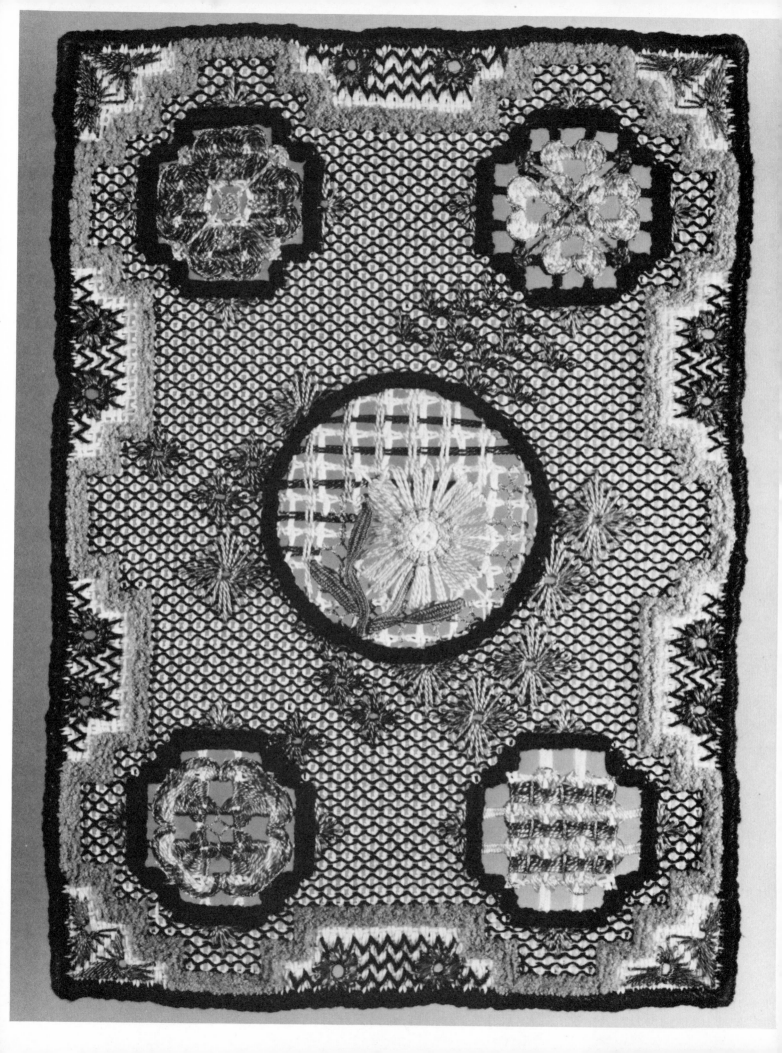

KEY TO STITCHES
AND THREADS
Sampler II

Sampler II involves isolated shapes of filet worked with pearl and crochet cotton, metal, and silk chenille on 10/inch white mono canvas. The finished size is 8½ inches by 11¾ inches. See the accompanying key to identify the stitches and threads. The bold numbers with letters refer to the lesson and diagram where each stitch or pattern is located in *Filet*. The bold italic numbers refer to the threads, which are listed under Materials Employed.

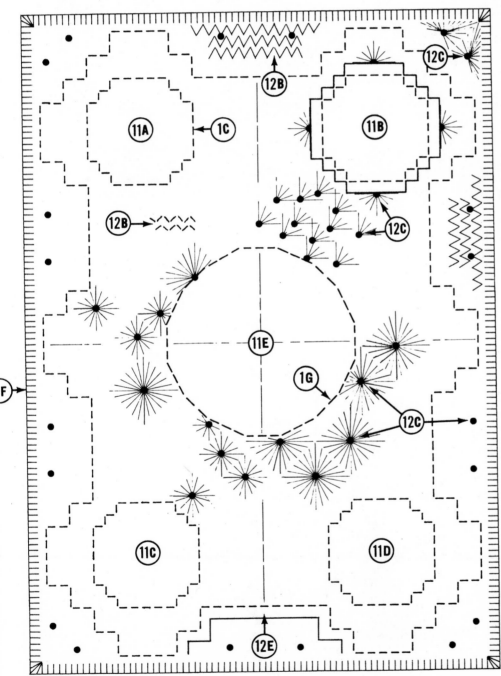

1 Canvas preparation, *4, 6*
1F Buttonhole Edge, *4*
1G Chain Stitch, *5*
11A Cloth Flower, *1, 3, 7, 10*
11B Double Petal, *1, 7, 10*
11C Darned Corners, *2, 3, 7, 10*
11D Woven, *2, 3, 8, 9, 10*
11E Chrysanthemum, *1, 2, 3, 7, 8, 9, 10*
12B Canvas Lace and Blackwork, *5, 6*
12C Eyelet Variations, *1, 2, 3*
12E Couching, *11, 12*

MATERIALS EMPLOYED

CANVAS
10/inch white mono, 12 inches wide by 16 inches high; edges bound

THREADS
1 DMC Pearl Cotton, size 3, 920 dark rust
2 DMC Pearl Cotton, size 5, 920 dark rust
3 DMC Pearl Cotton, size 5, 922 light rust
4 DMC Pearl Cotton, size 3, 823 navy
5 DMC Pearl Cotton, size 5, 823 navy
6 DMC Pearl Cotton, size 8, 310 black
7 DMC Pearl Cotton, size 5, 108 shaded yellow
8 DMC Pearl Cotton, size 5, 742 yellow
9 DMC Cordonnet Crochet Cotton, 6-cord, size 10, white
10 Lumiyarn Metal, size 1½, gold
11 Soie Chenille, yellow/gold color
12 Silk Sewing Thread, yellow

NEEDLES
Tapestry 18, 20

STRETCHER STRIPS
1 pair 12-inch   1 pair 16-inch

Sampler II

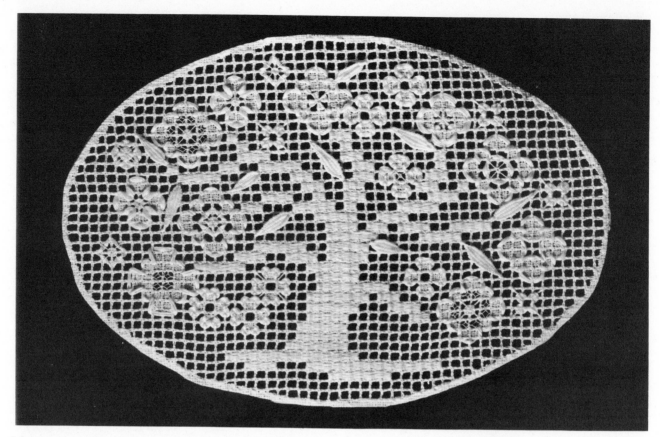

Mounted under glass as a tray cloth, the Tree of Flowers was designed and worked by Patti Baker Russell, who was inspired to create it while illustrating this section of *The Open Canvas*.

MASTER PATTERN
Tree of Flowers

The graph grids represent the filet network. All of the stitches are covered in these lessons. The design is worked on a 24/inch white congress canvas with readily available heavy-duty white cotton thread. The finished size is 8¾ inches by 5¾ inches.

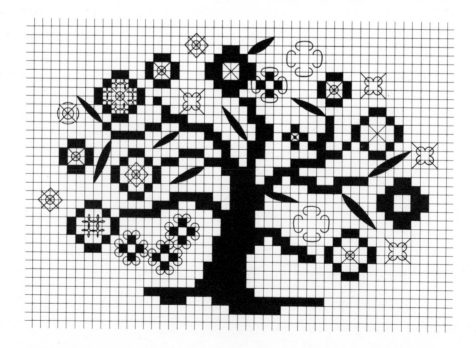

154 FILET–PATTERN DIAGRAM, BASKET OF FLOWERS

LESSON 1

CANVAS PREPARATION

THIS lesson contains the master patterns for both samplers. In addition, methods are supplied for establishing a complete network, as demonstrated by Sampler I, and for the five isolated shapes of Sampler II. In the first instance, the withdrawn elements are all unplucked and rewoven into the marginal canvas area. A quick way to temporarily dispose of them is to tape them down on the backface with paper tape. In the second sampler, five different edgings are demonstrated as borders for the isolated shapes of filet. A less formal edging method for a more contemporary design is simply to tack the withdrawn elements down on the backface with a sharp needle and matching thread. Because of the loose open weave of canvas, you must find a way to prevent further unraveling of the withdrawn elements; on finely woven fabric, this is less crucial.

MASTER PATTERN, SAMPLER I

The master pattern for Sampler I shows the network of elements that remains after alternate pairs of elements have been withdrawn from both directions of the entire ground. The heavy black outlines define the paired elements that are incorporated in stitch patterns in the subsequent lessons. The withdrawing is accomplished before "framing up" (stretching the canvas on the frame). In this sampler, a network of twenty-four pairs of elements by thirty-six pairs remains, which means that to follow this pattern you should start with a rectangle of forty-eight by seventy-two elements. Making sure to leave 1½-inch margins, outline a rectangle of these dimensions with a basting thread or disappearing ink. See **1A** for withdrawing and reweaving the elements and **1B** for overcasting the network. The master pattern appears on the next page.

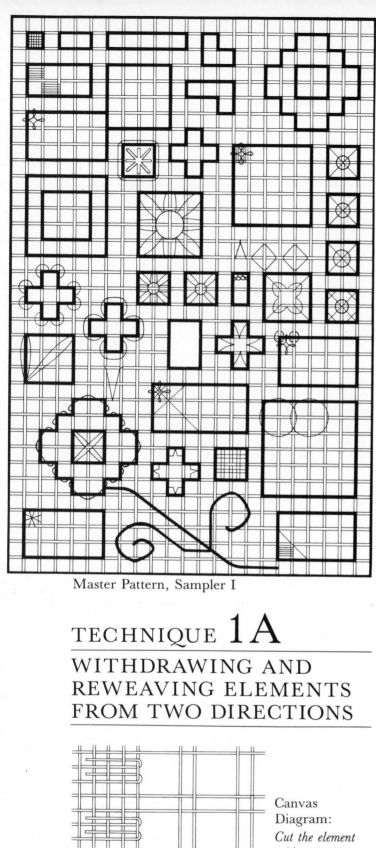

Master Pattern, Sampler I

TECHNIQUE 1A

WITHDRAWING AND REWEAVING ELEMENTS FROM TWO DIRECTIONS

Canvas Diagram: *Cut the element midway, pluck it out, and weave it into the marginal elements on the backface.*

Start the withdrawing process with the shorter elements, either warps or wefts. In Sampler I, you

withdraw the wefts first. To establish an even count of warps and wefts, which produces matching open squares on all sides, withdraw the two center elements first. Cut one of the center elements in the middle and unweave it to the margin, just beyond the marked perimeter. To unweave, pluck the element out with a tapestry needle or awl. Reweave on the backface by threading a tapestry needle with the element, passing over the first marginal element, and then under and over several others. Clip off the excess. This disposes of the withdrawn elements until the work is completed, at which time they are cut off altogether. They are kept at this time to prevent the canvas from distorting. Repeat the unweaving and reweaving on the other side. Then cut, withdraw, and reweave the other center element. Complete the withdrawing from one direction at a time.

STITCH 1B

OVERCASTING THE NETWORK

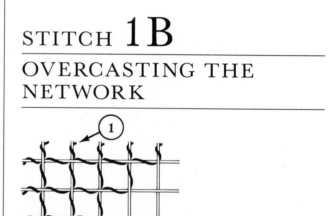

Stitch Diagram: *Travel in steplike diagonal rows.*

Draw the pairs of elements together by overcasting them in diagonal rows. Use a thread that matches the canvas and that is a little finer than the elements. Unstripped six-ply embroidery floss* run through beeswax is used in Sampler I and Cordonnet crochet cotton in Sampler II. Work with the canvas stretched on a frame. The canvas will not be taut until the overcasting is completed. Start to work in the upper left corner, descending in steplike zigzag rows using a scooping motion. Since descending is usually easier, turn the work after each row. Keep the needle in a diagonal position as you scoop under each intersection of paired elements. Secure and connect the threads in the woven margins.

* It is unnecessary to align the individual threads for this procedure. Rather, the working thread should resemble the twisted canvas element; it should become an integral part of the network.

Master Pattern, Sampler II

MASTER PATTERN, SAMPLER II

This master pattern for Sampler II involves five isolated shapes from which canvas elements are withdrawn in both directions to establish a network for the stitches of filet. The first segment of the canvas preparation, outlining and withdrawing the elements, is done before framing up. However, when dealing with areas that are closer together than the ones in this sampler, open and stitch one shape at a time. You can withdraw the elements on or off the frame, but do all of the filet embroidery on the frame. To follow this master pattern, baste the long center lines on the canvas to provide matching reference points. Backstitch the outer border outlines and those of the five openings, employing thread to match either their respective embroidered borders or the canvas ground. The following diagrams show how to prepare the shapes for the darned and looped fillings of the lessons to come.

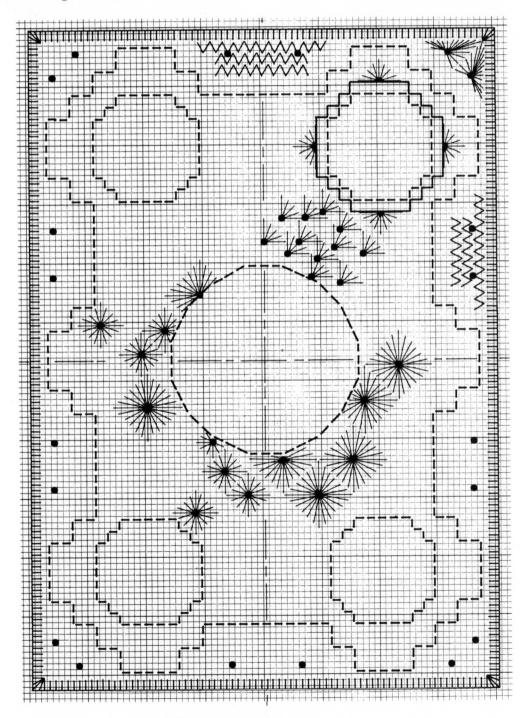

STITCH 1C

BACKSTITCH OUTLINE; CUTTING ELEMENTS

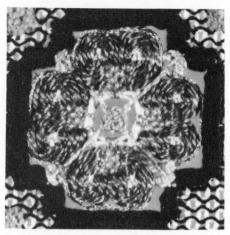

Sampler II: *The diagrams in 1C, 1D, 1E, and 1F illustrate how to prepare this squared shape.*

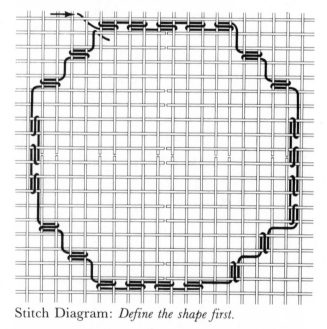

Stitch Diagram: *Define the shape first.*

This stitch diagram shows the backstitch outline that is indicated on the master pattern for Sampler II by a broken line. For each stitch, pass back two elements on the frontface and move ahead four on the backface. When you turn the corners, do not work slanted stitches on the backface; these would be seen when the shape was opened. Notice the locations for cutting the pairs of elements that are to be withdrawn. Cut them now, but do *not* withdraw them yet. First overcast around the shape, as in **1D**.

STITCH 1D

OVERCASTING THE BACKSTITCH OUTLINE

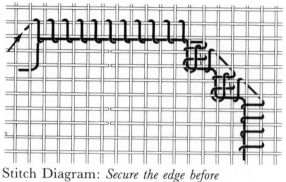

Stitch Diagram: *Secure the edge before withdrawing elements.*

For a square geometric shape such as this, a strong border is useful as a security measure. With straight overcast stitches, travel around the shape, including two rows of elements from the canvas ground and catching the backstitches in the process. If you do not want a border around a shape, employ fine matching thread or one-ply floss for the backstitches, and, using a sharp needle, overcast into the ground elements over just one row.

STITCH 1E

TACKING ELEMENTS DOWN ON THE BACKFACE

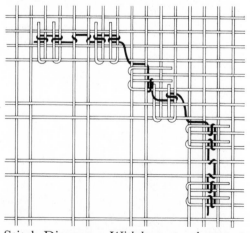

Stitch Diagram: *Withdraw one element at a time; then tack it down and trim it.*

After securing the elements around the edges of a shape, you are ready to withdraw and fasten down the cut pairs of elements. Turn the work to the backface. Withdraw one element at a time and tack it down over two rows of canvas with a backstitch, as shown. It is helpful to clip away the excess length of each element after it is tacked down. In this diagram, for the sake of clarity, the overcast backstitches of **1D** are not shown. Turn the work to the frontface to bind the edges (**1F**).

STITCH 1F

BINDING EDGES, FOUR VARIATIONS

BUTTONHOLE

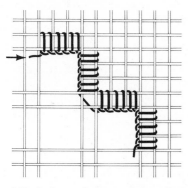

Work from left to right. Start a row by emerging at the edge on the frontface. Hold the working thread with the thumb of one hand and insert the needle into the backface at the top of the stitch. Emerge, pass the needle over the held thread, and draw it through to make the first stitch. Continue in this way.

DOUBLE BUTTONHOLE

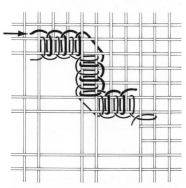

Space a row of buttonhole stitches far enough apart so that you can insert a second row between the stitches, to make festoons along the opposite side.

LONG ARM CROSS

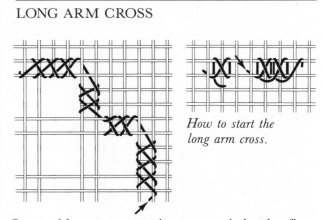

How to start the long arm cross.

Start with a compensating cross-stitch, the first arm of which heads in the direction of the row. The next complete stitch, the "long arm," passes over two elements.

Cross back over one element and advance over two each time for a close, padded edging.

SATIN

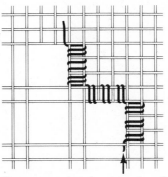

Overcast closely together between the elements. Line the stitches up side by side. Use as many stitches as you need.

STITCH 1G

CHAIN STITCH

Sampler II: *The diagrams in 1G, 1H, and 1I illustrate how to prepare this curved shape.*

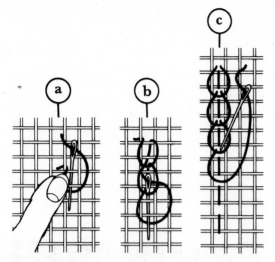

Stitch Diagram **a**: *Emerge, hold, insert, and emerge two away.*

Stitch Diagram **b**: *Draw up and repeat.*

Stitch Diagram **c**: *Work a chain over backstitch outlines.*

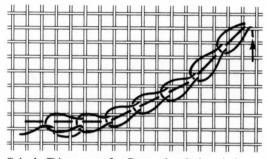

Stitch Diagram **d**: *Curve the chain stitches.*

Chain stitch outline is covered in **12B** of *Pulled Canvas*. In *Filet*, it is employed as a padding, to be whipped and then buttonholed. Start a chain, emerging on the frontface. Insert the needle back into the same hole, holding a loop of the working thread on the surface, and emerge again inside the loop (**a**), two elements away. Then draw up the working thread and continue in the same fashion (**b**). Chain outline can be worked over backstitches (**c**).

Chain stitch is particularly useful for outlining curved shapes. Stitch Diagram **d** shows a chain stitch worked over each outline backstitch of the central circular shape in Sampler II. This secures the shape so that paired elements can be withdrawn (**1H**).

STITCH 1H
TACKING DOWN

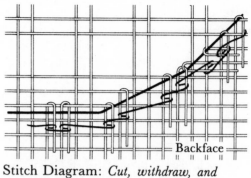

Stitch Diagram: *Cut, withdraw, and fasten on the backface.*

Cut the pairs of elements that cross each other in the center of the circle. Then cut alternate pairs along the center line, as in Stitch Diagram **1C**. Turn the canvas to the backface. Withdraw one element at a time, tacking it down with a backstitch as shown in this diagram. Clip away the excess length of each element after tacking it down to get it out of the way.

STITCH 1I
WHIPPED CHAIN STITCH

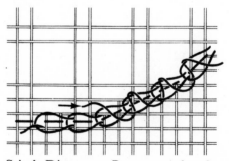

Stitch Diagram: *Pass over and under each chain.*

Whip a chain stitch outline by overcasting once around each chain without entering the backface. This procedure supplies a solid padding for the buttonhole edge seen in Sampler II. Work buttonhole stitches, as shown previously in **1F**, over the whipped chain without plunging into the backface. Your stitches should be perpendicular to the curve as you travel.

LESSON 2

CLOTH STITCH

A SQUARES

B TWISTING

C SIMPLE FLOWERS

D CROSSES

E LARGE SHAPES

C LOTH filling is also known as double darning, linen stitch, or *point de toile*. It resembles a regular plain weave in textiles, in which the threads of one direction pass over and under those that travel in the opposite direction, reversing their positions on adjacent rows. However, in filet, just as in *lacis*, the cloth stitch is woven within the open squares of the ground. Each square of cloth stitch has four warps and four wefts. Cloth stitch makes a light but solid filling that contrasts well with both the open network and any of the other fillings of *Filet*. It is a simple technique, as will be evident in the diagrams of this lesson. And it can be interesting to plot routes that employ a minimum amount of twisting or overcasting to get from one position to another.

STITCH 2A

SQUARES

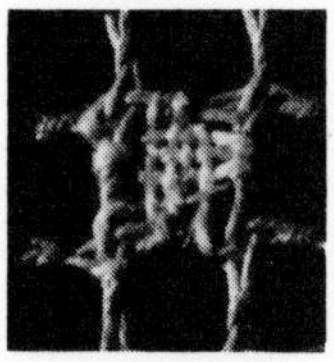

Sampler I: *Include the canvas network in the weaving.*

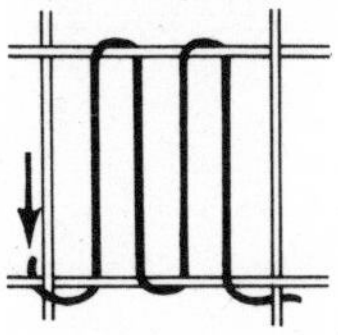

Stitch Diagram **a**: *Lay four warps, starting at a corner.*

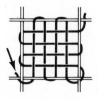

Stitch Diagram **b**: *Weave around a corner and darn the warps.*

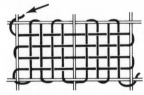

Sampler I: *Lay warps along the longer distances first; then fill the shorter ones.*

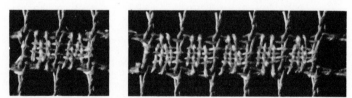

Stitch Diagram **c**: *Start in any corner.*

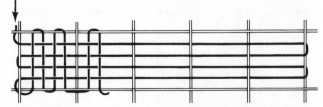

Stitch Diagram **d**: *Include any amount of ground, being sure to surround each intersection*

STITCH 2B
TWISTING

Sampler I: *Produce angular shapes without fastening off.*

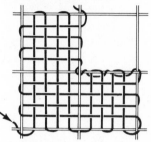

Stitch Diagram: *Overcast back when you reach a dead end.*

You can expand or reduce the number of cloth stitch squares to create patterns or pictures without having to fasten off and on when you arrive at what seems to be a dead end. This is accomplished by *twisting,* a method of overcasting back or forward over a filet. However, when you turn a corner or make a right angle, remember to overcast around the edges of the network as shown in this diagram; never make a diagonal stitch across an intersection. Also, do not move by twisting from one self-contained shape to another; fasten off and start again. Produce large squares of cloth stitch by weaving long warps over the shape and filling from the other direction. The large cloth stitch squares in Sampler I are a background for the needlewoven leaves of **6C** and **6D**, and for the bullion knots of **12A**.

STITCH 2C
SIMPLE FLOWERS

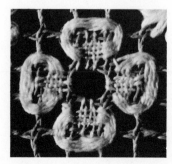

Sampler I: *Simple flowers.*

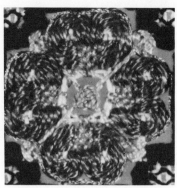

Sampler II: *Embellished flower motif.*

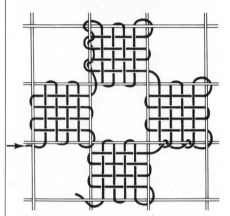

Stitch Diagram: *Pass from unit to unit with a minimum of twisting.*

To weave the cloth stitch grounds for the simple flower shapes of Samplers I and II, work four individual but connected squares around an open center. To understand the routes taken in these cloth stitch diagrams so that you can create your own patterns, draw several variations on paper. See which way works with the least amount of twisting from square to square.

STITCH 2D
CROSSES

Sampler I: *With a little maneuvering, you can fill a solid shape.*

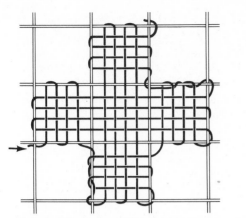

Stitch Diagram: *Think ahead as you lay the warps.*

To work a solid cloth cross as in Sampler I, start as for the flower (**2C**) but continue to lay the vertical warps for the upright part of the cross by twisting downward from the first square. Complete the lower square, then lay the warps for the right arm of the cross, fill across the three horizontal squares, and twist to fill the top square.

STITCH 2E

LARGE SHAPES

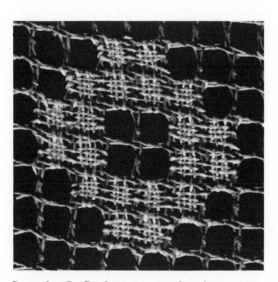

Sampler I: *Produce any angular shape.*

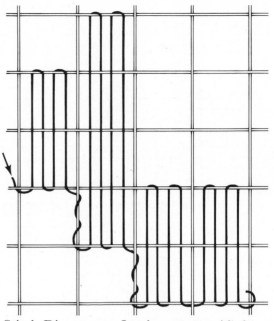

Stitch Diagram **a**: *Lay long warps with the help of some twisting.*

With a little experience, it is possible to fill any angular shape based on squares with the cloth stitch. In this large shape, a flower from Sampler I, you will be able to practice your maneuvering skills. In Stitch Diagram **a**, the warps are laid, with the help of some twisting, for one-quarter of the shape.

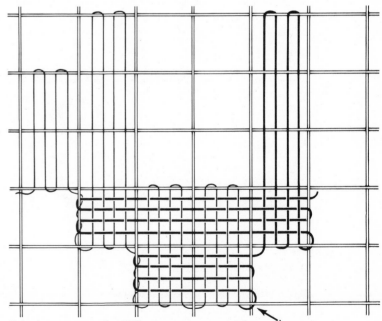

Stitch Diagram **b**: *Fill some squares, and lay some more.*

To weave the squares (**b**), pass around the lower right, hand corner and add the filling for the lower squares. Then lay the four vertical right-hand warps before completing the filling of the lower portion. With practice, these detours will become automatic. Old patterns such as this one were probably passed on from person to person, along with the easiest methods for working them.

The right side of the shape is completed first, and then the top segment (c). After completing the top, a decision is made as to whether to twist in steplike fashion to a position for completing the filling of the left side, or to start with a new working thread. The decision was made to employ a new thread, fastened on at the original starting location.

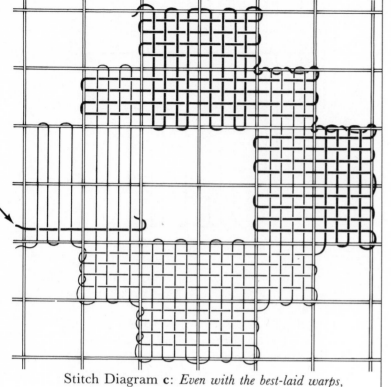

Stitch Diagram **c**: *Even with the best-laid warps, you may reach an impasse.*

LESSON 3

LADDER

A LADDER FILLING

B LADDER IN TWO DIRECTIONS

IN this lesson, ladder filling, the quickest and simplest of all filet work, is described. Also known as darning stitch, *point de reprise,* or tress stitch, ladder is in fact a form of loose needleweaving. The working thread passes over and under the filets as it travels back and forth either horizontally or vertically. No tension is exerted, so the work remains flat and the network square. The diagrams for ladder show a very abbreviated number of weaves in each square unit for the sake of clarity. Work sufficient rows to amply cover the network openings and to create solid, even squares of fabric.

STITCH 3A

LADDER FILLING

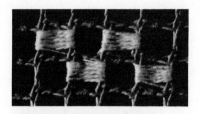

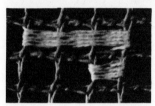

Sampler I: *Employ ladder filling in a pattern or as a solid filling.*

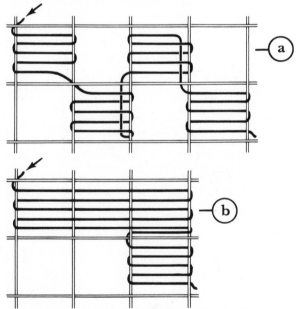

(a)

(b)

Stitch Diagrams: *You need to vary the process of passing from one square to another depending on the pattern you are filling.*

Fill single squares by passing over and under the filet on each side. Work checkerboard patterns in diagonal rows. Notice the various methods for passing from square to square (**a**): passing diagonally behind the network, up and down through the cores of weavings, or around the network corners. A larger area can be covered more easily with ladder filling (**b**). A tree is worked in ladder filling in the Tree of Flowers.

STITCH 3B

LADDER IN TWO DIRECTIONS

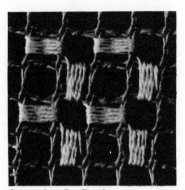

Sampler I: *Produce a pattern through alternation.*

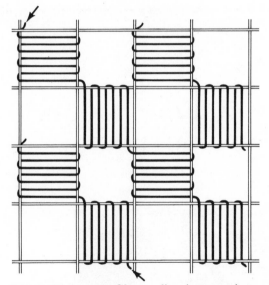

Stitch Diagram: *Change direction, passing around the corners in a consistent weave.*

Work ladder filling either vertically, horizontally, or in both directions. In this pattern from Sampler I, you can see how easy it is to travel in diagonal steps, changing the direction of the ladder filling in each square of the row.

LESSON 4

DARNING

A DARNED OUTLINE

B OVERCAST DARNED OUTLINE

C STALKS AND TENDRILS

D DARNED OUTLINE OR UNDERLAY

E DARNED BORDER

F DARNED CORNERS

G DARNED CORNER VARIATION

D ARNING—in *Filet,* a technique of passing over and under filets to create outlines—is used to soften the square shapes of cloth fillings and to create linear movement in the open network in the form of stalks, tendrils, and the like. Darning has many variations, a number of which are explored in this lesson. Once you become familiar with this rather simple process, you can adapt these techniques to suit your own purposes.

STITCH 4A

DARNED OUTLINE

Sampler I: *Soften the edge of square shapes.*

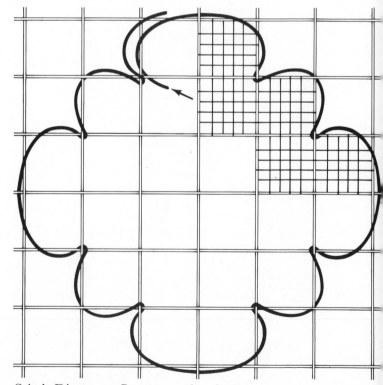

Stitch Diagram: *Pass over and under in sequence around the perimeter.*

Work darned outlines by traveling around a cloth-filled shape, employing the corners of the squares and passing over and under the filets in sequence. Darn a second journey for emphasis. This diagram shows how the large flower head in Sampler I is outlined. For other variations of darned outlines around similar large shapes, see the Tree of Flowers tray cloth.

STITCH 4B

OVERCAST DARNED OUTLINE

Sampler I: *Give texture to the lines.*

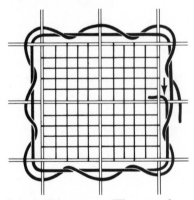

Stitch Diagram: *The second row of darning also overcasts the first darned row.*

Travel around the perimeter, passing over and under each of the filets. Work a second journey by reversing the over-and-under sequence. At the same time, pass under and over the working thread that falls between the filets of the first journey.

STITCH 4C

STALKS AND TENDRILS

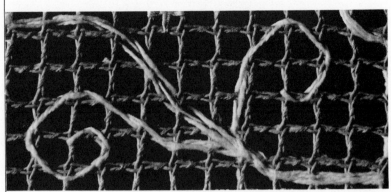

Sampler I: *Create linear movement.*

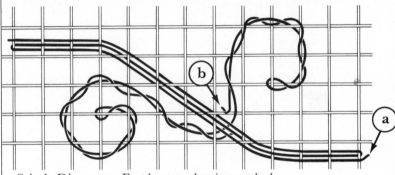

Stitch Diagram: *Employ two darning methods.*

The darned outlines of **4A** and the overcast darned outlines of **4B** are now used to form stalks and tendrils, creating movement in otherwise rather static patterns. To work the stalk or stem (**a**), pass over and under the filets; then reverse each journey for two more rows. To work the tendrils (**b**), pass over and under the filets, creating scrolls on each side of the stalk. Overcast this first journey on the return as you reverse the darning.

STITCH 4D

DARNED OUTLINE OR UNDERLAY

Sampler I: *Provide a strong border.*

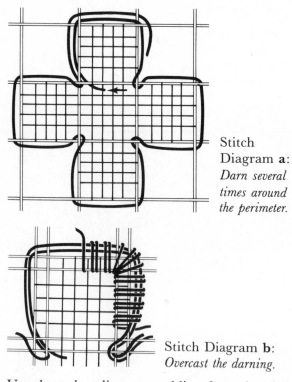

Stitch Diagram **a**: *Darn several times around the perimeter.*

Stitch Diagram **b**: *Overcast the darning.*

Use darned outlines as padding for satin-stitched edges, as shown here on the cross from Sampler I. Work two or three rows of darning around the perimeter of the cloth stitch shape (**a**). Then work the satin stitches over both the filets and the rows of darning (**b**). Move around the corners by gradually slanting the stitches in the new direction. Notice that two satin stitches are worked between each of the cloth stitch elements in this example.

STITCH 4E

DARNED BORDER

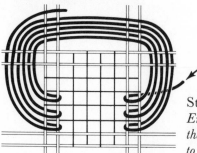

Sampler I: *Outline the three sides of each square.*

Stitch Diagram: *Employ the mesh of the cloth stitch squares to darn evenly.*

By darning a number of rows around the filets that surround the outer edges of the simple cloth stitch flowers of Lesson **2C**, you can produce rounded petal shapes. To work this darned border from Sampler I, employ the lower three holes of the cloth filling as you darn around each of the four cloth stitch squares.

STITCH 4F

DARNED CORNERS

Sampler I: *Outline the two corners of each square.*

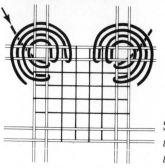

Stitch Diagram: *Employ the mesh at the corners of the cloth stitch squares.*

Darn around the outer corners of the four cloth stitch squares (see **2C**) that make the simple flower shape in Sampler I. Start each of these corners by emerging from a corner mesh hole of the cloth square. Darn around the corner filets, emerging each time from a cloth mesh. You can move from corner to corner by passing under the filets on the backface.

STITCH 4G

DARNED CORNER VARIATION

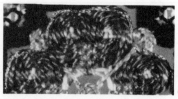

Sampler II: *Outline each half of each square.*

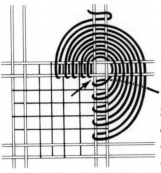

Stitch Diagram: *Employ all of the mesh at the top and sides of the cloth stitch squares.*

In this darned corner variation, each of the cloth mesh holes along the sides of the square is occupied once, and each of the cloth mesh holes across the top is occupied twice. Start the darning by emerging from the upper corner hole and darn around the four filets five times. A pattern diagram for the entire motif can be seen in **11A**.

LESSON 5

LOOPSTITCH

A SINGLE LOOPSTITCH

B LOOPSTITCH GROUND

C LOOPSTITCH BORDER

LOOPSTITCH, also called *point d'esprit*, interlocking lace stitch, and ghost stitch, is an open, lacy stitch quite unlike the weavings shown in the previous lesson. It was not used in the traditional *lacis* patterns on a true net ground, but it is commonly seen in the netted lace and drawn work of later periods. In this lesson, a loopstitch filling and border are shown. You will find three more examples of loopstitch in combination with other stitches in Lesson **9**, where fillings are demonstrated. Loopstitch also appears in *Pulled Canvas* and *Hardanger*.

STITCH 5A

SINGLE LOOPSTITCH

Sampler II: *Fill open center squares.*

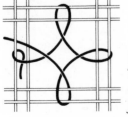

Stitch Diagram: *Throw the working thread over a perpendicular filet and emerge to the left.*

This diagram shows single loopstitch used in the centers of these two motifs from Sampler II. Fasten on at the backface of a filet, on the left side of the open square. Emerge to the left of the filet, throw the working thread up over the top filet, and emerge, crossing over the working thread. Throw the working thread over the filet on the right, and emerge, crossing over the thread again. Throw the working thread over the filet at the bottom, and emerge, crossing over a third time. Throw the working thread to the left between the two elements of the filet, above the first loop made. You are actually working four buttonhole stitches around the open space.

LOOPSTITCH GROUND

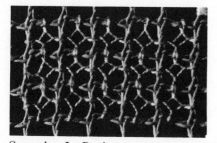

Sampler I: *Produce an open lace filling.*

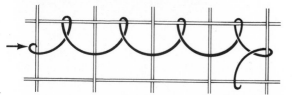

Stitch Diagram **a**: *Throw the thread over the top filets and the end one.*

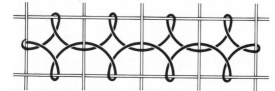

Stitch Diagram **b**: *Return, throwing the thread over the lower filets and passing under the vertical filets.*

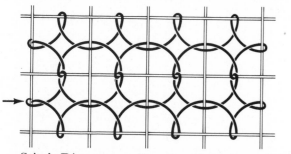

Stitch Diagram **c**: *Pass through the loops of the previous journey.*

A loopstitch ground is composed of interlocking rows of loopstitches. Start by fastening on at the left (**a**), and travel across the row of open squares, throwing loops over the top filet of each square. At the end of the row, loop around the vertical filet. Stitch Diagram **b** shows the return journey, in which you throw loops over the lower filet, passing over the festoons of the first journey and behind the vertical filets as you return to the starting point. Next, start another row of loops just like the first row (**c**). Each time you throw over the top

filet, pass the working thread through the loop of the previous row, thereby interlocking the rows.

LOOPSTITCH BORDER

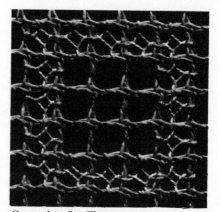

Sampler I: *Turn corners neatly.*

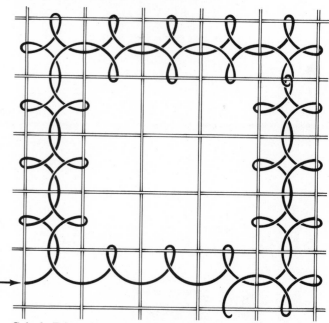

Stitch Diagram: *Be sure to interlock the loops in the upper right and lower left corners.*

This loopstitch border is worked in two stages. In the first stage, you complete two adjacent sides, or a right angle. In the second stage, you complete the remaining two sides. Start in a corner and loop around each outer filet to the diagonally opposite corner. There, loop around the right and bottom filets of that last square and loop back to the starting point, as in **5B**, Stitch Diagram **b**. On arriving at that first square, continue into the second stage by looping around each of the inner filets of the remaining two sides. Interlock a loop into the upper right-hand corner loopstitch and travel back to the starting point, where you interlock once more.

LESSON 6

NEEDLEWEAVING

A PYRAMID

B MALTESE POINTS

C LEAF WITH STEM

D LEAVES WITH TWO VEINS

E CROSSED LEAVES

THE needleweaving in this lesson is worked over surface warps. The warps are laid by throwing the working thread above the network and looping it around or into the filets at either end. The actual needleweaving never enters the net ground but is raised above it. The warps can be thrown at any angle and over any number of squares. There can be double warps for heavier texture or many single warps for lighter or wider work. Tension can be adjusted to shape the weaving, and the needlewoven shapes can be made to overlap. These numerous options make needleweaving a very satisfying technique for creative needleworkers. The first two diagrams are for pyramid shapes that can be used in geometric designs; the next three lessons show four variations for working leaf shapes. See *Needleweaving* for another method of working leaves.

STITCH 6A

PYRAMID

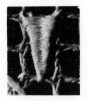

Sampler I: *Needleweave triangles on the surface.*

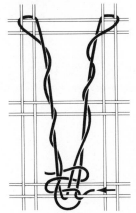

Stitch Diagram: *Throw and overcast a V shape and needleweave it away from yourself.*

Pyramids are worked in canvas filet by casting a pair of surface warps in a V shape and then needleweaving them. They can point in any direction and can be of any size. Turn the work so that the point is toward you, and emerge between the two elements of a horizontal filet. Cast the right spoke by passing under the upper right vertical filet and overcast back, entering the filet at the starting point. Emerge at the base of the V and cast a left spoke; overcast back in reverse of the right spoke. Pass under the base of the V and emerge from the filet ready to needleweave. Insert the needle into the V and pass under the left spoke. Pass over the left spoke and into the V. Pass under the right spoke. Pass over the right spoke and into the V. Continue to needleweave back and forth, maintaining an even tension and shaping the V.

STITCH 6B

MALTESE POINTS

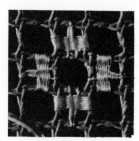

Sampler I: *Work four units around an open mesh square.*

Stitch Diagram: *Include the side filets after needleweaving half a pyramid.*

Maltese points are similar to pyramids except that after half of the pyramid is woven, the filets on either side of the V become additional warps. In Sampler I, four Maltese points are worked around a center square. Instead of starting at the point of the V, start at the upper right corner, emerging at the top of the filet. Pass the working thread between the two elements of the filet to secure it, then pass over the middle of the bottom filet, emerging above it. Secure the working thread between these two elements and throw a left spoke in reverse of the right one. Then overcast back. Loop around the point of the V and start the needleweaving over the spokes. Halfway up, begin to pass over and under the filets in proper sequence while still needleweaving the spokes.

STITCH 6C

LEAF WITH STEM

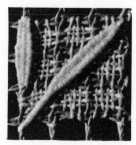

Sampler I: *Needleweave pairs of thrown warps; then coil a stem.*

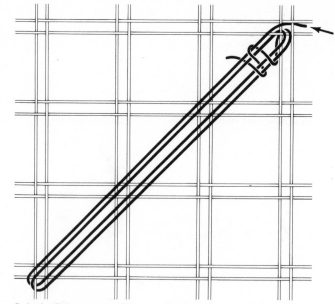

Stitch Diagram: *Throw the thread back and forth diagonally across three squares; turn the canvas and needleweave.*

Double warps are thrown at a 45-degree angle across three squares for a leaf with stem, as in Sampler I. Emerge for the tip of the leaf at the top right corner. Throw the working thread across the three squares and loop around the lower left corner as shown. Throw the working thread back into the upper filet hole and repeat the entire process, emerging on the right of the new warps ready to needleweave. It is usually easier to needleweave away from yourself, so turn the canvas at this time. Start the needleweaving snugly at first; then gradually loosen the tension to add width to the leaf. As you approach the stem section, gradually tighten the tension again. Work the stem by tightly overcasting around all four warps; this is called coiling. In this leaf, you have a single vein, because the paired warps divide the leaf in the middle.

STITCH 6D

LEAVES WITH TWO VEINS

Sampler II: *This two-veined leaf has been twisted before fastening off.*

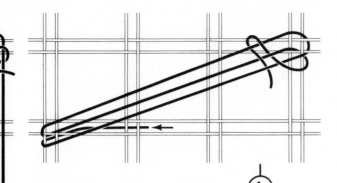

Stitch Diagram **a**: *Throw straight warps parallel to the filets.*

Stitch Diagram **b**: *Throw oblique warps across three squares.*

The needleweaving in these two diagrams is worked over three single warps, resulting in leaves with two veins. Throw the warps as shown in each of the diagrams. Then turn the canvas to needleweave away from yourself. As in **6C**, adjust the tension to shape the leaves. Start by weaving snugly, then gradually loosen the tension to add width, then gradually tighten the tension again. In Stitch Diagram **a**, the warps are thrown parallel to the filet for a straight leaf (see photograph **6C**). The warps are thrown at an oblique angle (**b**) and the leaf is twisted before being fastened off in Sampler II. If this twist does not hold, the leaves can be secured with a few small, invisible stitches.

STITCH 6E
CROSSED LEAVES

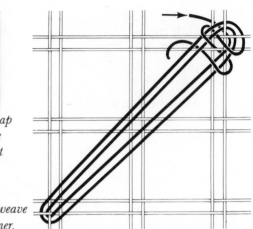

Sampler I: *Overlap leaves and vary the tension for different effects.*

Stitch Diagram: *Throw and needleweave from the same corner.*

A crossed leaf technique can be used to make flower centers, as in Sampler I. Use double warps for heavier texture. In this diagram, the warps start at the upper right, as does the needleweaving. Start the second overlapping leaf at the lower right. When you needleweave the second leaf, be careful not to catch the bottom one. You can vary the shape of these leaves by adjusting the tension; they can also be positioned differently or used to enrich a ground with a geometric pattern of diagonal crosses.

LESSON 7

STARS

A FOUR-POINTED STAR

B SIX- OR EIGHT-POINTED STAR

C SUPER STAR

THREE variations of stars are demonstrated in this lesson. The working thread can be thrown on the surface of the network in four possible directions; it is secured by passing diagonally under the corners of the squares. The resulting long ovals of laid threads are then drawn together at the center by several revolutions of weaving. Use a tapestry needle or awl to trace the passage of the working thread in the stitch diagrams.

STITCH 7A
FOUR-POINTED STAR

Sampler I: *Cross laid threads; then pass over the four segments and under the filets to darn the center.*

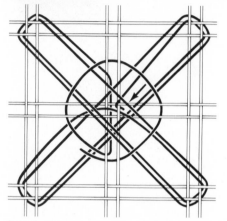

Stitch Diagram: *The central intersection of the filets is used to secure the working threads.*

In this diagram, a simple star is laid over four squares of the network. Emerge from the very center of the net and lay the working thread twice in a diagonal direction, passing under the corners of the squares at either end. Employ the central intersection to hold the working thread in place as it changes direction. After laying the thread twice around the corners in this direction, pass vertically under all of the laid threads. Emerge at the base and pass over the laid threads and under the filets in two more revolutions.

STITCH 7B
SIX- OR EIGHT-POINTED STAR

Sampler I: *Add vertical and/or horizontal laid threads to crossed ones.*

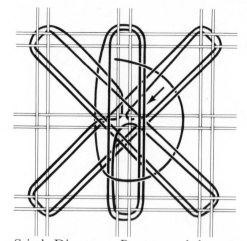

Stitch Diagram: *Darn around the center, passing under the diagonal rays and over the straight rays or filets.*

To work a six-pointed star, lay an additional pair of working threads around the vertical filets. Employ the central intersection to hold the working thread in place as it changes direction. To work the small eight-pointed star shown in the photograph, lay horizontal pairs of working threads as well before collecting all the threads at the center. To darn the circle at the center, pass under the diagonal rays and over the vertical rays and the horizontal filets. If you are working an eight-pointed star, pass over the horizontal rays instead of the filets.

STITCH 7C
SUPER STAR

Sampler I: *Work a large, bold medallion over sixteen squares.*

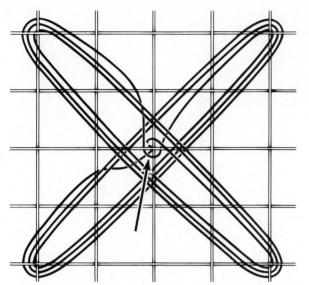

Stitch Diagram **a**: *Start and end the crossed rays in the center.*

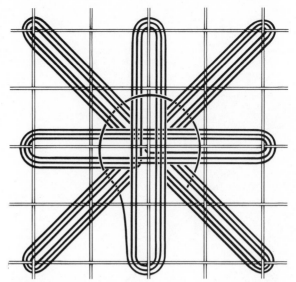

Stitch Diagram **b**: *Then work a horizontal ray and a vertical ray.*

This bold, eight-pointed star is worked over sixteen squares. Emerge from the center and lay the working thread three times in each diagonal direction, passing under the corner squares at the far ends (**a**). Employ the center mesh to hold the thread as you change direction. Lay horizontal and vertical threads, and then draw all eight points together by passing under and over the rays (**b**).

LESSON 8

SPOKES, WHEELS, AND RIBS

A SPOKES FROM THE CENTER

B WOVEN AND DARNED WHEELS

C RIBBED AND REVERSE RIBBED WHEELS

D RIBBED AND REVERSE RIBBED DIAMONDS

E REVERSE RIBBED PYRAMID

F DARNED RIM

G DARNED CORNERS WITH SPOKES

H SPIDER FROM A CORNER

I DARNED CORNERS WITH SPOKES, VARIATION

THIS lesson expands on the various ways to employ filets and thrown warps in darning circles, diamonds, pyramids, or other simple shapes. These additional supports are referred to as spokes. They resemble those of Lesson **6** in *Hemstitching*. When spokes are thrown diagonally across each other, becoming radiating warps for variations of woven circles at their centers, the resulting patterns are referred to as spiders, and the circles thus formed are called wheels. Two methods for spiders are shown here, along with techniques for working the wheels. The same weaving methods employed in producing wheels can be applied to intersecting filets; two diamond shapes are illustrated that are produced in this manner. A single vertical spoke can also be ribbed to produce a pyramid, and radiating spokes can be laid that do not converge in the center.

STITCH 8A

SPOKES FROM THE CENTER

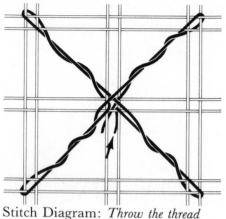

Stitch Diagram: *Throw the thread over each corner and overcast back.*

To throw spokes for the wheels that follow, emerge from the center of a box of four squares. Throw a spoke to the lower right and pass over the far corner. Emerge and overcast back to the center, throw the working thread to the upper left, and pass over that corner. Emerge, overcast back, and emerge from the center. Throw a spoke to the lower left and pass over the corner. Emerge and overcast back to the center. Throw the working thread to the upper right and pass over that corner. Overcast back to the center. You are now in position to work a center wheel.

STITCH 8B

WOVEN AND DARNED WHEELS

Sampler I: *Pass over the spokes and under the filets for several revolutions.*

Stitch Diagram **a**: *Each revolution of a woven wheel is the same.*

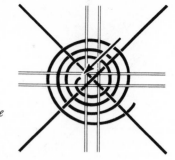

Sampler I: *Alternate the over/under sequence for a darned wheel.*

Stitch Diagram **b**: *When there are even numbers of warps, pass under two of them in each revolution.*

To *weave* a wheel (**a**), work each revolution in the same way. To *darn* a wheel (**b**), it is necessary to change the order of passing with each revolution. Frequently, there are an even number of radiating warps. It is therefore necessary to pass consecutively under a spoke and a filet with each revolution of a darned wheel in order to change the passing sequence. Do not pass *over* two warps, as this shows on the frontface; it is imperceptible in the work when you make a long pass on the backface.

STITCH 8C

RIBBED AND REVERSE RIBBED WHEELS

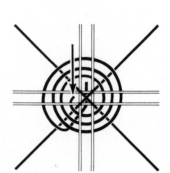

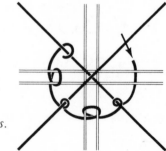

Sampler I: *Backstitch around the radiating warps.*

Stitch Diagram **a**: *Pass under two and back over one.*

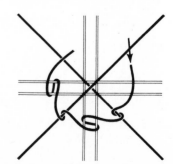

Sampler I: *Work an upside-down backstitch.*

Stitch Diagram **b**: *Pass over two and back under one.*

Work a ribbed wheel (**a**) by traveling around the center of the spokes and filets with backstitches. Work the backstitches by moving ahead clockwise, passing under two warps (a filet and a spoke), and moving back counterclockwise, passing over one warp (a filet or a spoke).

As its name implies, the procedure for working the reverse ribbed wheel (**b**) is the opposite of the preceding ribbed wheel. Move ahead clockwise with long stitches, passing over two warps (a filet and a spoke); move back counterclockwise, passing under one warp (a filet or a spoke).

STITCH 8D

RIBBED AND REVERSE RIBBED DIAMONDS

 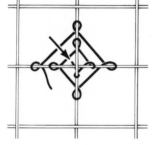

Sampler I: *Travel with long passes on the backface for the ribbed diamond.*

Stitch Diagram **a**: *Start in the center and backstitch around the four filets.*

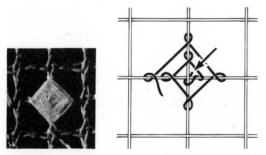

Sampler I: *Travel with long passes on the frontface for the reverse ribbed diamond.*

Stitch Diagram **b**: *Traveling in the same direction, reverse the backstitches.*

STITCH 8E

REVERSE RIBBED PYRAMID

 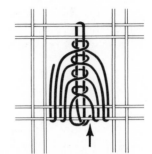

Sampler I: *Darn both sides of a single filet around a center spoke.*

Stitch Diagram: *Throw a spoke and then encircle it as you pass from side to side.*

Work reverse ribbed pyramids over a vertical filet, similarly to the reverse ribbed diamond of **8D**. Or, as shown here, throw a spoke between two filets to support the pyramid. To throw the spoke, emerge at the bottom of the lower filet; pass over it and under the top one. Then pass back over the top filet and under the lower one. To work the reverse ribbing, cross back and forth, passing over and under the lower filet on both sides after you encircle the spoke.

STITCH 8F

DARNED RIM

 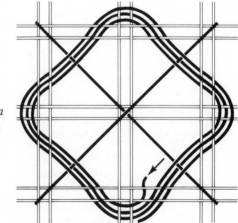

Sampler I: *Produce a softened diamond with a spider and a center wheel.*

Stitch Diagram: *Pass over and under the spokes and filets.*

Work this darned rim after you have produced a spider, as in Stitch **8A**, with the spokes thrown across two squares of the network. Darn a rounded diamond shape by passing over and under filets and spokes. Work the softened points of the diamond by passing outside of filet intersections. Notice that at the base of the diamond, the working thread has been passed under the filet twice. Do this to reverse the sequence of passing when there are an even number of warps. The ribbed wheel is shown in **8Cb**.

STITCH 8G

DARNED CORNERS WITH SPOKES

Sampler I: *Employ the ends of spokes.*

Stitch Diagram: *Throw the spokes from each corner and include them in the darning.*

In this motif from Sampler I, spokes radiate from the corners of an open square, where they are incorporated in the darned corners. Start by throwing a spoke from the corner of one square diagonally across another square. Pass over and under the far corner and overcast back to the first square. Then darn the corner evenly, passing under and over filets and spokes. Overcast a filet to arrive in position to throw subsequent spokes and to darn the other corners.

STITCH 8H

SPIDER FROM A CORNER

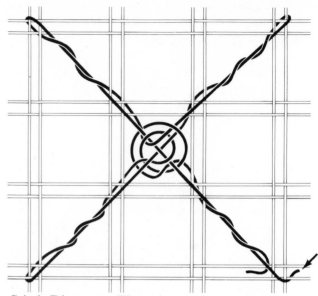

Stitch Diagram: *Throw four spokes and darn a center wheel.*

When there is no center mesh to assist in producing a spider, you can start at a corner. Throw a spoke from the lower right corner diagonally across the squares and pass over the far corner. Emerge and overcast to the center. Throw a spoke to the upper right corner and pass over the far corner; overcast to the center. Throw a spoke over the lower left corner and overcast to the center. Darn a wheel around the center and overcast the lower right spoke back to the starting point.

STITCH 8I

DARNED CORNERS WITH SPOKES, VARIATION

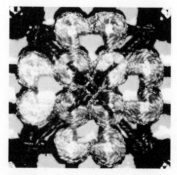

Sampler II: *Throw a spider and darn sixteen corners.*

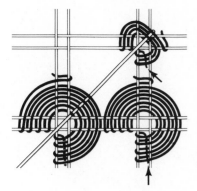

Stitch Diagram:
*Darn the four center
corners, then the
eight filet corners,
then the tips of the
spokes with the filets.*

To work the first part of this motif, complete the spider from Stitch **8H**, which occupies nine squares. You can see a pattern diagram for the complete motif in **11B**. Darn four corners of the open center square, incorporating the spokes as in Stitch Diagram **8G**. Darn the other eight filet corners. Lastly, darn the corners at the ends of the spokes.

LESSON 9

FILLINGS

A LOOP AND LADDER

B SMALL CIRCLES AND LOOPSTITCH

C LARGE CIRCLES

D LADDER AND SPOKE

E BASKETWEAVE

F CROSSED LOOPSTITCH

G CHECKER

S INCE the network ground of canvas filet is composed mainly of squares with negative space, the repeat patterns contributed by filling stitches are very important to maintain interest as well as density in the large positive areas. Fillings are demonstrated in this lesson. Some are composites of stitches already shown. You can enliven them by employing contrasting colors, values, and textures. Try using some of the stitches from other lessons in repeat patterns for fillings, such as the spider and ribbed units from Lesson **8**. Later, in Lesson **11**, you will see examples of many stitches combined into single motifs.

STITCH 9A

LOOP AND LADDER

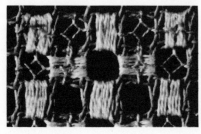

Sampler I:
*Combine two
fillings in a
repeat pattern.*

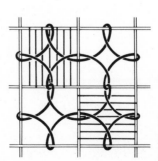

Stitch Diagram: *Work the
ladder filling, then the
loopstitch units over it.*

Loop and ladder is a composite of ladder in two directions, Stitch **3B**, and loopstitch ground,

Stitch **5B**. First cover the desired area with a ladder filling. Then work units of four loopstitches over four squares, leaving spaces of two squares between units.

STITCH 9B
SMALL CIRCLES AND LOOPSTITCH

Sampler I: *Combine a dense filling of circles with a light, interlacing one.*

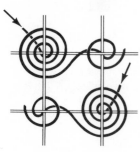

Stitch Diagram **a**: *Darn counterclockwise when the row travels to the right, and clockwise when it goes to the left.*

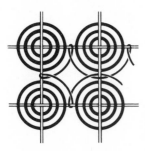

Stitch Diagram **b**: *Fit the loops over the filets between the circles.*

Travel across one row from the left, darning the network in counterclockwise revolutions, and the next row from the right in clockwise revolutions (**a**). Pass over the horizontal filets and under the verticals, with the connecting thread on the front-face. First fill the space with circles. Then work a loopstitch ground (**5B**) to fit neatly in the center of each square (**b**).

STITCH 9C
LARGE CIRCLES

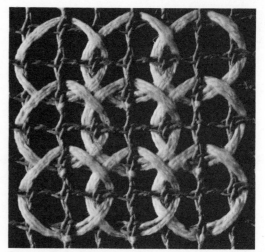

Sampler I: *Fill large areas with this bold pattern.*

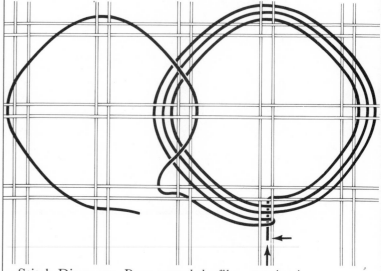

Stitch Diagram: *Darn around the filets, passing in either direction and overlapping wherever circles meet.*

Darn these overlapping large circles, traveling across three rows of horizontal and vertical filets. This is a very large pattern and it needs to be repeated a number of times (see Sampler I) to be appreciated. Employ the space between the two elements of a filet for securing and holding the working thread when you start each circle. Notice how the adjacent circles overlap both horizontally and vertically.

STITCH 9D
LADDER AND SPOKE

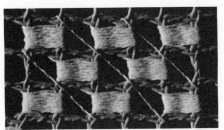

Sampler I: *Combine a ladder checkerboard with long diagonal lines.*

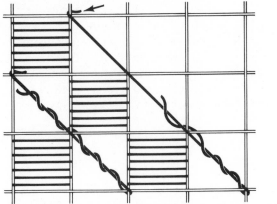

Stitch Diagram: *Complete the diagonal rows of ladder filling; then bisect the open squares with spokes.*

First, cover the desired area with ladder filling (Stitch **3A**). Then work overcast spokes in the diagonal rows of open squares. To work a spoke, secure the working thread at the upper left corner of an open square. Throw it across a diagonal row of open squares, passing over the intersecting warps; loop it around the corner of the lower right square. Overcast snugly back to the starting point, passing under each of the intersections on the way.

STITCH 9E
BASKETWEAVE

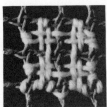

Sampler I: *Imitate the network ground.*

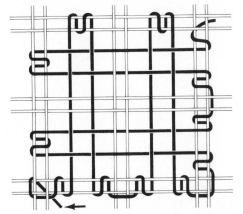

Stitch Diagram: *When changing direction, overcast the filet.*

Basketweave creates a fabric in the open squares similar to that of cloth stitch. It differs in that you now provide two warps and two wefts in each square instead of four. Also, each time you change the direction of the working thread, you overcast a filet; each time you pass a filet when changing direction or turning a corner, you work an extra overcast. Use a contrasting working thread to emphasize the woven texture.

STITCH 9F
CROSSED LOOPSTITCH

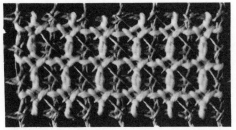

Sampler I: *Combine two light, interlaced fillings.*

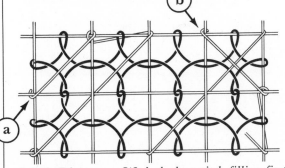

Stitch Diagram: *Work the loopstitch filling first; then complete the diagonals in two separate stages.*

To work this crossed loop filling, start by filling the squares with loopstitch (**5B**). Complete the cross-hatching in two separate stages. In the first stage weave the working thread across the network in diagonal journeys that slant from lower left to upper right (**a**). Pass over the loopstitches and under the filets. In the second stage, weave across the network from upper left to lower right (**b**). Pass under the loopstitches, over the first working thread, and over the filets.

STITCH 9G
CHECKER

Sampler I: *Produce a lacy checkerboard effect.*

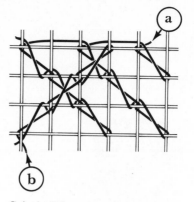

Stitch Diagram: *Work in two stages of diagonal rows. Work each row in two journeys.*

Proceed in two separate stages of intersecting diagonal rows. Work each diagonal row in two journeys (see *Pulled Canvas,* Stitch **8E**). To work the first stage, travel in rows that slant from the upper left to the lower right (**a**). Then ascend, passing over the descending stitches to finish the first stage of the diagonal rows. Complete the checkers by crossing the squares from lower left to upper right and back again (**b**).

LESSON 10

BUTTONHOLE

A BUTTONHOLE FILLING

B BUTTONHOLE STAR

C DOUBLE BUTTONHOLE EDGE

D LOOPED PICOT

SOME diverse uses for buttonhole stitches are demonstrated in this lesson. Far from being solely an edging technique, buttonholing is the basic stitch of needle lace, the simplest form of which is shown here. Liberties have been taken to adapt it to *Filet,* but only in the means of attaching the stitches around the edges. Buttonholing can also be employed to produce a motif, an example of which is the buttonhole star. A double buttonhole edge is shown surrounding a completely opened rectangle in the network. A double buttonhole stitch is also worked around the outer edges of Sampler I. A second edge of buttonholing is then worked into the festoons of the double buttonholes, and a looped picot is worked at each filet. This tenth lesson concludes Sampler I, with the exception of the bullion knots that appear in **12A**.

STITCH 10A
BUTTONHOLE FILLING

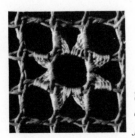

Sampler I: *Fill squares with needle lace.*

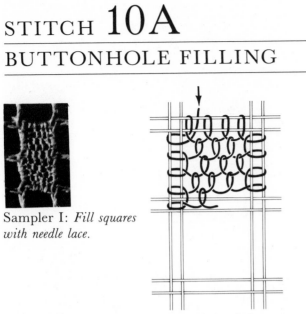

Stitch Diagram: *Attach the buttonhole stitches only at the outer filets.*

Work buttonhole filling over any number of squares; in this diagram a rectangle two squares high is being filled. Ignore the horizontal filet that separates the two squares. Start by fastening on and passing under and over the top of the left filet. Buttonhole four times from left to right across the top filet. To move from row to row, buttonhole twice over the side filets. Buttonhole the second row from right to left, looping over and under the festoons of the first row. Work three buttonhole stitches in each row, reversing the direction of travel on each journey. (Four stitches were made over the filet of the first row to match the four loops on the sides of the square.) You can see more buttonhole filling in *Reticello and Hedebo.*

STITCH 10B
BUTTONHOLE STAR

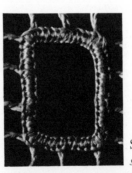

Sampler I: *Combine darned corners with the buttonhole stitch for a star motif.*

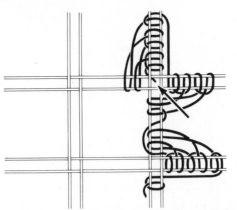

Stitch Diagram: *Pass over and under the filets of a center square between pairs of buttonhole stitches.*

This buttonhole star motif may look complicated, but it is easy to stitch once you grasp the technique. Move around the motif in a clockwise direction, turning your work or the diagram as you complete the amount shown. Start by buttonholing up the top of the vertical filet, passing under and over the horizontal filet of the center square between each pair of buttonhole stitches. Work as many as will fit, and then start the second point. Notice the connecting thread between the second and third points of the star. When you are connecting two parallel filets, you must make an overcast to get to the starting location of the next point.

STITCH 10C
DOUBLE BUTTONHOLE EDGE

Sampler I: *Bind an opened space within the network.*

Sampler I: *Bind an outer edge.*

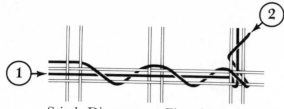

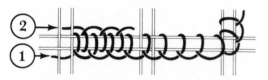

Stitch Diagram **a**: *First, lay a thread along the filets. Then overcast the perimeter.*

Stitch Diagram **b**: *Space buttonhole stitches around the outside; then fit stitches between them in a second journey.*

To produce either of these double buttonhole edges from Sampler I, start the process by laying a working thread across the edge filets, hooking around the network at the corners. Then overcast the laid thread. Both of these steps are shown in Stitch Diagram **a**. Buttonhole around the perimeter with the festoons on the outside; space the stitches sufficiently far apart to allow for a second journey of buttonhole stitches (with festoons on the inside) to intervene (**b**). For the sake of clarity, the threads worked in Stitch Diagram **a** are not shown in Stitch Diagram **b**.) If you are binding a space that is to be opened inside the network, you cut the filets that cross this space close to the bound edge before working the second journey of buttonhole stitches. If you are binding an outer edge, work both rows of buttonhole stitches first. Then remove the canvas from the stretcher frame. Clip away the excess canvas on the backface, close to the outer edge. If you are adding the picot edge (Stitch **10D**), do not clip away the excess canvas until you have completed the picots.

STITCH **10D**
LOOPED PICOT

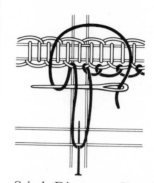

Stitch Diagram: *Pass the thread under the pin and then up over the filet; emerge and buttonhole the long loop.*

There are various kinds of picots (see Glossary) that you can work while buttonholing an edge. This looped picot buttonhole edge is one of the simplest. You can see other picots in *Hardanger* and *Reticello and Hedebo*. In Sampler I, this additional edge of buttonhole stitches is worked in contrasting pink thread over the festoons of the double buttonhole edge, with a picot at each vertical filet (see the bottom photograph, Stitch **10C**). To produce a looped picot, insert a pin into the elements or network at the point where the picot is to be caught. Work a buttonhole stitch as shown in the stitch diagram, and then pass the working thread under the pin. Enter the backface into the festoon of the previous row in the sampler, and emerge to work a buttonhole stitch over the long loop, which completes the picot. After completing the looped picot edge, clip away the excess canvas at the buttonholed edge or, as in the sampler, to the length of the picot.

LESSON 11

MOTIFS—COMBINED TECHNIQUES

A CLOTH FLOWER

B DOUBLE PETAL

C DARNED CORNERS

D WOVEN

E CHRYSANTHEMUM

THIS lesson consists mainly of pattern diagrams for the five motifs shown in Sampler II. It demonstrates the many ways you can combine the techniques already explored in previous lessons. However, the center chrysanthemum motif includes a new technique for throwing a spider with an eight-sided festoon around it as the support for a flower. Stitch diagrams and instructions are therefore included. These isolated geometric shapes and their fillings, along with some improvised ones, have been used in the darned cardigan, which appears in the color section of this book.

MOTIF 11A

CLOTH FLOWER

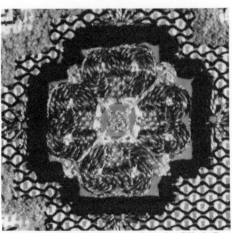

Sampler II: *Produce a densely filled flower shape.*

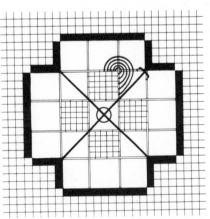

Pattern Diagram: *Work cloth stitch squares; throw a spider with a center wheel; darn the corners, spokes, and outline.*

To work this motif, proceed in the given order, following the lessons indicated.

Cloth stitch simple flowers: Stitch **2C**.

Spider from a corner with a wheel: Stitch **8H**.

Darned corners of spokes: Stitch **8I**.

Darned corner variation: Stitch **4G**.

Darned outline: Stitch **4D**.

MOTIF 11B
DOUBLE PETAL

Sampler II: *Leave the squares open.*

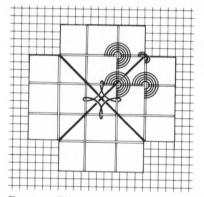

Pattern Diagram: *Throw a spider; darn the corners, spokes, and outline; loopstitch the center.*

To work this motif, proceed in the given order, following the lessons indicated.

Darned corners with spokes: Stitch **8I** (this combines **8G** and **8H**).

Darned outline: Stitch **4D**.

Single loopstitch: Stitch **5A**.

MOTIF 11C
DARNED CORNERS

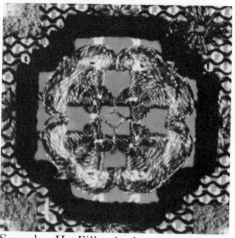

Sampler II: *Fill only the corner squares.*

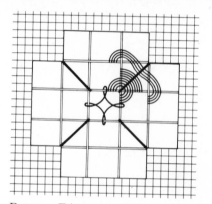

Pattern Diagram: *Throw corner spokes; darn the corners, corner squares, rims, and outline; loopstitch the center.*

To work this motif, proceed in the given order, following the lessons indicated.

Darned corners with spokes: Stitch **8G**.*

Section of darned rim: Stitch **8F**.*

Darned outline: Stitch **4D**.

Single loopstitch: Stitch **5A**.

* Improvise on examples given.

MOTIF 11D
WOVEN

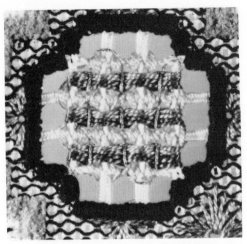

Sampler II: *Produce a textured fabric.*

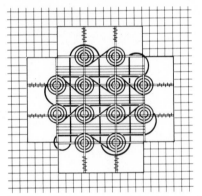

Pattern Diagram: *Fill with small circles, long ladders, large cloth stitch, and fine needleweaving.*

To work this motif, proceed in the given order, following the lessons indicated.

Small circles: Stitch **9B**.

Ladder filling: Stitch **3A**.

Cloth stitch: Stitch **2A**. (In this motif, the nine squares are treated as one open square.)

Needleweave the remaining network.

MOTIF 11E
CHRYSANTHEMUM

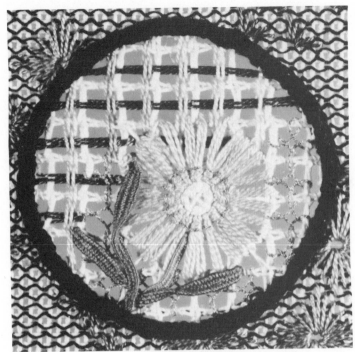

Sampler II: *Stitch a little picture in an opened circle.*

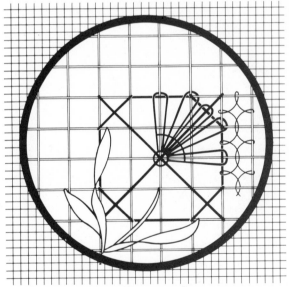

Pattern Diagram: *Throw a support structure, work a flower with leaves, weave a trellis, and frame the flower.*

To work this motif, proceed in the given order, following the lessons indicated.

Spider with festoon: Stitch Diagram **a** (following page).

Petals: Stitch Diagram **b** (this page).
Needlewoven leaves: Stitch **6D**.
Ladder filling: Stitch **3A**.
Loopstitch border: Stitch **5C**.

Sampler II: *Provide support for a flower.*

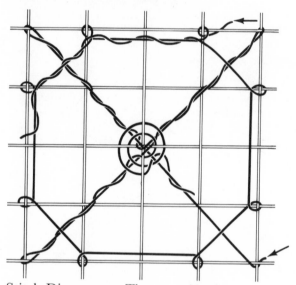

Stitch Diagram **a**: *Throw a spider from the corner across four squares; then throw an eight-sided festoon.*

To provide a supporting structure for the chrysanthemum, proceed in two separate stages. First throw a spider from a corner across four squares and darn a center wheel of four or five revolutions

before overcasting back to the starting corner. Then throw an eight-sided festoon by passing around the network, making festoons in the eight locations shown in this stitch diagram; overcast back to the starting point. The center wheel in this diagram is abbreviated for the sake of a clearer illustration; note the wheel in the photograph. Refer to the darned wheel in **8B** for further instructions.

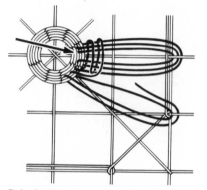

Stitch Diagram **b**: *Start each petal by emerging on the frontface between revolutions of the center wheel.*

Emerge for each of the sixteen petals between revolutions of the darned wheel and throw the working thread out to the eight-sided festoon. Pass under the filet intersections indicated on the pattern diagram and return, passing into the backface close to the emerging thread. Come to the frontface and, aligning the working threads, lay two additional threads in this manner. After the last journey, pass under and over all the laid threads of the petal twice, close to the center, to draw them together. Notice in the pattern diagram how the petal made at a 45-degree angle passes around the spoke and festoon, which gives a round shape to the flower head. As in the sampler, after all the petals are completed, you can emphasize the flower center by adding a circle of gold backstitches worked where each petal is drawn together.

LESSON 12

SURFACE STITCHES AND FINISHING

A BULLION KNOTS

B CANVAS LACE AND BLACKWORK

C EYELETS

D WEAVING BACK OUTER EDGES

E COUCHING

T HIS last lesson provides a potpourri of contrasting or complementary techniques that complete the two canvas filet samplers. Shown first are bullion knots, which supply a dense raised contrast to many forms of open work. They appear here on a cloth stitch square from Sampler I. Bullion knots are shown again in *Reticello and Hedebo*. The canvas lace ground of Sampler II is demonstrated next. Although no canvas elements are deflected or withdrawn, this Victorian imitation of lace belongs in *The Open Canvas* because the open mesh is the focus of the technique. The eyelet variations of Sampler II are members of the *Pulled Canvas* family of stitches; here they are superimposed on the canvas lace. The outer edges of Sampler II are finished by weaving canvas elements from the unworked margins back into the canvas. The resulting texture becomes the background for counted thread stitches and more eyelets. Finally, another raised technique, that of couching, is employed as an outline to frame the inner section of Sampler II. The buttonhole edge that completes this sampler has previously been explained in **1F**.

STITCH 12A
BULLION KNOTS

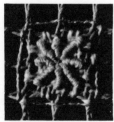

Sampler I: *Contrast the open work with raised work.*

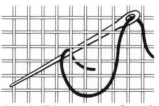

Stitch Diagram **a**: *Start by emerging at the base. Draw the thread through, enter at the top, and emerge again at the base.*

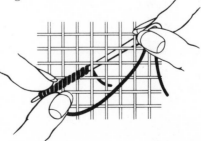

Stitch Diagram **b**: *Hold the eye of the needle securely and wind the thread clockwise. Hold those coils firmly!*

Stitch Diagram **c**: *Coax the needle through and draw up the thread. Now pull the thread to adjust the coils.*

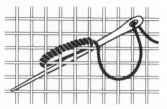

Stitch Diagram **d**: *Enter the backface as in* **a**. *Emerge in position for another bullion, at this location or another.*

Bullion knots are easy and delightful to work—with a little practice. Make sure to hold the coils firmly, and use a long needle with a round eye, such as a milliner's needle, so that you can easily slide it through the coils. If you want a highly raised stitch, use more coils than will fit. This is the same diagram as in the *Reticello and Hedebo* section. The bullion knots in the filet sampler are worked over a cloth stitch square.

STITCH 12B

CANVAS LACE AND BLACKWORK

CANVAS LACE

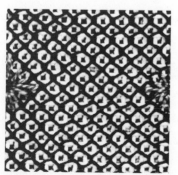

Sampler II: *Simulate a black lace background.*

This ground cover employed in Sampler II is an example of canvas lace work, which was introduced in the middle of the nineteenth century. It is typically Victorian in that it involves one needlework technique imitating another.

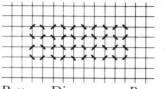

Pattern Diagram **a**: *Reverse the slants in adjacent rows.*

Stitch Diagram **a**: *Work a half cross over every other element. Fill the spaces with a return journey.*

Travel across each row in two journeys. First, work half cross-stitches, slanting in one direction over every other element intersection. Return with half cross-stitches slanting in the opposite direction. Reverse the stitch slant in each row to establish this diamond pattern.

BLACKWORK

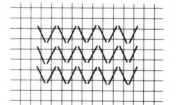

Sampler II: *Borrow an old counted-thread-on-fabric technique.*

Pattern Diagram **b**: *The rows are all alike, and each occupies two horizontal elements.*

As its name implies, blackwork is traditionally worked in black thread, on an evenly woven fabric. The stitches used are double running and backstitch. Blackwork is usually worked over two elements, and the little repeat patterns are endless in variety.

This zigzag blackwork pattern is not worked on Sampler II until the elements are woven back into the canvas along the outer edges, as shown in **12D**. It is shown here because of its relationship to the canvas lace pattern. See the master pattern to position the work on the sampler.

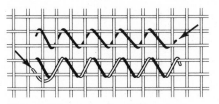

Stitch Diagram **b**: *Fill each row in two journeys, traveling in opposite directions.*

STITCH 12C

EYELETS

Sampler II: *Converge in the same space but emerge in a pattern at the perimeter.*

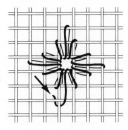

Stitch Diagram: *Emerge at the perimeter. Enter the center hole and give a slight tug; move in consecutive order.*

Eyelets are examined fully in *Pulled Canvas,* as they are units of satin stitches that deflect the canvas elements. However, eyelets provide a secondary pattern on the canvas lace ground of Sampler II, and the technique is briefly shown here. As you can see on the sampler, you can easily change the pattern of eyelet units by varying the shape of the perimeter.

Start by locating the center hole; then enlarge it with an awl or the points of your closed embroidery scissors. Work satin stitches around the shape, giving the working thread a slight tug after entering the center to emphasize the hole. Fasten off by passing the needle around the shape under the stitches on the backface. See the master pattern to locate all the center holes for the eyelets.

TECHNIQUE 12D

WEAVING BACK OUTER EDGES

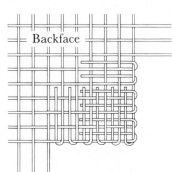

Canvas Diagram: *Weave back consistently on the same side of the elements.*

Remove the canvas from the stretcher frame and cut away the bound edges. Withdraw all the horizontal elements at the lower edge up to the position of the buttonhole edge, shown on the master pattern for Sampler II. Weave each element back into the canvas up to the completed background. Another woven pattern will emerge on the canvas. Work the other sides in the same way. Work on the backface and clip away excess elements, as shown in the above diagram for a complete corner. If you are working Sampler II, stitch the blackwork segments (**12B**), then the round eyelets, variations of **12C**. Blackwork and eyelet holes are shown on the master pattern. Complete the buttonhole edge of the entire perimeter (**1F**).

STITCH 12E
COUCHING

Sampler II: *Provide a softened border with rich texture.*

Couching is a system for laying a decorative thread on the work surface and tacking it down with another, finer thread. Couching is employed when the selected thread cannot be comfortably fed through the ground fabric, as in the case of Japanese gold or silver thread, where the thin wrapped paper coating would shred away from the cotton core. It is also employed when the selected thread is costly, as in the case of silk chenille—half the yardage can be saved by employing this thread on the surface only. Couching metal threads to fill solid shapes is an embroidery skill requiring practice. However, you can easily employ some simple couched outlines, as in the above stitch diagram

from *Pulled Canvas*, and on Sampler II, where several rows of couched silk chenille provide a soft border.

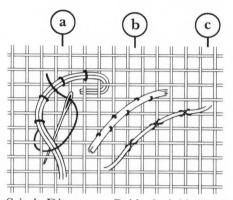

Stitch Diagram: *Guide the laid threads with one hand; stitch them down with the other.*

Couch outlines in any of the three methods shown here. Most couching is started by anchoring the tail end of the decorative (couched) thread on the backface and securing it there; it is fastened off in the same manner. If you employ a richly textured chenille thread, you can secure the ends invisibly on the frontface. To complete Sampler II, couch down the chenille along the backstitch outline shown on the master pattern, laying four threads in two journeys. Overcast at ¼-inch intervals (**a**), employing a closely matching silk thread for couching down.

BOOK FIVE

HARDANGER

Selected elements are cut and withdrawn from both directions in geometric shapes that have been bound by blocks of satin stitches. The opened spaces and the remaining elements are embroidered with darned and looped stitches. Surface stitches embellish the unopened foundation fabric.

CONTENTS

INTRODUCTION

Hardanger embroidery is easily mastered. The major requirement is that you be accurate in counting stitches and elements. This is important in all counted-thread techniques, but particularly so here, because Hardanger is based completely on right angles and squares. If you like counting, you will relish the precision of this simple but exacting work. Once you master it, you will find that it combines well with other types of embroidery.

You can explore basic Hardanger techniques by completing the sampler provided, starting with the master pattern in Lesson **1** and entering the work as you progress with the lessons. It is a good idea to first familiarize yourself with Hardanger by reading the introductory material, which includes information about its history, general procedures, and equipment. The sampler can also serve as a jumping-off point for those interested in experimentation. A neck ruff worked in a Hardanger border pattern is included to suggest some additional uses for this highly organized form of open canvas work.

Once you become familiar with Hardanger, counting will become second nature to you; so be persistent. Eventually, you will find that you will be able to set the work free, creating delightful and unique patterns.

A THIMBLEFUL OF HISTORY

Hardanger is named for the Hardanger district on the west coast of Norway, a land of inlets and fjords that flow between steep cliffs. This somewhat forbidding landscape is where the technique as we know it today developed and prospered. Its roots are said to be in ancient Asia and Persia, where it was worked on fine gauze netting in colored silks and worn by the nobility. When it reached Norway and the other Scandinavian countries, however, just prior to 1800, it evolved into a traditional folk embroidery.

At first it was worked on very fine white cloth, fifty threads to the inch, with matching white thread. Its strictly geometric patterns were used to decorate household linens, blouses, caps, and particularly the aprons that are so much a part of a peasant costume. Gradually, Hardanger was worked on coarser fabrics with weaves of twenty-eight and twenty-two threads to the inch. And when Scandinavian immigrants brought Hardanger to America (by the turn of the century, it had become very popular), it was worked on mono canvas as well as on cloth.

SOME NEEDLE POINTS

Hardanger is very easy to recognize. Blocks of satin stitches, called kloster blocks, make battlemented enclosures (see Glossary) that reinforce the cut edges of open spaces that are in turn filled with webs, spokes, festoons, and wheels. Secondary to the embellished open spaces are very simple geometric patterns worked on the foundation fabric. Also typical of Hardanger are scalloped edges of buttonhole stitches.

Hardanger is a highly ordered, organized technique. Everything is accomplished according to plan; the order of the various procedures is set. First, a master pattern must be consulted, which can be acquired or planned on graph paper. Then, the pattern is set on the fabric by working the kloster blocks and the surface embroidery; this is done with the canvas stretched on a frame. Next, if it is difficult to cut and withdraw the elements on the frame, the canvas can be removed from it, and selected elements—those that lie between the satin stitches—cut and withdrawn. Finally, the work is returned to the frame and the open spaces are filled. After the work is completed, the canvas is removed from the frame, final finishing is done, and the excess canvas is cut off.

Hardanger worked on canvas differs from Hardanger worked on a denser, softer fabric in that it is necessary to conceal connecting threads on the backface so that they are not visible through the open mesh. This is accomplished by weaving through the backface of the blocks and bars. The easily counted mesh and the firm body of the canvas are so helpful in learning Hardanger techniques that they compensate for this extra care.

The kloster blocks that are peculiar to Hardanger are often invaded by spokes and loops.

Since klosters are always composed of an odd number of stitches, you must decide which side of the satin stitch at the center of the block to enter when you are throwing the working thread. Also, when you use canvas for Hardanger, as in the sampler, be sure to pass over two horizontal elements as you enter between the satin stitches into the backface. The stitch diagrams of Lesson 3 should clarify these points.

WORKBASKET SUPPLIES

Ever since Hardanger was westernized it has been traditional to relate the working thread closely to the ground fabric, employing a white, neutral, or pastel palette. However, with the advent of dyed canvas and Hardanger cloth, vibrant color combinations are becoming popular. For special colors, consider dyeing either the canvas or the working threads—or both.

CANVAS
Hardanger can be worked on a variety of fabrics as long as they meet certain requirements. The warps and wefts must be of equal weight and spaced evenly apart. A perfect square should result when these elements are withdrawn. Mono canvas fits all these requirements and works quite well. Use any size mesh in any color. You can also paint your canvas, but be sure the color is permanent in case the work requires steaming or cleaning at a future time. Size 24/inch canvas closely matches 22/inch Hardanger cloth, and the two can be used interchangeably.

STRETCHERS
Use interlocking wood stretcher strips for a working frame. Tack the canvas down as taut as possible. You may want to remove the work to open the canvas and then to return it to the frame for the open work. Sewing the canvas to a taped bar is therefore not recommended. You will want to turn the work over many times to secure and conceal working threads, so a stand is not practical.

NEEDLES AND OTHER TOOLS
You will need tapestry needles in sizes to suit both weights of thread. Use size 20 for the size 5 pearl cotton, size 22 for the size 8 cotton, and sizes 24 and 26 for finer twisted threads. Very sharp pointed embroidery scissors are extremely important to cut the elements cleanly and thus avoid the ragged stubs that can protrude from the kloster blocks. An awl or stiletto is a valuable tool for expanding eyelet holes and can be employed in counting stitches and elements.

THREADS
Hardanger embroidery requires two weights of working thread and is most beautifully worked with two different textures. For the satin stitches of the kloster blocks, for the buttonhole edge, and for the simple geometric surface stitches of the unopened canvas, a soft, slightly twisted thread or pearl cotton that is slightly heavier than the elements is best. This thread encourages the stitches to blend together and cover the canvas nicely. For the filling stitches and the bars within the webs, a finer thread is preferable. A twisted thread is best, but may not be as easy to find as the finer pearl cotton, which, in addition to its other virtues, can be had in an identical color to its heavier cousin. Two weights of pearl cotton is a popular choice. However, DMC 6-cord Cordonnet Crochet Cotton, which now comes only in white and ecru, silk twist, fine linen, and DMC 3-cord Cebelia Crochet Cotton are prettiest for the fine open work. Experiment with various threads in various weights. Size 5 Pearl Cotton, a heavier thread, and size 8, a finer one, are the usual choices for 24/inch canvas or 22/inch Hardanger cloth. Do not overlook metallic threads, which can sometimes be found in soft sewing textures.

KEY TO STITCHES AND THREADS
Sampler

The Hardanger sampler is worked with pearl and crochet cotton on 18/inch white mono canvas, painted red. The finished size is 6¼ inches by 6¼ inches. See the accompanying key to identify the stitches and threads. The bold numbers with letters refer to the lesson and diagram where each stitch or pattern is located in *Hardanger*. The bold italic numbers refer to the thread, which is listed under Materials Employed.

1A Scalloped Buttonhole Edge, *2*
1B Outer Buttonhole Edge, *5*
1C Kloster Blocks, *2*
1D Kloster Blocks Expanded, *3*
1E Square Eyelet, *7*
1F Rivières, *4*
2A Overcast Bars, *6*
2B Needlewoven Bars, *6*
2C Loopstitch Bars, *6*
2D Oblique Loopstitch Bars, *8* or *9*
2E Needlewoven Bars with Post Stitch Picots, *8*
3A Corner Spokes with Festoon Stitch, *1*, *8*, *9*
3B Branched Spokes, *1*, *6*
3C Double Spokes, *8*, *9*
3D Divided Bars with Twisted Loopstitch, *8*
4A Woven Wheel, *5*, *7*
4B Darned Wheel, *7*
4C Ribbed Wheel, *7*
4D Reverse Ribbed Wheel with Darned Embellishment, *5*, *7*

MATERIALS EMPLOYED

CANVAS
18/inch white mono; 10 inches square; edges bound

THREADS
1 DMC Pearl Cotton, size 3, white
2 DMC Pearl Cotton, size 3, 744 yellow
3 DMC Pearl Cotton, size 3, 800 blue
4 DMC Pearl Cotton, size 5, white
5 DMC Pearl Cotton, size 5, 744 yellow
6 DMC Pearl Cotton, size 5, 800 blue
7 DMC Pearl Cotton, size 5, 906 green
8 DMC Cordonnet Crochet Cotton, 6-cord, size 30, white
9 DMC Cebelia Crochet Cotton, size 30, blue

NEEDLES
Tapestry 18, 20, 22

STRETCHER STRIPS
2 pairs 10-inch

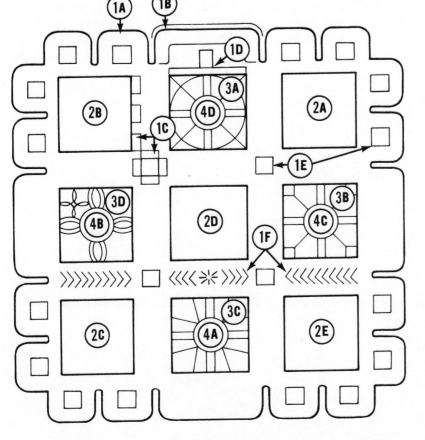

KEY TO STITCHES AND THREADS
Neck Ruff

The bold numbers and letters refer to the lesson and diagram where each stitch can be located in *Hardanger*. Use the following list for quick identification. The working threads are all DMC Pearl Cotton; the sizes and colors are below. The double faggot ground is from *Pulled Canvas* and is diagramed there in Stitch **7B**. Small seed pearls are sewn between the seven-stitch kloster blocks at the long straight edges.

1A Scalloped Buttonhole Edge, size 5, 553 lavender
1B Outer Buttonhole Edge, size 8, 553 lavender
1C Kloster Blocks, size 5, 553 lavender
1D Kloster Blocks Expanded, size 5, 498 red
1E Square Eyelet, size 8, 350 coral
2B Needlewoven Bars, size 8, black 310
7B Double Faggot Ground (in *Pulled Canvas*), size 8, 554 lavender

A scalloped Hardanger border can be added to many items of clothing or home furnishings. Shown here is a ruff, or ruffled collar, made from a simple Hardanger border pattern. The key indicates the stitches and threads. A master pattern for the border is included in Lesson **1**. To make the collar shown here, you will need a width of 24/inch congress canvas cut and bound, 9 inches by 28 inches, in beige. Center a narrow ribbon pattern of textured stripes about eight to ten elements wide and twenty-four inches long in surface canvas work. Then work the border with eleven repeats on either side. Sew a bias tape facing on the backface along the ribbon pattern. Feed a wire circlet through it. Tack a grosgrain ribbon over the gathered tape to hold the gathers in place. Wire circlets can be purchased in craft shops; they come with hook closures. Another, simpler solution is to feed a velvet ribbon through the casing and tie the collar closed.

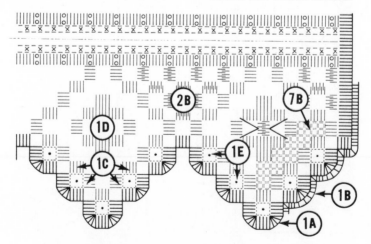

LESSON 1

CANVAS PREPARATION

MASTER PATTERN, SAMPLER

MASTER PATTERN, NECK RUFF

A SCALLOPED BUTTONHOLE EDGE

B OUTER BUTTONHOLE EDGE

C KLOSTER BLOCKS

D KLOSTER BLOCKS EXPANDED

E SQUARE EYELET

F RIVIERES

G CUTTING SELECTED ELEMENTS: THE FIRST CUT

H CUTTING SELECTED ELEMENTS: THE SECOND CUT

THIS lesson deals with preparation of the canvas for the open work in the remaining lessons. Strangely, you start this phase of work with what is usually accomplished last—binding the outer edges. This helps you to establish an accurate stitch count with the border, and the rest of the work then falls neatly in place. This procedure is not followed for all Hardanger embroidery, but it is the simplest way to produce a small canvas work such as this. Study the master pattern for the sampler and the neck ruff; then proceed to the first set of diagrams to work the scalloped buttonhole edge. After completing all of the surface work shown in Stitch Diagrams **1A** through **1F**, remove the canvas from the frame to cut and withdraw the elements (**1G** and **1H**).

MASTER PATTERN, SAMPLER

To design or work a Hardanger embroidery, it is necessary to have a master pattern (see page 202). The heavier lines around the scalloped edge indicate the buttonhole stitches; the finer lines around the squares indicate the satin stitches of the kloster blocks; the black dots signify the center holes of the square eyelets; and the arrowheads indicate the rivières. These are the stitches to be worked on the stretched canvas in Lesson **1**. Notice that all of the spaces to be opened are bound by kloster blocks or buttonhole stitches before any cutting and withdrawing is done. As you complete each block or set of buttonhole stitches, count them carefully; it can be extremely discouraging to find an error when you are further along! Start the sampler by basting the center lines on the canvas to provide matching reference points. Then, work the scalloped buttonhole edge, referring to Stitch Diagram **1A**. Follow the lessons in sequence to complete the sampler, returning to **1B** to add the outer buttonhole edge.

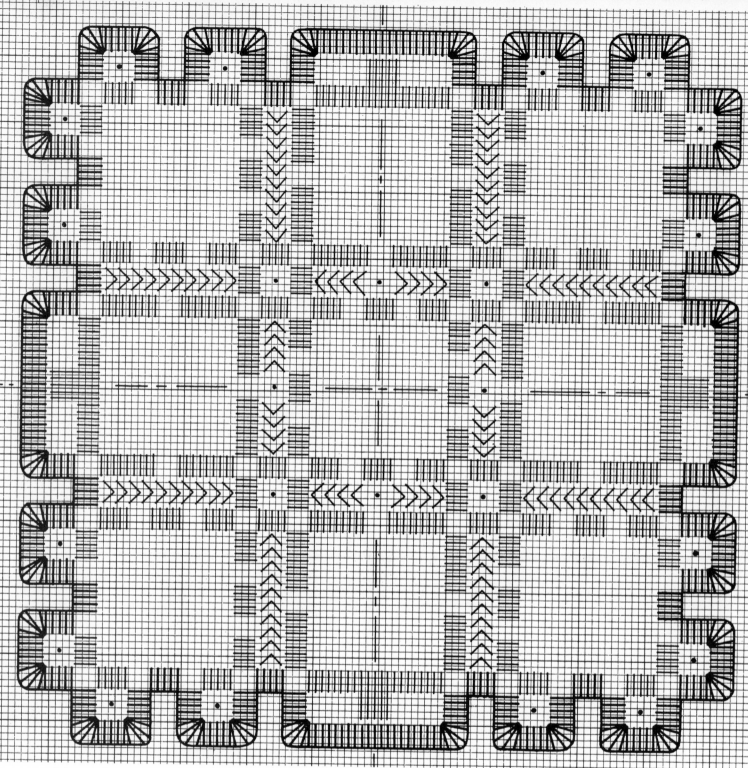

Master Pattern, Sampler

MASTER PATTERN, NECK RUFF

Opposite is the master pattern for the Hardanger border of the neck ruff. All the stages of work are shown in this diagram. Complete the surface work first, while the piece is on the frame. This includes the scalloped buttonhole edge, indicated by the heavy lines; the kloster blocks, indicated by the thinner straight lines; and the square eyelets, indicated by black dots. The squares indicated by double lines are the double faggot ground from *Pulled Canvas* (**7B**). If you are making the ruffled collar, be sure to work some sort of simple design between the two halves of the ruff, in the spaces indicated by the x's in the pattern diagram. The next phase of the work is accomplished off of the stretcher. Withdraw the elements from the festooned web: cut and withdraw all four horizontal elements, then cut and withdraw four vertical elements on either side of the four center elements. Next cut and withdraw the selected elements of the open squares defined by the needlewoven bars and kloster blocks (see **1G** and **1H**). Return the work to the stretchers and work the needlewoven bars (**2B**) and the festooned web with corner spokes, similar to **3A**. Remove the work from the stretchers and work the outer buttonhole edge (**1B**). Cut away the excess canvas. Finally, add an overlay of satin stitches to the festooned webs.

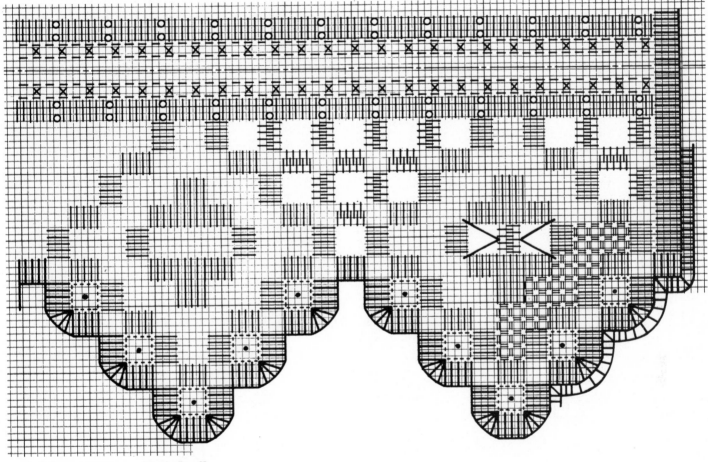

Master Pattern, Neck Ruff

STITCH 1A

SCALLOPED BUTTONHOLE EDGE

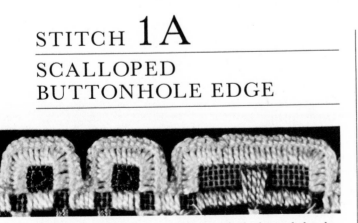

Sampler: *Start the embroidery with the buttonhole edge.*

First, stitch a scalloped buttonhole edge around the entire perimeter to define the outer shape of a small canvas Hardanger embroidery.

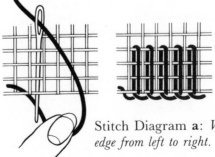

Stitch Diagram **a**: *Work a buttonhole edge from left to right.*

Although the buttonhole stitch is most conveniently worked from left to right, it may be worked from right to left as well. But be sure to maintain a consistent direction for each phase of work. (See *Hemstitching,* **1B**.)

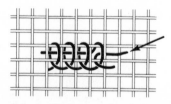

Stitch Diagram **b**: *When you run out of thread, add a new one imperceptibly.*

Insert the old working thread into the backface as shown. Pass the needle through a number of loops; but do not cut away the old thread end yet. Weave a new working thread into the canvas from the right and emerge on the frontface at the base of the last stitch, at the very spot where the needle would normally emerge. Now adjust the tension of the old working thread, secure it on the backface, and trim it.

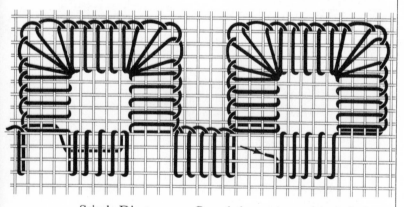

Stitch Diagram **c**: *Round the corners and include the adjacent kloster blocks.*

When the kloster blocks and the scalloped edge are to be worked with thread of the same size and color, stitch them in the same journey to save additional fastening on and off. There are several ways to turn the corners of the scallops so that they will be rounded. In this stitch diagram and in the sampler, the corner stitch and the second one from the corner on each side are eliminated; this both maintains a pleasant curve and prevents overcrowding. The scallops of the Hardanger collar ruff are rounded by shortening or eliminating some of the corner stitches; see that master pattern for details.

STITCH 1B
OUTER BUTTONHOLE EDGE

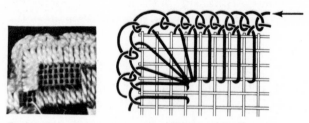

Sampler: *A second row of buttonhole stitches secures the edge.*

Stitch Diagram: *Enter the festoons of the previous row.*

At the conclusion of a Hardanger embroidery, you can add a second row of buttonhole stitches outside of the first to provide a neat and secure edge. This lesson is somewhat out of place, since this second buttonhole edge should be the last stitch you accomplish on the sampler. But it is included here so that the relationship between the two buttonhole edges can be easily grasped.

Remove the canvas from the frame. Stitch from left to right, entering a festoon of the first scalloped buttonhole edge with each new loop. After completing the second row of buttonhole stitches, turn the work to the backface and carefully clip off the canvas elements close to the first row of buttonholing.

STITCH 1C
KLOSTER BLOCKS

Sampler: *Provide matching kloster blocks on opposite sides of the elements to be withdrawn.*

Kloster blocks are the primary stitch units on which all the open work of Hardanger depends. Each block is composed of an odd number of satin stitches—five, seven, nine, or more. An even number of elements is later cut and withdrawn from between opposite kloster blocks. To secure the edges, there must always be matching kloster blocks on *opposite sides* of the space from which the elements are to be cut and withdrawn.

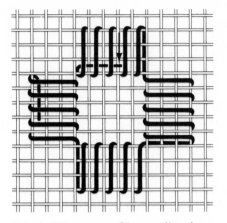

Stitch Diagram: *Change direction at right angles, sharing stitch holes.*

Kloster blocks always change direction at right angles to one another. To accomplish this, make sure that the first stitch of a new block shares a hole with the last stitch of the previous block. In this stitch diagram, the blocks are worked in a clockwise direction; the small squares at the four corners of the center square of the sampler should be stitched in this manner. Although square eyelets are worked within this square by deflecting elements in the sampler, you could cut and withdraw all the elements from a unit like this one. If you are working the sampler, complete the kloster blocks that surround the four large squares in the corners and the center square at this time as well.

If you are fastening off behind a kloster block, carefully secure the thread by darning back and forth. Be sure to pass around the first and last stitches.

STITCH 1D

KLOSTER BLOCKS EXPANDED

Sampler: *Work long kloster blocks that rise gradually or jump suddenly into a peak.*

Kloster blocks can be expanded to include any odd number of satin stitches. In the sampler, four of the large squares are bound on the outer edge with blocks of twenty-one satin stitches. You can see pattern diagrams for each of them in Lesson 3. At the middle of these expanded blocks, five satin stitches jump to twice their height. You can also work center stitches so that they rise gradually to form a point; in either case the rise is called a festoon. Each of the remaining three sides of these squares consists of two kloster blocks composed of nine satin stitches each.

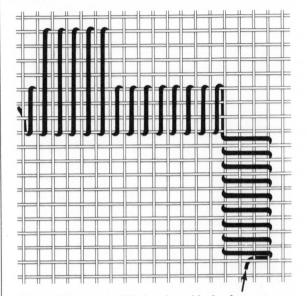

Stitch Diagram: *Work a long block of twenty-one satins with five large ones in the center.*

To follow this stitch diagram, start by stitching a block of nine satin stitches on the right side; then turn the corner to work the long block of twenty-one satins. Begin this long block with eight stitches of normal height, work five of them at twice this height, and then drop to complete the block with eight of normal size. Next, turn the corner, work a block of nine, and complete the remaining sides. The four large squares worked in this way in the sampler will have eight elements cut and withdrawn from each corner, leaving a large cross in the center of four elements crossing four more. This cross is clearly shown in Lesson 3.

STITCH 1E

SQUARE EYELET

Sampler: *These stitches provide strong accents.*

Square eyelets are particularly useful stitch units for this form of open work because Hardanger is a system that is based on square spaces. Work densely packed backstitched square eyelets inside each of the scallops of the buttonhole edge (**1A**); center a simple eyelet in a rivière (**1F**); or, instead of opening a small kloster block, deflect the elements with a square eyelet, shown here.

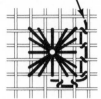

Stitch Diagram: *Backstitch around the eyelet to cover the canvas elements.*

Square eyelets are units of consecutively worked satin stitches that enter a center hole from around a square perimeter. Prepare the hole first with an awl or the pointed ends of embroidery scissors by gently spreading the canvas elements apart. Start with a vertical satin stitch. Maintain a medium tension to emphasize the hole, but try not to lose the rhythm of the satin stitches. Travel around the perimeter, completing the eyelet by passing the needle under and around the stitches on the backface. To work the square eyelet in this diagram, pass around the perimeter in a second stage, working a backstitch over each element. Notice that each square eyelet in the center of a rivière is composed of only eight satin stitches.

Stitch **1F**
RIVIERES

Sampler: *Embellish the surface with bands of satin stitches.*

The surface embellishment on Hardanger embroideries consists mainly of traditional geometric patterns worked in satin stitches. Since the focus here and in the sampler is on the open work of Hardanger, only narrow strips of solid canvas have been provided for surface embroidery. However, these strips become ideal spaces for embroidered bands, sometimes referred to as rivières. The rivières shown here consist of pairs of overcast stitches that slant like arrowheads, leading the eye into the center of the sampler. Simple square eyelets are centered on each of the four sides of the large center square.

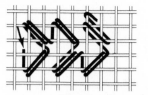

Stitch Diagram: *Point two pairs of slanted overcasts into a shared hole, slightly deflecting the elements.*

Work two pairs of diagonal overcasts to point into the same shared hole. Notice that you are emphasizing the points of the arrows by slightly deflecting the canvas elements.

TECHNIQUE **1G**
CUTTING SELECTED ELEMENTS: THE FIRST CUT

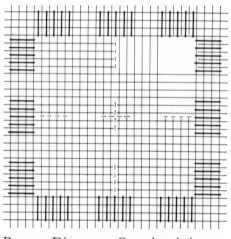

Pattern Diagram: *Cut selected elements midway between opposite kloster blocks.*

Each selected element is cut twice (you can remove the canvas from the stretchers for **1G** and **1H** if you like). Make the first cuts midway between matching opposite kloster blocks. Cut one element at a time, unweaving each half back to the kloster block. Complete the cutting and unweaving from one direction, then proceed with the other. To unweave, pluck the element out with an awl or the tip of a tapestry needle. This pattern diagram shows the location of the first cuts for the webs shown in Lesson **2**, where you will find diagrams showing them completely opened. The sampler's remaining webs appear in Lesson **4**.

TECHNIQUE 1H
CUTTING SELECTED ELEMENTS: THE SECOND CUT

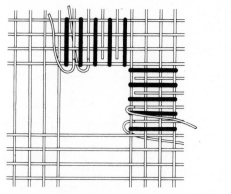

Canvas Diagram: *Make the second cut at the kloster blocks on the front- and backface.*

Make the second cut at the kloster block. In Hardanger it is easy to achieve a clean, close cut, preventing any unattractive stubs from poking out of the kloster blocks. You can determine on which face of the canvas to make the cut by bending each element back over the kloster block. When a withdrawn element lies on top of a horizontal canvas element, it can be cut closer if cut on the frontface. Complete the cutting of the elements on one face, and then turn the canvas and cut the remaining ones on the backface. To cut closely, hold the scissors so that they lie flat on the work.

LESSON 2

WEBS

A OVERCAST BARS

B NEEDLEWOVEN BARS

C LOOPSTITCH BARS

D OBLIQUE LOOPSTITCH BARS

E NEEDLEWOVEN BARS WITH POST STITCH PICOTS

F NEEDLEWOVEN BARS WITH CHAIN STITCH PICOTS

WEBS are the networks of crossed elements that remain within the kloster enclosures after selected elements are withdrawn. A web consists of at least one unit of four elements crossing four others. At the intersection of crossing units, a square of canvas remains in its original state. The canvas should be returned to the frame prior to this lesson, in which five of the sampler webs are filled. The remaining long elements in the webs are called bars. Five different systems are shown for drawing together the four elements of the bars. Only one of the two picot methods diagramed in this lesson appears on the sampler. The second method is a simple alternative.

STITCH 2A

OVERCAST BARS

Sampler: *Maintain even tension and a consistent stitch slant.*

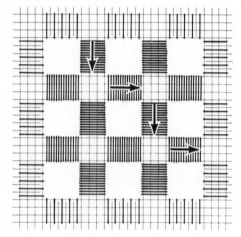

Pattern Diagram: *Overcast the bars snugly and evenly.*

Employ an even tension as you fill the bars of the sampler; each one is overcast eight or nine times. Maintain the same stitch slant by wrapping the elements consistently in the same direction; accomplish this by turning the work with each diagonal row or reversing the direction of the overcasting. (Turning the work will also let you work away from yourself, which is easier.) The arrows in the pattern diagram show the direction of travel of the second steplike row.

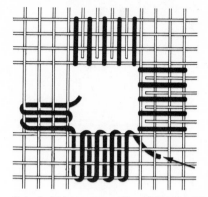

Stitch Diagram: *Travel in steplike diagonal rows.*

Emerge on one side of the first bar. Overcast the four elements to draw them neatly and snugly together into coils that fill the bar. Emerge again at the base of the next bar of the steplike diagonal row. When working bars, try at first to position the canvas so that you overcast or needleweave away from yourself. You will find that this makes it easier to control the elements and keep the work even.

STITCH 2B

NEEDLEWOVEN BARS

Sampler: *Work flat, even bars with neatly squared corners.*

Neck Ruff: *Fill triangles with needlewoven bars.*

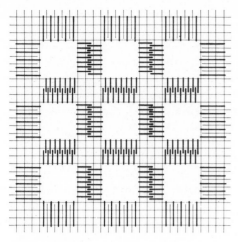

Pattern Diagram: *Darn the bars snugly and evenly.*

Employ webs of needlewoven or overcast bars to produce simple, bold open work. Needlewoven bars fill the steplike triangular spaces in the Hardanger neck ruff. More delicate webs can be worked with very fine pastel canvas and working thread.

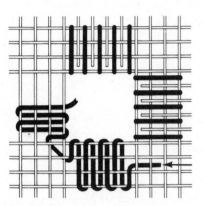

Stitch Diagram: *After the first "short" stitch, insert the needle between pairs of warps.*

To start a bar, emerge on the frontface between pairs of elements. Pass over one pair of warps, then under all four elements and emerge on the other side. Fill the rest of the bar by inserting the needle from the frontface between pairs of warps. Complete the bar by passing over the warps closest to the next bar in the steplike diagonal row. Emerge once more between the pairs of warps for the first weave only. By starting each bar in this manner, you can produce sharp corners. You can slant diagonal rows in either direction.

STITCH 2C
LOOPSTITCH BARS

Sampler: *Center loopstitch units in alternate open squares.*

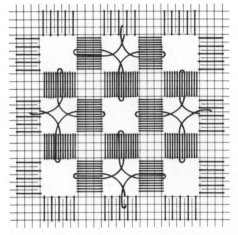

Pattern Diagram: *Work the loopstitch units in alternate rows.*

A loopstitch is a unit of four buttonhole stitches, each of which loops around the four bars of an open square or into a kloster block. Be consistent in passing over and under so that all loopstitches in a web match. Work the loopstitches while overcasting or darning the bars in alternate rows, as shown in the stitch diagram.

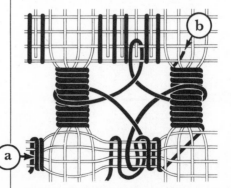

Stitch Diagram: *Overcast one and a half bars of the second diagonal row; then throw a loopstitch unit.*

To fill a web of loopstitch bars as in the pattern diagram, start by overcasting the two bars of the first ascending row (**a**). Overcast the first bar of the next, descending row (**b**) and half of the second bar. Emerge from the base on the frontface and throw a loop over and under the bar to the right. Throw the second loop into the kloster block and emerge. Throw the third loop over and under the completed bar on the left. Complete the unit by passing over the first thrown thread and under the bar; complete the bar. Overcast one and a half more bars and work another unit; this time you invade a kloster block on the left. Continue in steplike rows, working the loopstitches in every other row. Loopstitch bars can also be needlewoven, in which case the thrown loops invade the space between the pairs of woven elements.

STITCH 2D

OBLIQUE LOOPSTITCH BARS

Sampler: *Throw loopstitches into the corners of alternate open squares.*

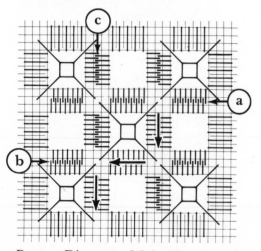

Pattern Diagram: *Work oblique loopstitch units on alternate rows.*

An oblique loopstitch is a unit of four loops thrown into the centers of four corner mesh squares. Several overcasts are worked around the thrown loops each time they emerge; you can determine the number of overcasts by the weight of the thread. For best results, employ a fine twisted thread, such as DMC Cordonnet Crochet Cotton or a twisted silk thread.

A row of oblique loopstitches is worked along with a row of needlewoven bars (**a**); then a row of bars (**b**) is worked without loopstitches. Combine the two stitches again (**c**), and finish with two needlewoven bars and a single independent loopstitch in the lower right corner.

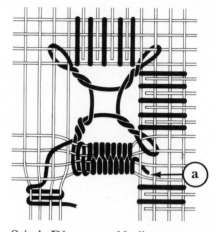

Stitch Diagram: *Needleweave a complete bar, then throw loops into the four corners.*

To fill the web of oblique loopstitch bars shown in Pattern Diagram **2D**, start by needleweaving the first bar of the descending row (**a**) as shown in this stitch diagram. After completing the last stitch of the bar, throw a loop to the lower right corner and into the center of the mesh square; emerge on the right of the thrown thread, and overcast it to the left several times. Throw two more loops in a counterclockwise direction in the same way. Complete the unit by overcasting the first thrown thread and entering the center of the last mesh square. A fourth loop quite unexpectedly appears as you draw the working thread through to the frontface in position to needleweave the next bar.

STITCH 2E

NEEDLEWOVEN BARS WITH POST STITCH PICOTS

Sampler: *Accent each side of needlewoven bars.*

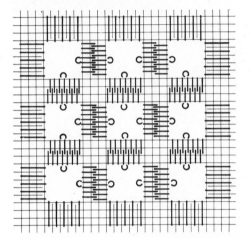

Pattern Diagram: *Needleweave half a bar, work a picot on each side, complete the bar, and continue the journey.*

Post stitch picots are worked identically to French knots. The only difference between them is that French knots lie on the surface of the work; picots are French knots seen in profile on the edge of the canvas. Pairs of picots are shown in this web on either side of all the needlewoven bars. Produce them halfway down each bar as you travel in steplike diagonal rows. The pattern in the negative space is particularly effective.

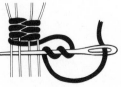

Stitch Diagram: *Wind the thread around the needle twice before passing under the paired warps.*

Complete a weave at the center of the bar. Wind the working thread twice around the shaft of the needle and pass the tip of the needle under two warps, in position for the next weave. Hold the coiled thread in place with one hand and draw the needle through with the other to complete the weave. There should now be a tight coil in profile on one side of the bar. Give the canvas a full turn and follow this diagram for a post stitch picot on the other side of the bar.

STITCH 2F

NEEDLEWOVEN BARS WITH CHAIN STITCH PICOTS

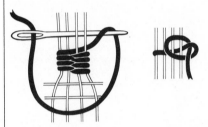

Stitch Diagram **a**: *Pass under the right warps and work a chain stitch.*

Stitch Diagram **b**: *Pass under the left warps and work a chain stitch.*

As in Stitch **2E** (post stitch picots), complete the weave at the center of the bar. Pass the needle between the paired warps, pointing to the right. Pass the working thread over and under the tip of the needle (**a**). Draw the needle and thread completely through to make a snug knot.

Pass the needle between the paired warps pointing to the left. Pass the thread over and under the tip of the needle (**b**). Draw the needle and thread completely through to make a snug knot. Resume the needleweaving, being careful not to displace the picot.

LESSON 3

SPOKES AND FILLINGS

A CORNER SPOKES WITH FESTOON
STITCH

B BRANCHED SPOKES

C DOUBLE SPOKES

D DIVIDED BARS WITH TWISTED
LOOPSTITCH

THIS lesson illustrates four webs with larger open spaces; only four bars, in the shape of a cross, remain in the center of each. Although the stitch diagrams are drawn with overcast bars, they can also be needlewoven. The fourth web of the lesson, however (**3D**), *must* be worked with needle-weaving. Three kinds of spokes are demonstrated. The spokes of this lesson are working threads that are thrown, like the radii of a circle, from the middle of the center mesh square to various locations around the perimeter of the web, where they emerge and are overcast back to center. Two variations of loopstitch are also demonstrated. In the first example (**3A**), festoon stitches surround a web and form a ring; in the second, twisted loop-stitches distort four pairs of narrow needlewoven bars in a pleasing pattern (**3D**).

STITCH 3A

CORNER SPOKES WITH FESTOON STITCH

Sampler: *Join the four single spokes and the four overcast bars in a ring.*

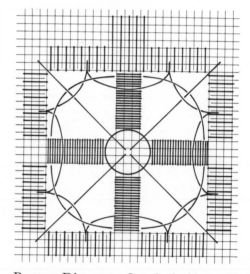

Pattern Diagram: *Invade the kloster blocks five satin stitches in from the corner mesh squares.*

Produce the web shown here in four stages. First, overcast the bars of the opened web. Then throw the spokes into the four corners from the center mesh square. Next, in a clockwise direction, festoon stitch around the four sides of the web, invading each kloster block and passing over spokes and bars. Then travel around again *counterclockwise*, passing under spokes and bars but over festoons to produce a twisted ring. See Lesson **4** for the last stage, the center wheel.

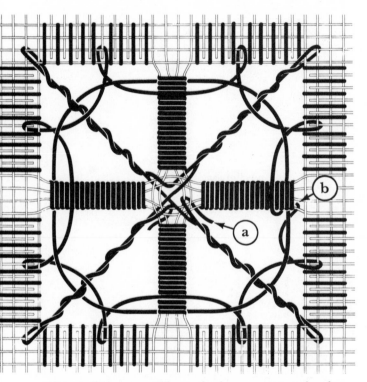

Stitch Diagram: *Throw the four overcast spokes from the center. Festoon stitch around the perimeter.*

To produce the spokes, emerge from the center mesh square (**a**) and throw the working thread into the center of the lower right mesh square. Emerge and overcast to the center a set number of times. Emerge again and throw a spoke into the upper left; overcast back. Produce the other two spokes in the same way, as shown in this stitch diagram. Work the festoon stitch in a separate stage, fastening on behind a bar at the perimeter (**b**). Throw the working thread into each kloster block in a regular pattern, passing over the spokes and bars. When you arrive at the starting bar, pass under and over it and work the return journey, traveling in the opposite direction (notice that no festoons are made this time around). Employ enough tension to pull the festoons into a circle. Fasten off under the starting bar.

STITCH 3B
BRANCHED SPOKES

Sampler: *Throw single spokes that are divided in two.*

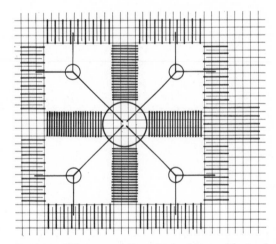

Pattern Diagram: *Invade the kloster blocks four satin stitches in from the corner mesh square.*

Overcast the bars of the web first. Throw each of the four spokes from the center into the kloster blocks on the two sides of each segment. Darn a small wheel at the fork before overcasting back to center.

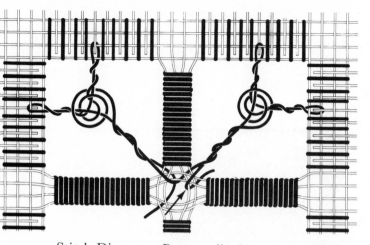

Stitch Diagram: *Darn small wheels at the fork of the two branches before overcasting back.*

Work the branched spoke in the upper right segment of the web first. Emerge at the center and throw the working thread into the top kloster block. Emerge on the right of the spoke and overcast back twice. Throw the working thread into the right kloster block an equal distance from the corner. Emerge below and overcast back twice. Darn a small wheel by passing over the long spoke, under the left branch, and over the right branch. Darn once more around and overcast the single spoke back to the center; emerge on the frontface to start the branched spoke to the left. Turn the work to follow the diagram for the other half of the web.

STITCH 3C
DOUBLE SPOKES

Sampler: *Throw spokes that radiate around a center wheel.*

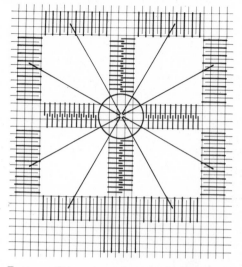

Pattern Diagram: *Invade the kloster blocks over two long canvas elements four satin stitches from the corner.*

Overcast or needleweave the bars first. Then throw two overcast spokes from the center into the kloster blocks on the two sides of each segment.

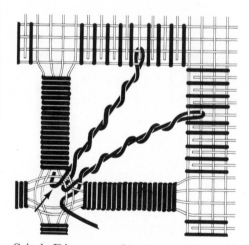

Stitch Diagram: *Overcast the matching spokes in the same direction.*

Work the double spokes in the upper right segment of the web first. Emerge at the center and throw the working thread into the top kloster block. Emerge on the left of the spoke and overcast to the right a set number of times back to the center. Emerge and throw the working thread into the right kloster block. Emerge above the spoke and overcast an equal number of times back to center. Work the remaining segments in the same manner in clockwise sequence.

STITCH 3D

DIVIDED BARS WITH TWISTED LOOPSTITCH

Sampler: *Pull the narrow woven bars into graceful curves with loopstitches.*

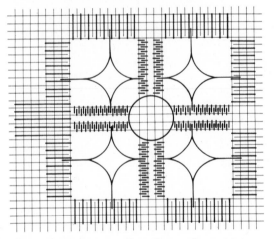

Pattern Diagram: *Complete each segment individually.*

Complete each quarter of this web in separate stages. Needleweave the two narrow bars and throw the twisted loopstitch unit of each segment in a single journey. The loops that are thrown into the narrow bars spread them gracefully into a centrally balanced pattern.

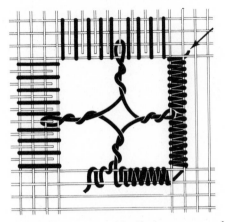

Stitch Diagram: *Needleweave one and a half narrow bars; then throw a twisted loopstitch unit.*

Work the upper left corner of a web to follow this diagram. Separate the vertical bar and needleweave two single elements to the center mesh square. Needleweave half of the divided bar perpendicular to the first. Start a twisted loopstitch by throwing the working thread into the middle of the completed bar. Emerge on the right of the thrown thread. Produce a twisted loop by overcasting the thrown thread several times (three in the sampler). Gently tug the twisted loop to pull the bar out of alignment. Throw the working thread into a kloster block, emerge, and overcast. Work the next twisted loop in the same way. Complete the unit by overcasting the first thrown thread and needleweaving the rest of the bar. Turn the work to follow this diagram for the remaining segments.

LESSON 4

WHEELS

A WOVEN WHEEL

B DARNED WHEEL

C RIBBED WHEEL

D REVERSE RIBBED WHEEL WITH DARNED EMBELLISHMENT

THIS lesson deals with the center wheels worked around the converging bars and spokes within a web. The wheels offer a round focal point that contrasts with the angularity of the webs. After you conclude this lesson, the Hardanger sampler will be almost completed. You may then remove it from the frame for the last time, add a second row of buttonhole edging as described in **1B**, and cut away the excess canvas. You might also want to add a second layer of satin stitches to the kloster blocks, blending these stitches into the existing ones to produce a slightly padded, shiny border. This overstitching was done on the small festooned webs of the neck ruff.

STITCH 4A
WOVEN WHEEL

Sampler: *Pass two bands of different colors around the center mesh square; then add an eyelet.*

Pass over the spokes and under the bars for several revolutions. In the sampler, a few more revolutions were then woven in another color, passing over the bars and under the spokes.

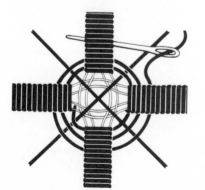

Stitch Diagram: *Employ the spokes and bars as radiating warps.*

STITCH 4B
DARNED WHEEL

Sampler: *Alternate the rounds of weaving; pass over and under, then under and over.*

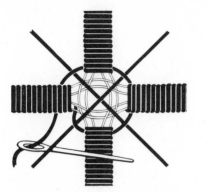

Stitch Diagram: *Pass under two warps once in each revolution.*

Darn a wheel by passing over one radiating warp, (either a needlewoven bar or a thrown spoke) and under the next in one revolution. In the next revolution, warps that were passed under will be passed over, and vice versa. Since there are an even number of radiating warps, in order to change the sequence on each journey, pass under two consecutive warps—a spoke and a bar. This will maintain the darned quality of the wheel. Never pass over two warps, as this long pass is visible when made on the frontface. Note the needle passing under a second warp in this stitch diagram.

STITCH 4C

RIBBED WHEEL

Sampler: *Produce a ribbed texture with backstitches.*

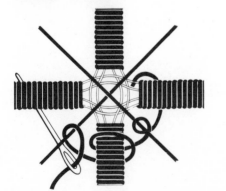

Stitch Diagram: *Pass under two warps as you move ahead and over one as you move back.*

Produce a ribbed wheel by traveling around the center mesh square with backstitches. Pass under two warps as you move ahead and over one as you move back.

STITCH 4D

REVERSE RIBBED WHEEL WITH DARNED EMBELLISHMENT

Sampler: *Produce a densely textured wheel; then add a decoration in a contrasting color.*

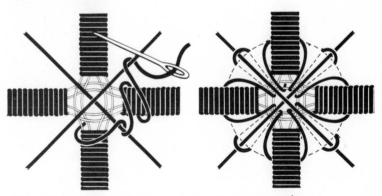

Stitch Diagram **a**: *Pass ahead over two warps and back under one.*

Stitch Diagram **b**: *Employ the center mesh to darn around the bars and spokes.*

As its name implies, this wheel is produced in reverse of the preceding one. Pass over two warps as you move ahead and under one as you pass back (**a**). To work the darned embellishment (**b**), emerge from the center mesh square, pass over the wheel, under the bar, then back over the wheel and into the center. Next, pass under the wheel, over the spoke, then back under the wheel and emerge from the center. Alternate these two movements around the wheel.

BOOK SIX

RETICELLO AND HEDEBO

In reticello, all but four elements crossing four others are withdrawn from large squares; the crossed elements are needlewoven to become the framework for geometric patterns of buttonholed and overcast bars. In Hedebo, all the elements are withdrawn from characteristic rounded shapes that are filled with geometric patterns worked in a distinctive knotted buttonhole stitch.

CONTENTS

INTRODUCTION

Because they are so similar in concept, reticello and Hedebo are explored in the same section of *The Open Canvas*. In fact, Hedebo might never have existed if it were not for reticello. Both techniques are based on withdrawing elements from both directions and filling the spaces with simple geometric forms of needle lace. Each has its own distinct style. A sampler is provided to illustrate all of the techniques and as a practice piece for those who care to follow it. If you employ the master pattern as a guide, you can execute the stitches in sequence with the lessons. Most of the lessons start with a pattern diagram of a reticello or Hedebo shape that shows the location of the stitches diagramed in the lesson. The lessons themselves are planned to progress in a logical sequence, and they conclude with the completion of the sampler.

You should note that in many of the stitch diagrams in this book, it seems as though two colors of thread—black and white—were used. The colors were employed to distinguish each journey; you should be using the same working thread throughout, unless you make a decision to change colors yourself.

A THIMBLEFUL OF RETICELLO HISTORY

Reticello lace was made chiefly between 1480 and 1620. It is believed to have originated in the Ionian Islands, which lie between Greece and Italy. Greek point lace, the ancestor of reticello, was one of the first needlemade laces. The earliest Greek point was worked in geometric patterns of straight lines; half circles, triangles, and wheels were later introduced, and finally coarse lace fillings were added. By the middle of the sixteenth century, Venice had become the center for reticello lace and, by the end of the century, reticello was being produced all over Italy, as well as in France, England, Spain, Flanders, and Germany. The rapid spread of reticello was due to the publication of several pattern books that provided lace designs to be worked by ladies of the leisure class. The first pattern book was by Mathio Pagan, pub-

lished in 1542. The most famous books, *Lacis* and *Point Coupé* (the name reticello came later), were by Federic Vinciolo and were published in Paris in 1587.

Research into early lace designs, workmanship, and modes of weaving has been greatly assisted by the study of paintings, legal documents, and the already mentioned pattern books. Detailed renderings of lace are seen in the portraits of the sixteenth-century Florentine school. Inventories still exist listing lace among the treasured possessions of cathedrals and wealthy families of this period. Sumptuary laws, which were prohibitions against the wearing of lace, were enacted in 1530. These laws dictated who could wear the lace, the width of the lace, and even the age of those allowed to wear it; lace was a symbol of wealth and nobility, and the wealthy and noble were determined that it remain so.

The earliest reticello was stiff and formal, used chiefly for ecclesiastic vestments and shrouds. Later, reticello was used for wearing apparel, and the patterns became more solid and ornate. By the seventeenth century, an attempt was made to create pictorial designs that included people, animals, and buildings. The results were somewhat unsuccessful, since the work retained its stiff, geometric quality.

There have been several revivals of Greek point and reticello lace techniques. Most notable are the movements of John Ruskin and the Amelia Ars Society. John Ruskin was an English painter, poet, writer, and social reformer. In 1884 he instigated a linen industry and crafts revival program in the Lake District of England to encourage handwork and help relieve poverty in the area. To spin flax brought from Belgium, he had spinning wheels made from old blueprints. Lace patterns were brought from Italy and were used to decorate the hand-spun linen with cutwork, drawn work, reticello, and needleweaving; this work became known as Ruskin work or Greek lace.

In the 1920s, the Amelia Ars Society—a crafts program organized to revive the native crafts of the area—was founded in Bologna, Italy. The society produced reticello lace, employing many of the same patterns shown in the old sixteenth-century Vinciolo design books.

A THIMBLEFUL OF HEDEBO HISTORY

Hedebo originated at the middle of the eighteenth century in the barren heaths of Denmark. Pronounced "hay'-the-bow," the term is a contraction of heather born—people who live on the heath. It is interesting to note that this delicate lace embroidery was done by people whose principal work was digging and drying peat. Hedebo passed through three stages of development. The embroidery of the first period, from 1760 to 1820, was not as open or as delicate as was subsequent work. The opened shapes were patterned after the flowers and leaves of the wood carvings on domestic furniture. And the spaces were filled with a withdrawn-element embroidery* similar to that shown in the first few lessons of *Filet*, inspired by early netted lace patterns and similar to Russian drawn work. The opened shapes were outlined in chain stitch. They included semicircles, hearts, crescents, leaves, cones, and pears, and were found on men's shirts, women's underclothes, and household linens. The surface embroidery was worked with a medium weight linen thread that all but covered the dense, handwoven linen ground fabric.

The second stage of development occurred between 1820 and 1850. More formal reticello squares and fillings were added to the rounded, conventional shapes of the first period, and the amount of surface embroidery was greatly reduced. The center motif shown on the sampler, a large square divided in quarters by needlewoven bars, is of this period.

In the final stage, from 1850 through the turn of the century, Hedebo changed drastically. The opened, rounded shapes continued to be filled with the lacy designs adapted from reticello. Now, however, all of the embroidery was done on mass-produced linen that was often provided with stamped-on patterns. Hedebo at the turn of the century was used for tablecloths, table centers, doilies, trims on bed linens and towels, and for women's collars and blouses. Little surface embroidery remained; simple designs were worked in satin stitches and eyelets.

SOME NEEDLE POINTS

Although reticello is considered a true lace because so little ground fabric remains, it actually

---

* Alternate groups of elements were withdrawn evenly in both directions from a linen ground, the remaining elements were overcast, and the resulting network filled with darned and looped stitches.

incorporates both withdrawn element embroidery, known by embroidery scholars as *punto tagliato*, and *punto in aria*, a subsequent development that abandoned the ground fabric completely. Only square or rectangular skeletons of foundation fabric are left to become the framework for the same bars, picots, and buttonhole fillings used in *punto in aria* laces. Reticello is easily recognized by the needlewoven frameworks and formal geometric patterns of straight lines, diagonals, triangles, circles, and arcs. Basically, reticello is an insertion lace, bound on both long, straight sides by the remaining elements of the foundation fabric. Four-sided stitches are traditionally employed as secondary edgings to the buttonholed or overcast cut edges.

Although similar in concept, Hedebo is distinctly different from reticello in both technique and pattern. No elements of the ground fabric remain; the rounded spaces are achieved by slashing and folding back sections of the shape to be withdrawn, and a specialized Hedebo buttonhole stitch is employed exclusively. The distinguishing feature of Hedebo buttonholing is a little knob at the top of each vertical stitch that sharpens its appearance and emphasizes the connecting festoons between the stitches. Hedebo buttonhole stitch is always worked from left to right, and the festoons are overcast back from right to left. Another distinction between the two techniques is that the needlewoven bars so typical of reticello are absent from the Hedebo of the later period. The chain stitch outline of the Hedebo shapes on the sampler is borrowed from the earlier period.

The term *slashing* is used here to indicate that a cut is made and the canvas is folded back, rather than being completely trimmed away. The curved shapes of Hedebo are slashed in at least two directions, and the canvas is finger-pressed to the backface, carefully maintaining the curved line made by the split stitch outline. To slash the canvas, cut the elements that bisect the shape to be opened at 45-degree angles.

WORKBASKET SUPPLIES

CANVAS
Interlock is a very suitable foundation for canvas reticello and Hedebo. The double warp construction prevents the rapid fraying so typical of mono canvas. Also, the elements themselves are composed of fewer plies than are those of mono canvas, resulting in a much lighter weight fabric. This is very helpful in Hedebo preparation, where the canvas is slashed and folded to the backface.

Interlock lacks the strength of mono canvas, which may be a hazard in some other forms of open canvas work, but it is perfectly suitable for reticello and Hedebo, since the edges of the canvas are carefully reinforced. However, when selecting interlock canvas, look for a superior quality with smooth elements and without too much starch. Congress canvas, because of its close weave and lightweight elements, is also suitable for this work.

THREADS

For the padding stitches covered by buttonholing, described in Lesson **1**, and for much of the surface embroidery, use a soft, lightly twisted cotton such as DMC Broder Special (article number 107). This is a lovely, soft thread that blends into the canvas but still retains its twisted character where it is needed. As of this writing, it comes in two convenient sizes, 12 and 16, and in eighty-two colors. For the buttonhole stitches, a more twisted thread is preferable. Again from DMC, you can choose Cordonnet Crochet Cotton, 6-cord, also known as Cordonnet Special, article 151. This fine twisted thread is used for lace making and comes in various sizes, from 10 to 50, but only in white and ecru.

STRETCHERS

Use interlocking wood strips to assemble a stretcher frame. Tack down the bound canvas as tightly as possible. This simple framing method makes it easy to turn the work over to fasten down working threads, and you can easily remove the canvas from the stretcher during the progress of the work if you so desire.

NEEDLES AND OTHER TOOLS

You will need tapestry needles in appropriate sizes for most of the work. Use crewel needles for the double running stitch and the split stitch, and for piercing through bars. Use millinery needles for making bullion knots; these needles have small eyes, are very long, and can easily slide through the coils of working thread. You will also need a columnar tool such as a pencil, knitting needle, or crochet hook of appropriate girth around which a ring of thread is wound for the Hedebo rings shown in Lesson **8**.

COLOR

Canvas can be colored with oil or acrylic paint, or with dye. The reticello and Hedebo sampler has a dyed background of deep blue to provide a strong accent for the white embroidery. You can brush on the dye or dip the canvas in a dye bath. For the sampler, two shades of Deka Permanent Dye were blended, numbers 400 light blue and 411 dark blue. The reticello and Hedebo shapes were first defined with working thread, as described in Stitch Diagrams **1A**, **1B**, and **1G**. Then the dye was brushed from the outer edge to these outlines. Thus, no deep color appeared under the crisp white edgings.

KEY TO STITCHES AND THREADS
Sampler

The reticello and Hedebo sampler is worked with cotton thread on 18/inch white interlock canvas. The finished size is 7½ inches by 7½ inches. See the accompanying key to identify the stitches and threads. The bold numbers with letters refer to the lesson and diagram where each stitch or pattern is located in *Reticello and Hedebo*. The bold italic numbers refer to the threads listed under Materials Employed.

1A Double Running Stitch, *1*
1B Overcast Stitch, *1*
1C Buttonhole Stitch, *4*
1D Four-sided Stitch, *3*
1F Needlewoven Bars, *2,4*
1G Backstitch Outline, *1*
1H Split Stitch Outline, *1*
1I Stem Stitch Outline and Filling, *1*
1K Hedebo Buttonhole Edge, *4*
1L Chain Stitch Outline, *4*
2 A, B, C, D Independent Reticello Bars, *4*
3 A, B, C, D, E Simultaneous Bars with Picots, *4*
4 A, B Reticello Lace, Open Buttonhole, *4*
4 C, D Reticello Lace, Venetian Cloth, *4*
5A Loose Needleweaving with Buttonholed Ring Picots, *4*
5B Point d'Angleterre, *4*
6A Two Hedebo Bars, *4*
6B Three Hedebo Bars, *4*
7A Loose Hedebo Filling with Detached Pyramid, *5*
7B Four Joined Pyramids, *5*
7C Straight Bars, *5*
7D Mixed Fillings, *5*

8A Detached Rings, *5*
8B Detached Ring with Pyramids, *5*
8C Eyelets, *1*
9A Double Stem, *1*
9B Bullion Knots, *1*
9Ca Ring Bullion Rosette, *4*
9Cb Buttonhole Eyelet Rosette, *4*
9Cc Woven Rosette, *4*
9Cd Reverse Woven Rosette, *4*
10 A, B Hedebo Edge, *2, 3*

MATERIALS EMPLOYED

CANVAS
18/inch white interlock; 12 inches square; edges bound

THREADS
1 DMC Embroidery and Cutwork, size 16, white
2 DMC Embroidery and Cutwork, size 16, 334 medium blue
3 DMC Embroidery and Cutwork, size 16, 797 royal blue
4 DMC Cordonnet Crochet Cotton, size 20, white
5 DMC Cordonnet Crochet Cotton, size 30, white

NEEDLES
Tapestry 24
Crewel 8
Millinery 5

COLORS:
Deka Permanent Dye, 400 light blue; 411 dark blue; use sable brush size 5

STRETCHER STRIPS
2 pairs 12-inch

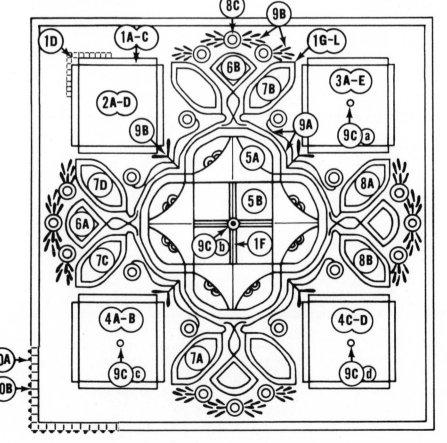

LESSON 1

CANVAS PREPARATION

T HIS first lesson demonstrates various procedures for marking, padding, edging, opening, and bordering reticello and Hedebo shapes. Different methods are employed for the two styles, all adapted for canvas from traditional linen openwork techniques. If you are working the sampler, a master pattern is provided here with instructions for transferring the design outlines onto canvas. Separate pattern diagrams are then supplied for each shape to identify the locations of all the procedures. All of the pattern diagrams are followed by stitch diagrams that illustrate these steps.

MASTER PATTERN, SAMPLER

The master pattern for the reticello and Hedebo sampler shows outlines for all the opened shapes and the placement of surface embroidery. To get started, baste center lines on the stretched canvas to provide matching reference points. Follow the preparation of the four reticello squares from the double running outline of **1A** through the needlewoven bars of **1F**. Then prepare the Hedebo shapes, starting with the backstitch outlines of **1G** and proceeding through **1L**, the chain stitch outline that completes the first lesson. Continue through the lessons, filling the shapes in sequence. When you arrive at the eyelets (**8C**), follow this pattern for their placement. You will also want to refer to it for the positioning of the stem stitch outlines in **9A**, the bullion knots of **9B**, and the Hedebo edge of Lesson **10**.

Master Pattern, Sampler

Open Four-sided Border
Hedebo Picots and Fold Line

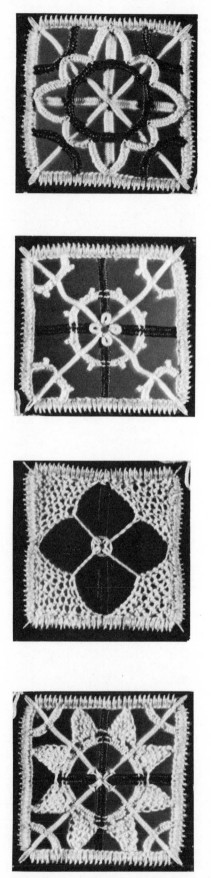

PATTERN DIAGRAM, RETICELLO SQUARES

This pattern diagram is for stitches 1A, 1B, 1C, 1D, 1E, and 1F.

In these diagrams, you can see some of the stages of canvas preparation. The double running stitch outline is completely covered by densely packed overcast stitches, which provide a white padded band for the buttonhole stitch edge. The buttonhole stitches are worked over one more row of canvas than the overcasting, and stand out sharply. The border of four-sided stitch just outside of the buttonhole edge is classic in reticello; it strengthens the edge functionally and aesthetically. Finishing the needlewoven crosses that remain in the opened squares is the first step toward filling each square.

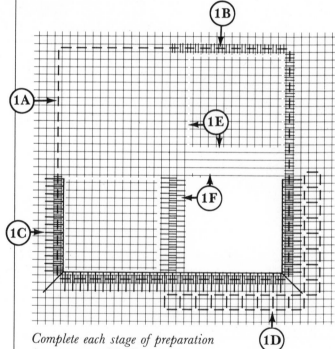

Complete each stage of preparation in sequence with diagrams.

This pattern diagram shows the location of each stage of canvas preparation for a reticello square. The letters correspond to the stitch diagrams that follow.

Sampler: *These four reticello squares surround the central Hedebo motif.*

STITCH 1A
DOUBLE RUNNING STITCH

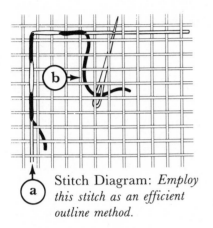

Stitch Diagram: *Employ this stitch as an efficient outline method.*

Travel in two journeys over the same path. Pass over and under an even number of elements in one direction (**a**). Then return over the same line of stitches (**b**), filling the spaces left by the first journey. Use a tapestry needle for the first journey and a crewel needle for the return in order to pierce the first row of stitches. Double running stitch can be seen on the darned cardigan, shown in the color section, where it was used in the blackwork fillings.

STITCH 1B
OVERCAST STITCH

Stitch Diagram: *Provide a dense padding for the buttonhole stitch edge.*

Overcast two horizontal canvas elements on either side of the double running stitch outline around four sides of a reticello square. Work two overcasts between the vertical canvas elements to produce a smooth, compact line of stitches.

STITCH 1C
BUTTONHOLE STITCH

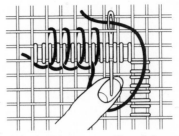

Stitch Diagram: *Travel from left to right, with festoons on the inside of the square.*

Work a buttonhole stitch between the canvas elements and over three rows of canvas around the sides of the reticello squares. Buttonhole from left to right, with the festoons on the insides of the squares, turning the canvas to complete each side. Work a diagonal buttonhole stitch in each corner. Position the stitches to fall between the two overcasts for a neat edge.

STITCH 1D
FOUR-SIDED STITCH

Stitch Diagram: *Travel all rows in a consistent direction.*

Travel in either direction. (The stitch is shown here worked right to left, over two vertical and two horizontal elements.) The vertical stitches slant slightly under tension, so be consistent in the direction you travel. Start with an upright stitch on the frontface, cross on the backface, and emerge to pass over two elements back into the starting point. Cross on the backface and emerge to pass over the same two elements at the top of the unit. Cross a third and last time to emerge in position for the first upright stitch of the next unit. Employ a little tension to emphasize the stitch holes.

TECHNIQUE 1E
CUTTING AND WITHDRAWING ELEMENTS

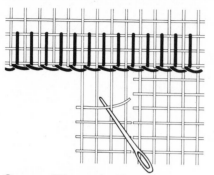

Canvas Diagram: *Do not cut the four center elements!*

Cut and withdraw the elements on the backface. Leave a large cross of four long elements that cross four others, dividing the reticello square into four smaller squares. In the sampler, there are twelve by twelve elements cut and withdrawn from each quarter segment. Start in a corner and clip each element along the buttonhole edge just inside of the festoons (only the buttonhole stitches of the edge are drawn here for simplicity's sake). Be sure not to clip the four center elements. Clip alongside center elements, as shown in this diagram and in the pattern diagram for the reticello squares at the beginning of this lesson. Use a tapestry needle to pluck out the short canvas elements that remain woven through the long ones.

STITCH 1F
NEEDLEWOVEN BARS

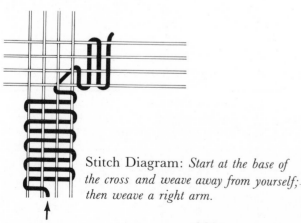

Stitch Diagram: *Start at the base of the cross and weave away from yourself; then weave a right arm.*

Needleweave the large cross that divides a reticello square into four smaller squares. Start at the base of a bar and needleweave pairs of warps up to the center mesh square. Then, turn the work and needleweave a bar that is at a right angle to the one just completed, working from the center out to the edge. Follow the same procedure for the remaining two bars. This is the same method described in *Hemstitching*, **7A**. Needleweave away from yourself, so that you can employ the needle as a shuttle to compress the stitches and align the warps. To start a bar, emerge on the frontface between pairs of warps. Pass over one pair of warps, then under all four elements, emerging on the other side. Fill the remainder of the bar by inserting the needle into the frontface between the pairs of warps, emerging alternately on the left and right sides of the bar. Complete the bar by passing over the two warps closest to the next bar to be worked. Emerge once more between pairs of warps for the first weave only. By starting bars in this manner, you can establish snug, square corners. (If the central mesh square is to be filled, you can pass on the backface from one bar to another any way you choose.)

PATTERN DIAGRAMS, HEDEBO SHAPES

These pattern diagrams are for Stitches **1G**, **1H**, **1I**, **1J**, **1K**, and **1L**.

Sampler: *This photograph shows a portion of the central Hedebo shapes; see page 224 for the entire motif.*

The central motif of the sampler includes open square shapes and needlewoven bars. It employs both reticello and Hedebo techniques. Notice here and in the following pattern diagram that the Hedebo buttonhole edge for this center motif is wider than the edges of the leaf and cone shapes.

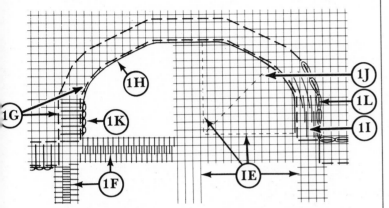

Pattern Diagram **a**: *A combination of reticello and Hedebo in the center motif of the sampler is shown in various stages.*

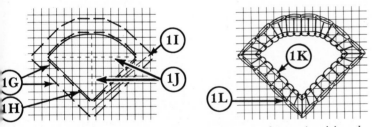

Pattern Diagram **b**: *Hedebo cone shapes (positioned between the leaves in the motif) before and after withdrawing elements.*

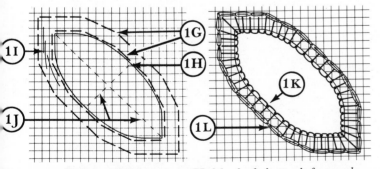

Pattern Diagram **c**: *Hedebo leaf shapes before and after withdrawing elements.*

These pattern diagrams show the location of each stage of canvas preparation for Hedebo shapes. Except for **IE** and **1F**, which refer back to reticello, the letters correspond with the stitch diagrams that follow.

STITCH 1G
BACKSTITCH OUTLINE

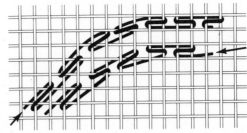

Stitch Diagram: *Provide guidelines for other stitches with a backstitch outline.*

Outline the curved shapes of Hedebo with two rows of backstitches. The inner row defines the open space; the outer row provides the necessary width for securing the folded canvas edge. Both of these rows are guidelines that are covered with subsequent stitching.

The backstitch is extremely useful for outlining on canvas. You can travel in either direction, following the angles and curves of all simple shapes. Notice the different angles of the stitches on the Hedebo pattern diagrams, as they pass back two elements on the frontface and forward four on the backface. See *Pulled Canvas*, Lesson **1**, for more about the backstitch.

STITCH 1H
SPLIT STITCH OUTLINE

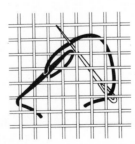

Stitch Diagram: *Produce sharp lines for folding.*

Work split stitches over the inner lines of backstitches in the Hedebo shapes. This outline acts as a guide for finger-pressing the slashed segments of the canvas to the backface. Advance on the frontface and retreat half that distance on the backface, piercing the long stitch as you emerge.

STITCH 1I
STEM STITCH OUTLINE AND FILLING

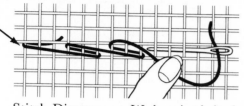

Stitch Diagram **a**: *Work a simple border.*

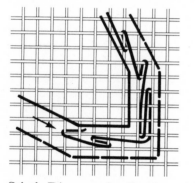

Stitch Diagram **b**: *Supply a padding for Hedebo buttonhole stitches.*

Supply padding for the Hedebo buttonholing to come by filling the space between the two rows of outlining with stem stitches. Advance with long stitches on the frontface and retreat with short ones on the backface. Travel from left to right, holding the working thread below the needle. When stem stitches are used as an underlay, they need not be precise. However, the stem stitch is also used as an outline or border stitch, as on the outer perimeter of the sampler just inside of the Hedebo four-sided edging covered in Lesson **10**. Stitch Diagram **a** illustrates a straight line of stem stitch. Notice that, as on the sampler border, the stitch passes over six elements on the frontface and three on the backface. Stitch Diagram **b** shows the shorter stitches used for padding between two rows of outline stitches.

TECHNIQUE 1J
SLASHING

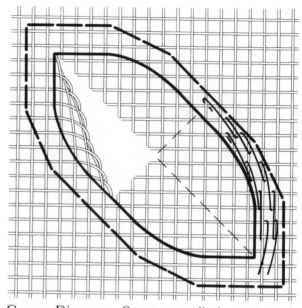

Canvas Diagram: *Cut at perpendicular angles and finger press to the backface.*

The sampler employs stitches from two periods of Hedebo. The leaf and cone shapes are typical of the later Hedebo period. To withdraw elements from these completely opened shapes, start by slashing the interior canvas elements at perpendicular angles. Finger-press the segments to the backface along the split stitch outlines. The larger central motif of the sampler combines reticello with Hedebo. Slash the canvas elements of each quarter-circle around this motif once to bisect it. Then cut the elements along the bars that are to be needlewoven. (Pattern Diagram **a** on page 231 illustrates this clearly.) Finger-press the segments to the backface along the split stitch outlines. Withdraw all the canvas elements from the four squares in the center, illustrated in Canvas Diagram **IE**. Needleweave all the bars in the large opened center shape of the sampler (see Stitch Diagram **1F**).

STITCH 1K

HEDEBO BUTTONHOLE EDGE

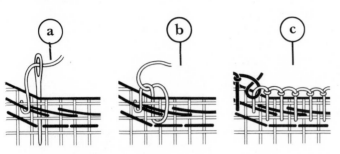

Stitch Diagram **a**: *Overcast the first stitch.*

Stitch Diagram **b**: *Pass the needle into the overcast from back to front.*

Stitch Diagram **c**: *Close a shape, passing from back to front and back again.*

The Hedebo buttonhole stitch is both an edging and a filling stitch. It is shown here as an edging for the Hedebo shapes. The festoons between the stitches are employed by fillings in subsequent lessons, so do not overcrowd the stitches. Place each stitch so that it lies perpendicular to the edge, with the festoons on the inside of the shape. Notice in the pattern diagram that the outer row of outline backstitch is used as a guide. Always work Hedebo buttonhole stitches from left to right. Work each stitch in two steps. Stitch Diagram **a** shows the first step. Emerge on the frontface at the base of the stitch. Loosely overcast the edge and emerge again on the frontface in position for the next stitch. Pass the needle through the loop at the top of the overcast from back to front (**b**), give a slight tug and the stitch is made. Actually, the first overcast shown here is an incomplete stitch. Complete it at the end of your journey around the shape (**c**) by passing the working thread through the loop at the top from back to front and back again.

STITCH 1L

CHAIN STITCH OUTLINE

Chain stitch an outline along the base of the Hedebo buttonhole edges to achieve a neat finish and to emphasize the graceful shapes. Stitch over

the backstitch outlines (see Stitch Diagram **c**). To work the chain stitch, emerge on the frontface and insert the needle back into the same hole while holding a loop of working thread on the surface with the thumb of the other hand (**a**). Emerge two elements away inside the held loop and draw up the working thread to complete the stitch (**b**). Work subsequent stitches in the same manner, emerging for each new one inside the loop of the last. To connect the last chain stitch to the first, complete the next to the last one and emerge as for the next stitch. Pass the needle under the first stitch (**d**) and then close the chain by inserting the needle back into the hole where you emerged (**e**).

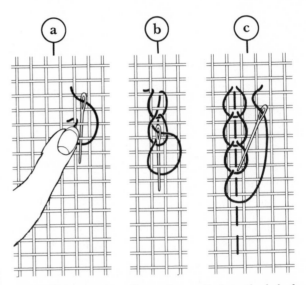

Stitch Diagram **a**: *Insert the needle into the hole from which you first emerged.*

Stitch Diagram **b**: *Emerge two elements away inside the chain.*

Stitch Diagram **c**: *Chain stitch over the backstitches.*

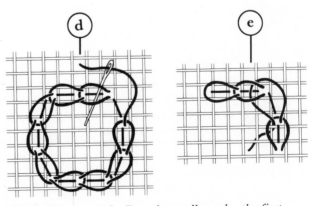

Stitch Diagram **d**: *Pass the needle under the first chain.*

Stitch Diagram **e**: *Close the last chain.*

LESSON 2

INDEPENDENT RETICELLO BARS

PATTERN DIAGRAM, **A** THROUGH **D**

A LONG SPOKES

B INDEPENDENT ARCS

C FULL CIRCLE

D SCALLOPS

THE four straight needlewoven arms of a cross that divide a large reticello square into four smaller ones are referred to as bars. In this lesson, other bars are also produced. First, long spoke bars are thrown diagonally across the large square, forming an X over the upright cross. Then, arc bars are thrown across the four corners; a circle bar is thrown around the center; and eight scallop bars are produced to connect all of the bars into an eight-pointed star. Matching sets of bars are worked in separate stages for this reticello square; this method simplifies the process and also provides an opportunity to change the color and texture of the working thread.

PATTERN DIAGRAM, A THROUGH D

This pattern diagram is for stitches **2A**, **2B**, **2C**, and **2D**.

Sampler: *Vary the working threads when stitching these spokes, arcs, circles, and scallops.*

This reticello square is typically divided in eight sections by the long diagonal spokes that cross the upright center cross. Corners, as shown here, are most frequently occupied by arcs that are bisected by the diagonal spokes. The center circle reverses the curve of the arcs, and in this motif supplies a framework to help support the scalloped bars.

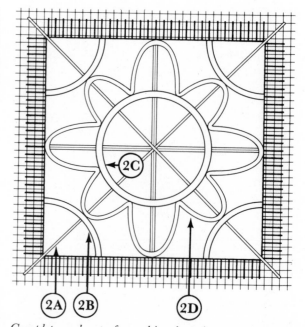

Complete each set of matching bars in a separate stage.

This pattern diagram shows the location of each independently worked bar. The letters correspond to the stitch diagrams that follow.

STITCH 2A
LONG SPOKES

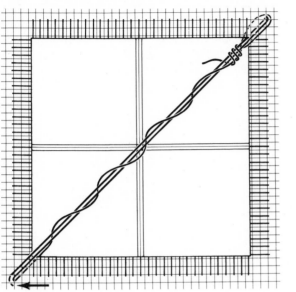

Stitch Diagram: *On the fourth journey, turn the work and snugly overcast back.*

To work the first spoke of this square, start by throwing the working thread diagonally across the square from lower left to upper right. Throw it back and forth a total of three times. Notice in the diagram that you overcast the first two throws several times on the third journey. Then work a fourth journey, snugly overcasting back to the starting corner. It is easier to work away from yourself, so turn the canvas for this last step. When overcasting, follow the twist of the working thread. Throw the second spoke so that it crosses and lies on top of the first one. Secure the crossing place in the center by piercing through the first spoke with a crewel needle on the first two throws.

STITCH 2B
INDEPENDENT ARCS

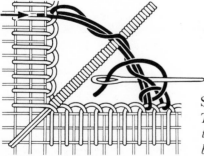

Stitch Diagram: *Throw the thread three times and then buttonhole back.*

Start an arc by emerging on the frontface a counted number of festoons from the corner, and throw the working thread under the spoke in an arc shape. Emerge from a matching festoon on the other side of the square. Throw the thread back a second time *over* the spoke and emerge at the starting point. Travel a third time, passing the working thread under the arc, over the spoke, and under the arc to emerge one festoon beyond the one now occupied. Buttonhole over the arc, moving from left to right, buttonholing over the two threads lying on the spoke. Complete the arc by joining the last buttonhole stitch one festoon outside of the starting point.

STITCH 2C
FULL CIRCLE

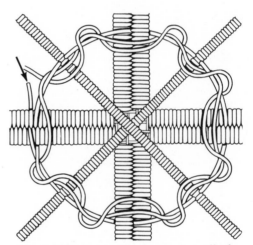

Stitch Diagram: *Use a crewel needle for the first revolution.*

Produce a full circle bar in four journeys. Start the first journey by emerging from the middle and the center of a needlewoven bar. Pass around in a circle, as shown in the pattern diagram for this lesson, piercing through the spokes and emerging from between the paired elements of the needle-woven bars. Complete the first journey by entering the starting bar. Pass around the circle two more times to establish a framework, overcasting the arcs and passing over both bars and spokes. Then buttonhole this round framework, which lies over the bars and spokes, with the festoons on the outside edge of the circle bar (see **2D**).

STITCH 2D
SCALLOPS

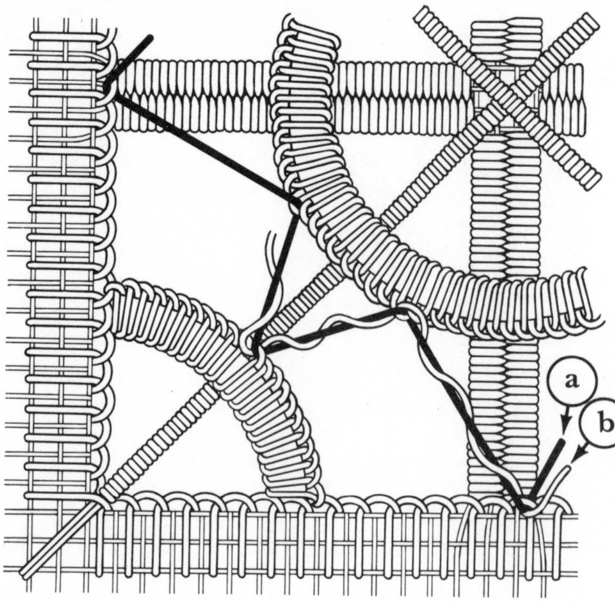

Stitch Diagram: *Throw the scallops, then overcast and buttonhole them.*

Work the scalloped bars in three journeys. Start the first journey by emerging from a buttonhole festoon at the base of a needlewoven bar (**a**). Throw the working thread across to the circle and emerge from the buttonhole festoon halfway between the needlewoven bar and the overcast spoke bar. Throw the working thread across to the corner arc and emerge from the buttonhole festoon that lies on the spoke. Complete the journey of scallops, emerging a second time at the base of the first needlewoven bar. Overcast the first journey with the same working thread (**b**), emerging each time from the same festoons. Complete the scallops on the third journey by buttonholing over this framework, with the festoons of the buttonhole stitches on the outer edge of the scalloped bar.

LESSON 3

SIMULTANEOUS BARS WITH PICOTS

PATTERN DIAGRAM, **A** through **E**

A SHORT SPOKES

B SIMULTANEOUS ARCS

C PICOTS, RIGHT TO LEFT

D PICOTS, LEFT TO RIGHT

E CIRCLE SEGMENTS

LESSON 3 differs from Lesson 2 in that all the components of a reticello square are worked in sequence, as a unit. After the first spoke is thrown, you overcast part of the way back to the center and then complete one corner arc only. Then you overcast a little more and proceed to finish a portion of the center circle. Each corner of the motif is thus worked in a continuous process with a spoke bar. You will also learn to make picots—a significant and charming addition to your needle lace repertoire.

PATTERN DIAGRAM, A through E

This pattern diagram is for stitches **3A**, **3B**, **3C**, **3D**, and **3E**.

Sampler: *Punctuate the arc bars with picots that soften the geometry.*

Although each of the four small squares is worked separately, the long spokes seem to cross at the center and the circle segments join to form a complete circle. A highly geometric design results when each of the corner spokes is divided in thirds by the arcs, and each half of the arcs is further divided by picots.

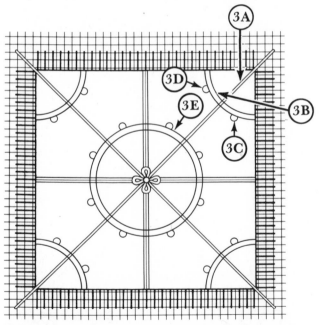

Complete the segments of each spoke bar in one stage.

This pattern diagram shows the spokes, arcs, picots, and circle segments of the upper right reticello square of the sampler. Each quadrant of this square is produced in one stage of work. The letters correspond to the following stitch diagrams that follow.

STITCH 3A
SHORT SPOKES

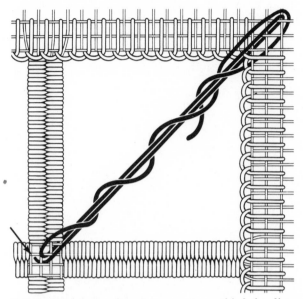

Stitch Diagram: *Snugly overcast one third the distance on the fourth throw.*

Throw a short spoke bar in four journeys. Start by emerging from the middle of the center mesh square, throw the working thread to the far corner, and emerge. Throw it back to the center and emerge again. Overcast back several times on the third journey to the corner. Emerge for the fourth journey and snugly overcast one third of the length of the spoke. (You can see this in Stitch Diagram **3B**.) You are now in position to begin an arc. Since it is easier to overcast snugly away from your body, you will want to reposition the canvas for each spoke bar.

STITCH 3B
SIMULTANEOUS ARCS

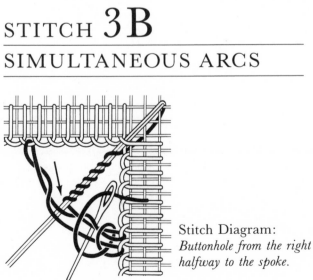

Stitch Diagram: *Buttonhole from the right halfway to the spoke.*

From the spoke you have just formed, throw the working thread to the right and emerge from a festoon a counted distance from the corner. Pass over and under the thrown thread and over the spoke; throw the thread to the left, and emerge from a matching festoon. Pass under the thrown thread and over the spoke; then throw the thread back to the right side, emerging from the festoon outside the one now occupied. Buttonhole half of the right side of the arc. You are now ready to make a picot.

STITCH 3C

PICOTS, RIGHT TO LEFT

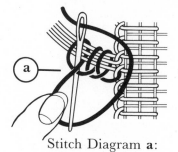

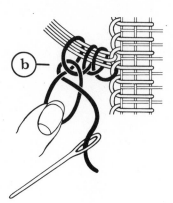

Stitch Diagram **a**: *Hold the thread and pass into the festoon with the needle over the thread.*

Stitch Diagram **b**: *Draw the needle through.*

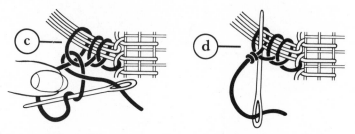

Stitch Diagram **c**: *Catch the thread over the needle.*

Stitch Diagram **d**: *Draw the thread through and enter the loop.*

Hold the working thread with the thumb of one hand, insert the needle back into the festoon, and emerge with the tip under the festoon and over the working thread (**a**). Draw the needle through, but continue to hold the loop (**b**). Insert the needle from the back of the held loop and catch the thread over the needle (**c**). Draw the needle through, producing two neat winds at the festoon. Insert the needle into the loop from the backface (**d**) and buttonhole to the spoke bar.

STITCH 3D

PICOTS, LEFT TO RIGHT

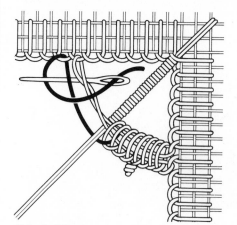

Stitch Diagram **a**: *Throw the thread and buttonhole halfway back.*

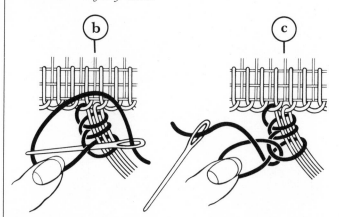

Stitch Diagram **b**: *Hold the thread and enter the festoon.*

Stitch Diagram **c**: *Draw the needle through.*

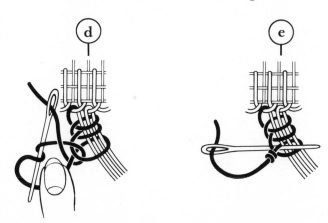

Stitch Diagram **d**: *Catch the thread over the needle.*

Stitch Diagram **e**: *Draw the thread through and enter the loop.*

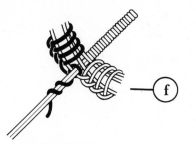

Stitch Diagram **f**: *Join the arc segments by passing around the spoke.*

Pass the working thread under the spoke and throw it to the left side. Buttonhole half of the remaining arc from left to right (**a**). Work the second picot in reverse of the first one (**b**, **c**, **d**, and **e**) and buttonhole to the spoke. Join the two arc segments by passing around the spoke (**f**). Snugly overcast another third of the spoke bar.

STITCH 3E
CIRCLE SEGMENTS

Stitch Diagram: *Turn the work to this position to work the left to right picots.*

For the circle segment, follow the process shown in **3B** and **3D**, but reverse the curve of the arc. Complete the spoke bar and fasten off.

LESSON 4

RETICELLO LACE

PATTERN DIAGRAM, **A** AND **B**

A THREE-CORNERED SPOKE

B OPEN BUTTONHOLE FILLING

PATTERN DIAGRAM, **C** AND **D**

C LOOSE BUTTONHOLE CIRCLE

D VENETIAN CLOTH STITCH PYRAMIDS

THE needlemade lace in this lesson is made up of detached buttonhole stitches. Open buttonhole filling and Venetian cloth stitch pyramids can be considered lace because they are almost completely free of the ground fabric, connected only at the edges to the buttonhole festoons. The first pattern, filled with open buttonhole filling, shows the simplest and most basic of the countless variations that can be achieved with buttonhole stitches. In this square, the consecutive rows travel back and forth, each looping into the festoons of the previous row. The second pattern, filled with Venetian cloth stitch pyramids, shows a denser, more even filling with detached sides. It differs from the first filling in that a working thread is carried across each row from right to left, and the buttonhole stitches loop over this as they travel only from left to right. The stitch diagrams for each pattern only show segments of the complete squares, since all segments are worked in an identical manner. The object in both cases is to gradually decrease the festoons with each row.

PATTERN DIAGRAM, **A** AND **B**

This pattern diagram is for stitches **4A** and **4B**.

Sampler: *Produce graceful shapes of needle lace in the four corners.*

The short spokes hold the long diagonal ones taut while the buttonhole fillings draw the diagonals into curves. The result is a curving dark flower shape in the negative space that is framed by the light needle lace.

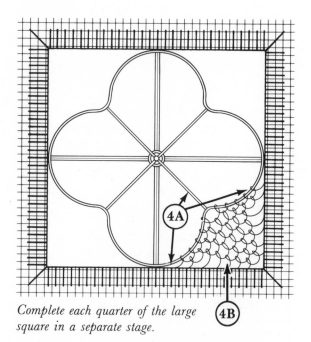

Complete each quarter of the large square in a separate stage.

This pattern diagram shows the location of the three-cornered spoke and the space that is filled with the open buttonhole filling. The letters correspond to the stitch diagrams that follow.

STITCH **4A**
THREE-CORNERED SPOKE

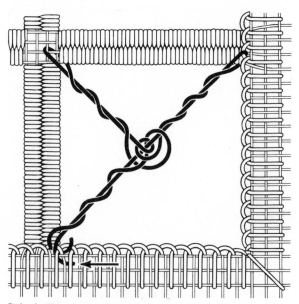

Stitch Diagram: *Throw the thread across a small square and into the center mesh.*

Throw a working thread diagonally across a small square from the base of a woven bar to the opposite corner. Emerge and overcast several times back to the center of the thrown thread. Secure the working thread here by passing over and under the thrown thread snugly, as in the diagram. Then for the third spoke, throw the working thread to the middle of the center mesh square and emerge. Overcast several times back to the middle of the long spoke. Secure the working thread here again by passing under and over the spoke and emerging from the loop just made. Overcast back to the starting point; do not fasten off.

STITCH 4B

OPEN BUTTONHOLE FILLING

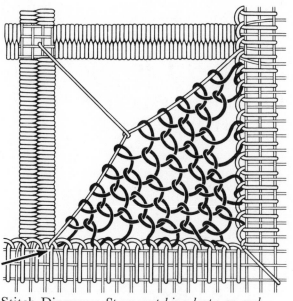

Stitch Diagram: *Space matching loops on each side of the center spoke.*

Loop each row of detached buttonhole stitches over the festoons of the previous row, reversing the direction of travel each time. In the sampler, there are ten stitches in the first row, nine in the second, then six, five, four, three, and two in the corner. Start at the left, using the working thread from the three-cornered spoke framework. Emerge from an edge festoon to the height of the open buttonhole stitches to be made. Space the stitches evenly, five on each side of the center spoke. Complete the row by entering a matching festoon on the other side. Overcast down to the next row. Work the second row from right to left. Complete the triangle as shown, ending with one or two stitches in the corner.

PATTERN DIAGRAM, C AND D

This pattern diagram refers to stitches **4C** and **4D**.

Sampler: *Hang eight needle lace triangles from a second circle.*

In this square, several techniques are combined to produce a more complicated design. Once you have mastered the methods for throwing supporting frameworks on which to hang needle lace and the technique for increasing and decreasing to create shapes, you are ready to work almost any reticello pattern.

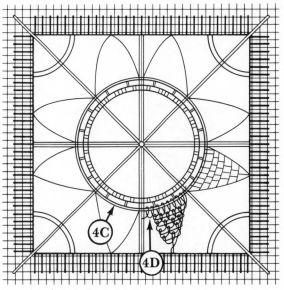

Complete the large square in three separate stages.

This pattern diagram shows the location of the three stages of work necessary to produce the design. First, each quarter of the square is filled with a simultaneous spoke, arc, and circle segment, as shown in **3A**, **3B**, and **3E**. Then, a second circle of loose buttonhole stitch is thrown just outside of the first circle. It is important to notice in this pattern diagram that the first circle has eight buttonhole stitches in each segment in anticipation of the second circle, **4C**, where two loose buttonhole stitches are evenly spaced. In the third stage, **4D**, the eight Venetian cloth stitch pyramids are evenly hung on the second circle.

STITCH 4C

LOOSE BUTTONHOLE CIRCLE

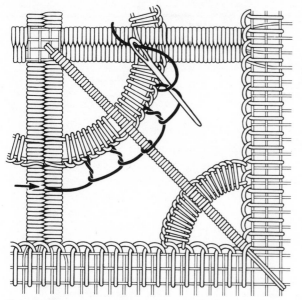

Stitch Diagram **a**: *Insert the needle from the back of each new festoon.*

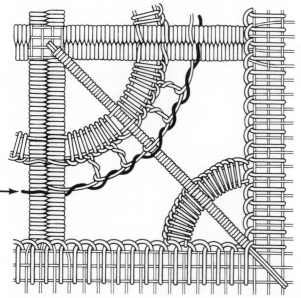

Stitch Diagram **b**: *Overcast the festoons, passing over the spokes and into the bars.*

Travel counterclockwise in two revolutions to complete a circle of loose buttonhole stitches. Start by emerging from the middle of a woven bar, the distance down from the circle bar of two rows of open buttonhole stitches. Work a large buttonhole stitch with one additional overcast into a festoon of the circle bar. Draw up the working thread to finish the stitch. Complete the first journey of this circle by working two loose buttonhole stitches in each of the segments at even intervals (**a**). Encircle each spoke and emerge from the woven bars as you travel around. On the second journey, overcast each festoon once, passing over the spokes and entering the bars (**b**).

STITCH 4D

VENETIAN CLOTH STITCH PYRAMIDS

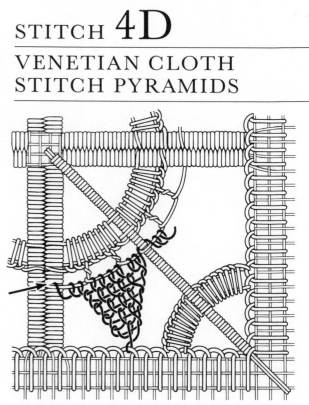

Stitch Diagram: *Buttonhole from the left over the carried thread.*

Emerge from a woven bar and buttonhole from left to right over one segment of the circle, taking two, then four, then two stitches if you are working the sampler square. Next, carry the working thread to the left side for the second row, entering the festoon and emerging as shown in this diagram. Work all rows in this manner, decreasing one stitch each time. After buttonholing the single stitch at the pointed end, pass under and over an edge festoon to secure the pyramid. Pass under the connecting thread and overcast back along the side of the pyramid to the loose buttonhole circle. Pass over this circle, under the spoke, and over the circle again to start the next pyramid. You can use a flat instrument such as a tongue depressor or letter opener under the pyramid to support it while working Venetian cloth stitches.

LESSON 5

RETICELLO WITH HEDEBO

PATTERN DIAGRAM, A AND B

A LOOSE NEEDLEWEAVING WITH BUTTONHOLED RING PICOTS

B POINT D'ANGLETERRE

RETICELLO squares and Hedebo rounded shapes are combined in this lesson, as demonstrated in the large center motif of withdrawn elements in the sampler. A method is shown for filling each of the two kinds of spaces, both of which employ the needlewoven bars described in Lesson 1. The loose needleweaving of 5A is repeated eight times to fill the rounded Hedebo shapes. This establishes a graceful frame for the four reticello square shapes and sets the stage for the delicate filling of 5B.

PATTERN DIAGRAM, A AND B

This pattern diagram is for stitches **5A** and **5B**.

Sampler: *Combine some techniques from both styles for the central motif of the sampler.*

The rounded spaces of the large central motif of the sampler are filled with pairs of gently curving triangles of loose needleweaving, each of which is embellished with two buttonholed ring picots. The four quarters of the large reticello square are filled with a netted lace called point d'Angleterre. A buttonholed eyelet, diagramed in **8C**, occupies the center mesh square.

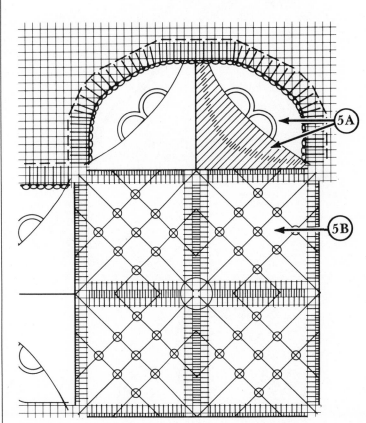

Complete each of the eight halves of the curved shapes, then each of the four squares.

The loosely needlewoven triangle shown in this pattern diagram at **5A** invades previously needlewoven bars on both straight sides: the base invades half of the bar it shares with the point d'Angleterre square, and the vertical side covers half of the bar it shares with another loosely woven triangle (the stitches of this triangle not visible in this diagram). When working each of these eight sections, turn the canvas to follow the diagrams. In the quarter of the large square shown at **5B**, you can see where the diagonally thrown grid divides each of the four side bars in thirds.

STITCH 5A

LOOSE NEEDLEWEAVING WITH BUTTONHOLED RING PICOTS

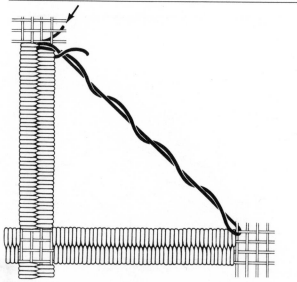

Stitch Diagram **a**: *Throw a supporting spoke across the space.*

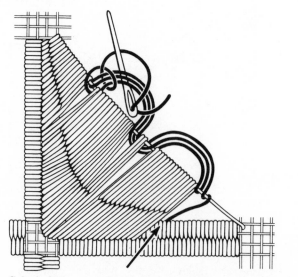

Stitch Diagram **b**: *Loosely needleweave three-quarters of the distance, then work two buttonholed ring picots.*

Start the supporting spoke (**a**) by emerging at the top of a needlewoven bar; throw the working thread diagonally across the opened space to the far end of a horizontal bar and emerge. Overcast back several times to the starting point. Loosely needleweave three-quarters of the triangle just formed and start the two buttonhole ring picots (**b**). Overcast the spoke and throw the first ring picot into the middle of the loose needleweaving, passing under and over the spoke again. Notice that two weaves are left between the two thrown picots to allow space for the buttonhole stitches to come. Throw the second ring picot into the loose needleweaving, dividing the remaining space in half. Loop around the spoke. Travel in two more journeys, following the same path to provide the supporting framework for the buttonhole stitches. These supporting threads should not be loose, as the buttonhole stitches round them out nicely. Buttonhole the rings, using enough stitches to fill them; then complete the loose needleweaving.

STITCH 5B

POINT D'ANGLETERRE

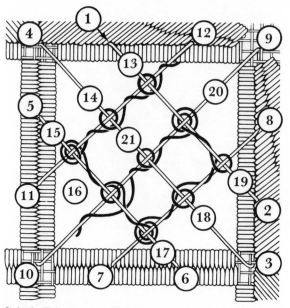

Stitch Diagram: *Throw a crosshatched framework, then weave small wheels on it.*

Complete each of the four small squares in two stages. Follow the first sequence of numbers in the stitch diagram, **1** through **12**, throwing the working thread across the square in one diagonal direction, then in the other, with long connecting threads on the backface. Emerge after **12** to begin the wheels. Start the second stage by overcasting to the first grid crossing at **13**. Pass over and under as in the diagram for each of the wheels; they are carefully planned to present a consistent pattern on the gridwork. Overcast to each grid crossing and pass around it as diagramed, following the numerical sequence. Complete the last wheel at **21**; then overcast twice back to **10**. Fasten off behind a needlewoven bar.

LESSON 6

HEDEBO BARS

A TWO BARS

B THREE BARS

H EDEBO bars are thrown across open spaces much as in reticello. The major difference is that a special Hedebo buttonhole stitch is employed, and this requires that you always proceed from left to right. Therefore, where you start each bar is determined by the number of throws and must be planned in advance. After you have studied these diagrams, you will understand the process. Charting your routes can be very satisfying; do not let this step discourage you.

STITCH 6A

TWO BARS

Sampler: *Fill Hedebo shapes asymmetrically.*

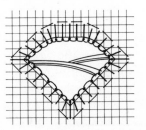

Pattern Diagram: *Throw the thread twice for each of these bars, starting at the left.*

Although Hedebo employs geometric formations much as reticello does, the rounded spaces do not often inspire the centrally balanced designs of the latter.

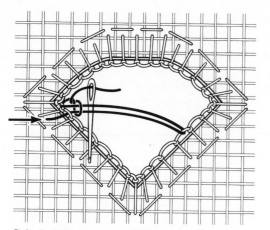

Stitch Diagram **a**: *Plan ahead to occupy two festoons for each side of a bar.*

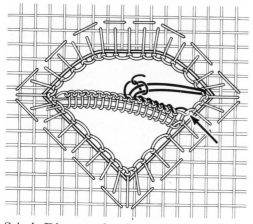

Stitch Diagram **b**: *Overcast back to throw a second bar.*

Start the first bar by throwing the working thread from a festoon in the left corner across the space to emerge from one on the right side (**a**). Throw the thread back, passing over and under the festoon below the starting one. Hedebo buttonhole over the thrown threads back to the right side again. Close the bar by passing over and under the festoon above the one already occupied.

Overcast the bar to one festoon from the center. Start the second bar (**b**) by throwing the working thread to the right corner. Emerge and throw the thread into the festoon to the left of the starting one. Hedebo buttonhole over the thrown threads and close the bar one festoon above the one already occupied.

STITCH 6B
THREE BARS

Sampler: *Employ arc bars to produce more cone shapes.*

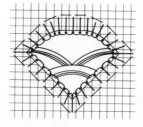

Pattern Diagram: *Throw the thread three times for each of these bars, starting at the right.*

The three bars in this cone shape are slightly heavier than the preceding ones, as they are worked over three thrown threads.

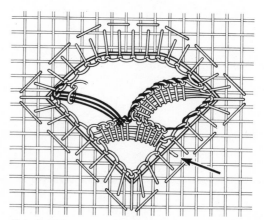

Stitch Diagram: *Complete the third bar in the center of the first by planning ahead.*

Start the first bar by throwing the working thread three times, starting at the right side, before buttonholing back from the left side. Then overcast the festoons along the right edge up to the right corner. Start the second bar by throwing the thread down to the first bar, emerging one festoon to the right of the center one on the top of that bar. Throw the thread back to the corner and return to emerge from the center festoon of the first bar. Hedebo buttonhole to a festoon above the occupied corner one. Overcast back to center and overcast one festoon to the left of center. Throw a bar to the left corner to match the one just completed, closing this third bar in the same center festoon of the first bar.

LESSON 7

HEDEBO LACE

A LOOSE HEDEBO FILLING WITH DETACHED PYRAMID

B FOUR JOINED PYRAMIDS

C STRAIGHT BARS

D MIXED FILLINGS

THE Hedebo buttonhole stitch is employed to produce the needle lace fillings of this lesson. The loose Hedebo stitch referred to in these diagrams differs from the usual Hedebo buttonhole stitch only in that, as its name implies, it is worked loosely and without the little tug after the stitch is completed. The detached pyramids of **7A** and **7B** relate to the Venetian cloth stitch (**4D**), where rows of buttonholing are worked from left to right over a carried thread. However, in these Hedebo lace fillings, you overcast the festoons back to start the rows from the left. The Hedebo pyramids, like those in reticello, are detached at the sides. In **7C**, straight bars are introduced, supplying another system for breaking up the opened spaces. In **7D**, a diagonal double bar, an arc bar, and a spider are worked together; techniques are often mixed in Hedebo embroidery.

STITCH 7A

LOOSE HEDEBO FILLING WITH DETACHED PYRAMID

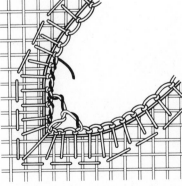

Sampler: *Vary the filling in each half of the space.*

Pattern Diagram: *Complete the loose Hedebo filling; then hang a pyramid on it.*

Notice that the loose buttonhole filling starts with a single stitch at a point of the leaf shape, and that a stitch is added with each row by working a stitch into each space. The detached pyramid decreases in a similar manner. Employ a double length of working thread to complete the two units without stopping.

Stitch Diagram **a**: *Overcast to the height of the first loose Hedebo buttonhole stitch.*

Stitch Diagram **b**: *Work the first row with a single stitch. Overcast back and up to row two.*

Start the filling by emerging at a point of the leaf shape (**a**). Overcast up the festoons on the left edge to the distance of a loose Hedebo buttonhole stitch (three overcasts are shown here and in the sampler). When overcasting, enter the festoons from the frontface.

Work the first row, consisting of a single stitch (**b**). Throw the working thread down to the starting festoon and emerge on the frontface. From the back, enter the loop just formed. You have just completed a loose Hedebo buttonhole stitch. Close the row by passing into a festoon on the right edge that matches the one occupied on the left edge. Overcast back to the left side and up the festoons to start another row.

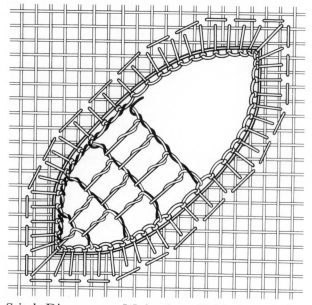

Stitch Diagram **c**: *Work a loose Hedebo buttonhole stitch in each space of a row, then overcast back and up to start another row.*

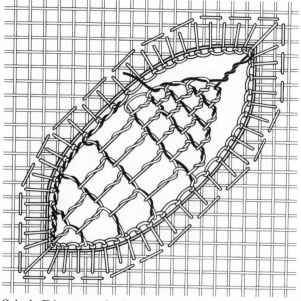

Stitch Diagram **d**: *Emerge twice in the first space of the first detached row, but only once in subsequent rows.*

Work four rows of loose Hedebo filling (**c**). All rows are worked as the first row. Increase by one space in each row by placing stitches in the spaces of the previous row.

Start the first row of the detached pyramid (**d**) by working a normal-size Hedebo buttonhole stitch into each open space of the loose Hedebo filling. Be sure to notice that you first pass under and over the connecting thread of the first open space before working the first Hedebo buttonhole stitch. Start each subsequent row by passing under and over this extra festoon along the left side of the pyramid so that you can easily overcast a journey down over it after completing the pyramid. Travel across the rows with a single Hedebo buttonhole stitch in each space, which automatically reduces the number of spaces in each row. Always work as many overcasts back on the return journey as you have worked Hedebo buttonhole stitches. When a single space remains at the peak, pass under and over the festoon at the tip of the leaf edge and overcast back to the pyramid and down the left side.

STITCH 7B
FOUR JOINED PYRAMIDS

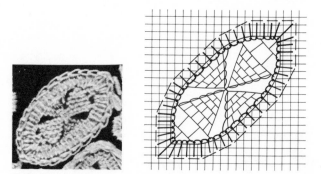

Sampler: *Focus attention on the fine, knotted texture of these triangular shapes.*

Pattern Diagram: *Hang the pyramids at the pointed ends of the leaf shapes on two rows of loose Hedebo buttonhole stitches.*

In this pattern, the leaf shape is divided to produce four pyramids of normal-size Hedebo buttonhole stitches. It is, however, necessary to provide two rows of loose Hedebo filling at the pointed ends. Work each pyramid independently in consecutive order; then draw them all together after completing the fourth one. Use fine thread for this pattern to show the knotted texture of the Hedebo buttonhole filling.

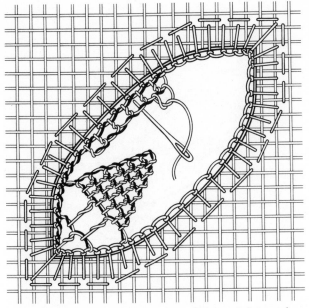

Stitch Diagram: *Loop into an additional festoon in the second pyramid to produce an edge to travel down.*

The first row of each pyramid has two stitches in each space; subsequent rows have one. Overcast back on each row the same number of times as there are stitches. Notice that an extra loop is always produced on the left of the pyramid. After you reach the peak, overcast down the left side and up the left edge of the leaf. The second pyramid is centered on the long side, and you work it directly into the festoons, with a single stitch in each. However, notice that you loop around the last festoon, rather than using a Hedebo buttonhole stitch, in order to produce the clean edge that you will need to overcast on your way down. To work the third pyramid, overcast around the second point of the leaf shape, turning the canvas so that you can follow the diagram. Work the fourth pyramid to match the second one, but on reaching the peak, overcast the four single stitches at the tops of the pyramids to draw them together. Then overcast down the side and fasten off.

STITCH 7C
STRAIGHT BARS

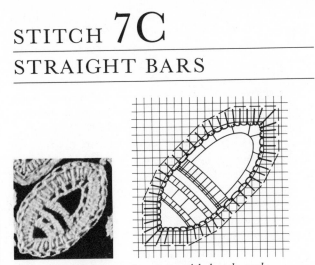

Sampler: *Break up the space with bands and open fillings.*

Pattern Diagram: *Complete the lower double bar, then a single bar, and hang a loose Hedebo edging on it.*

You can throw single or double straight or diagonal bars across Hedebo spaces, and then hang other shapes or open fillings on them to create a great variety of designs. In this pattern diagram, a straight double bar is thrown, then a single bar from which a loose Hedebo buttonhole edging is hung. In **7D**, you will see a diagonal bar with other fillings. The edging shown here can be used to fill circles and other rounded shapes. When planning an edging of loose Hedebo buttonhole stitches, distribute the stitches with regard to the negative spaces they create as well as the counted numbers of festoons they occupy.

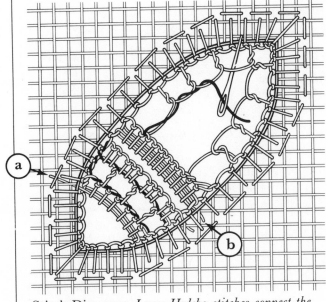

Stitch Diagram: *Loose Hedebo stitches connect the single bars.*

Start the double bar on the left side of the leaf (**a**). Throw the working thread across the space and back; emerge from the starting festoon. Overcast up one festoon; Hebedo buttonhole over the thrown threads to the right side. Overcast back and up two festoons. Work three loose Hedebo buttonhole stitches, evenly spaced as in the diagram, across the completed single bar. Overcast back and up one festoon. Complete the double bar with another row of Hedebo buttonhole stitches evenly spaced across it.

Start the single bar on the right side (**b**). Throw the working thread across the space three times and Hedebo buttonhole over it to the right side. Then work the loose Hedebo buttonhole stitches around the remainder of the leaf shape. Start this edging by overcasting back over two festoons of the single bar, to the height of a loose stitch. Then work the loose Hedebo buttonhole stitches, producing even spaces around the leaf shape. Emerge from a festoon at the other side of the single bar and overcast back to the starting side of the bar; fasten off.

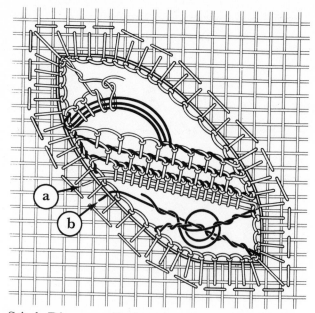

Stitch Diagram: *Produce the spokes of the arc bar while working the Hedebo buttonhole stitches.*

STITCH 7D
MIXED FILLINGS

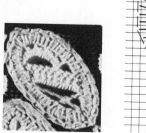

Sampler: *Break up the space with a diagonal bar; then fill it creatively.*

Pattern Diagram: *Complete a diagonal double bar, then hang an arc with rays on it, and fill the lower space with a spider.*

Hedebo embroidery provides open spaces and many interesting methods for filling shapes. In this pattern diagram, the diagonal double bar inspired the arc bar, which in turn inspired the rays of spokes. The remaining space seems to call for a leggy spider.

Throw a double bar on a diagonal across the space, starting on the left (**a**). Proceed as shown here, similarly to the straight double bar shown in **7C**, but work the Hedebo buttonhole stitches of the second and third rows slightly looser than those of the first bar. After completing the bar, overcast back half the distance to throw the arc bar. Throw the working thread three times as shown, then overcast up one festoon on the left side. Hedebo buttonhole two stitches and throw a spoke into the point of the leaf. Overcast back and Hedebo buttonhole two more stitches. Continue to fill the arc bar as shown in the accompanying pattern diagram. Complete this stage of work by overcasting to the left along the festoons of the diagonal bar.

Start the spider in the other point of the leaf, by throwing a spoke from upper left to lower right (**b**). Overcast to the center and throw a spoke to the left. Overcast to the center and throw a spoke to the right. Overcast to the center; pass under and over the spokes at the center to produce a small wheel. Then overcast back over the first thrown spoke to complete the spider.

LESSON 8

RINGS AND EYELETS

A DETACHED RINGS

B DETACHED RING WITH PYRAMIDS

C EYELETS

HEDEBO fillings that employ rings and pyramids are often worked in the hands, completely free of the foundation fabric. They are then set into the open spaces for which they have been planned, where they are fastened down in strategic locations. In this lesson, one leaf shape is shown filled with three rings and another one is filled with a single ring that supports two detached pyramids. Hedebo eyelets are also demonstrated here. These eyelets have larger center holes than those of pulled canvas work, where the canvas elements are merely deflected. Here, the center canvas elements are cut and pushed to the backface before the edges are bound. Hedebo eyelets are employed to accent the surface work that is shown in Lesson **9**. Warning: rings require practice but are habit-forming!

STITCH 8A

DETACHED RINGS

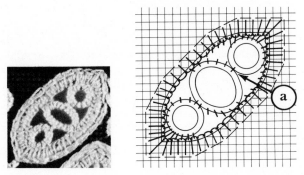

Sampler: *Complete the little rings in your hand; then set them in.*

Pattern Diagram: *Start by overcasting the two rings together at the arrow; follow the path of overcast stitches to secure them.*

Rings are started by winding the working thread around a columnar object of the desired circumference. Ovals are rings that are drawn to the sides of a space when fastened down. Select a pencil, knitting needle, Hedebo stick, or crochet hook and work a sample ring to determine the size

required by the space. In the sampler, a size I crochet hook was employed for the two small rings and a pencil for the larger center oval.

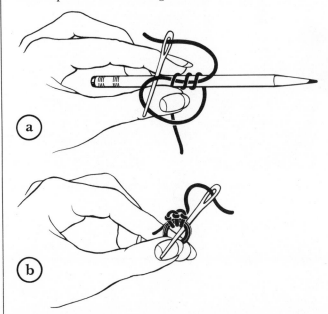

Stitch Diagram **a**: *Wind the thread three times and secure the ring with a Hedebo buttonhole stitch.*

Stitch Diagram **b**: *Completely cover and close the ring.*

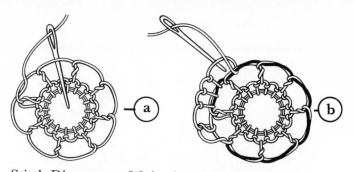

Start a detached ring by winding the working thread three times (**a**). Secure the ring with a Hedebo buttonhole stitch that passes around the three winds. Then gently slide the ring free.

Continue to Hedebo buttonhole the ring (**b**), completely covering the winding threads. Close the ring by inserting the needle from the front into the first festoon. Do not cut the end of the working thread. Later, when you set the rings in, position them so that the tail of thread can be fastened off at the side of the shape. Employ a long thread for the center ring shown here, so that you can join and fasten down all the rings with it. After you complete the three rings, overcast the center one to one of the smaller ones; then follow the overcasting path shown in the pattern diagram to fasten the rings in place (starting at **a**), or employ any path that seems logical.

*Stitch Diagram **a**: Work a loose Hedebo buttonhole stitch in every other festoon of the first ring.*

*Stitch Diagram **b**: Overcast each space but the last; then start a detached pyramid with five normal-size stitches.*

Employ a long working thread, thirty-six to forty inches long to avoid running out of thread.* Close a first ring of normal-size Hedebo buttonhole stitches by inserting the needle from the front into the first festoon. Then work a loose Hedebo buttonhole stitch into every other festoon (**a**), keeping a fairly slack thread between the stitches. Overcast into every space but the last one.

Start a detached pyramid (**b**) by emerging from the last space of the loose Hedebo circle. Work a normal-size stitch in this same space. Work three stitches in the next space and one in the last. Overcast the festoons back the same number of times as stitches for this and subsequent rows. Proceed as in Stitch Diagram **7B** until one stitch remains. Overcast down the left side and around the ring to be in position to work the pyramid on the opposite side from left to right. When you reach the peak of the second pyramid, attach it to the point of the leaf space before overcasting down the side of the leaf and securing the circle in the center. You can employ the backface of the leaf edge to travel to the other two securing positions. Six or eight detached pyramids spaced around a ring can make a star shape for an open circle.

STITCH 8B

DETACHED RING WITH PYRAMIDS

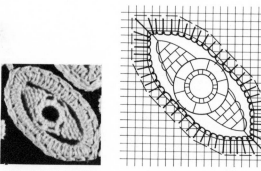

Sampler: *Complete a detached ring, hang two pyramids on it, and set it in place.*

Pattern Diagram: *Work sixteen stitches for the first ring, space eight loose stitches evenly around it; then hang two pyramids on it.*

In this pattern diagram, you can see how the detached pyramids start with five normal-size Hedebo buttonhole stitches in three of the spaces of the loose buttonhole circle. The entire unit is completed in the hand before overcasting it in place.

STITCH 8C

EYELETS

Sampler: *Punctuate the surface work with dots of negative space.*

* To add on thread midstream, enter a festoon with a new thread and stitch with both the old and new threads for six or seven stitches; then cut away the old thread.

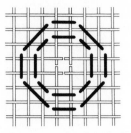

Canvas and Stitch Diagram:
Outline the eyelet with two rows of backstitch; then cut the center elements.

This is a combination stitch and pattern diagram for Hedebo eyelets. The placement for them on the sampler is shown on the master pattern in Lesson 1. First work two rows of backstitch outlines as shown here, passing over one or two canvas elements with horizontal, vertical, or diagonal stitches. Then cut the four center canvas elements. You can enlarge an eyelet, producing a larger open circle, by increasing the number of stitches around the eight sides and cutting additional horizontal and vertical canvas elements.

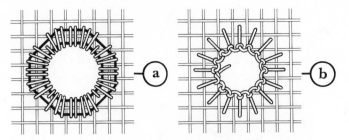

Stitch Diagram **a**: *Poke the cut elements into the backface; satin stitch over the backstitch outline.*

Stitch Diagram **b**: *Hedebo buttonhole stitch around the eyelet over the padding.*

Poke through the center hole with an awl or the points of closed embroidery scissors to push the canvas elements to the backface, thereby producing a large open circle. Satin stitch around the circle over the double outline (**a**), packing the stitches in closely and using short stitches to avoid square corners.

Work the festoons on the inside edge. Close the last festoon by emerging from the first one and inserting the needle back into the last one. Use the same soft working thread for all stages of the work to blend the stitches into a smooth ring.

LESSON 9

SURFACE STITCHES

A DOUBLE STEM STITCH

B BULLION KNOTS

C ROSETTES

THE flowing lines and raised texture of the surface work shown in this lesson provide a contrast to the knotted textures and dark spaces of reticello and Hedebo open work. The stem stitch is employed to emphasize the curved shapes of Hedebo. A second row of stem stitch is worked along the first row; the result looks much like a chain stitch, but it is more graceful. Two rows of identical stem stitches would provide a denser and even stronger line.

Bullion knots are very useful raised stitches, particularly when employed in pairs or clusters. They are shown in the sampler in conjunction with Hedebo eyelets, creating floral sprays. The ring bullions that follow are worked similarly; four of them form a rosette for embellishing the center mesh of a reticello square. These center meshes of canvas reticello often require further embellishment, and three additional rosettes are demonstrated here for that purpose.

STITCH 9A

DOUBLE STEM STITCH

Sampler: *Produce graceful, curving, counted-thread stitches.*

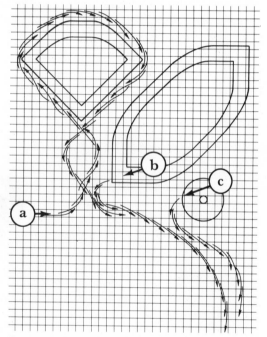

Pattern Diagram: *Follow the arrows for the first journey of each line of work.*

Work two journeys of stem stitches that share the same stitch holes. To open a space between the rows, work the first journey with the working thread held beneath the needle (a crewel stem stitch) and the second journey with the thread held above the needle (an outline stem stitch). Both are illustrated in *Hemstitching,* Stitch **2E.** In this pattern diagram, only a single journey is shown. Start (**a**) to outline the cone shape. Then

start (**b**) at the base of the leaf, to work the next outline, and then work a third outline (**c**). Notice that shorter stitches are worked where sharp curves are required. In the accompanying stitch diagram, you can see the beginning of the second journey (**2**).

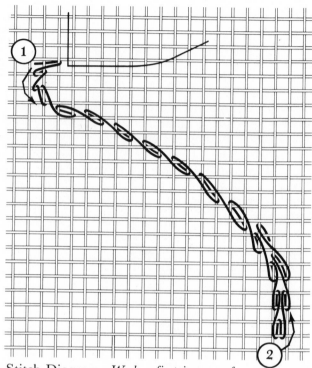

Stitch Diagram: *Work a first journey of crewel stem stitch and a return journey of outline stem stitch.*

After you have completed the first journey of a line (**1**), return over the same path, reversing the position of the working thread (**2**).

STITCH 9B

BULLION KNOTS

Sampler: *Cluster pairs and single knots to create floral arrangements.*

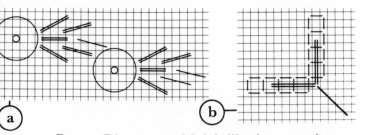

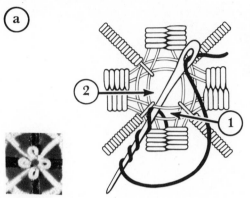

a

Pattern Diagram **a**: *Work bullion knots over four vertical canvas elements at various angles.*

Pattern Diagram **b**: *Work pairs of long straight bullion knots (the straight lines) over six canvas elements.*

Once you have established the four-sided outline of the reticello squares and the Hedebo eyelets, you can employ these diagrams for the exact placement of the bullion knots on the sampler.

Sampler: *Produce a rosette by working four ring bullion knots that meet in the center of a mesh square.*

Stitch Diagram: *Emerge at **1**, insert at **2**, emerge again at **1**, wrap clockwise, and then insert again at **2**.*

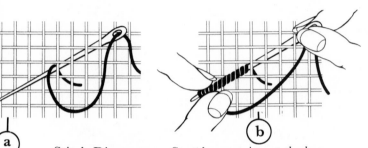

Stitch Diagram **a**: *Start by emerging at the base. Draw the thread through, enter at the top, and emerge again at the base.*

Stitch Diagram **b**: *Hold the eye of the needle securely and wind the thread clockwise. Hold those coils!*

Begin and end these bullion knots so closely together that they become round rings. Start by emerging one element from the center space of a mesh square (**1**). Insert the needle into the center, and emerge once more from **1**. Hold the eye of the needle securely and wind the thread around the tip in a clockwise direction. Hold the coils with one hand as you coax the needle through with the other. Draw the thread completely through, forming a ring by inserting the needle into **2** a second time. To produce a rosette, work four of these units, emerging at the start of each on a different side of the center square.

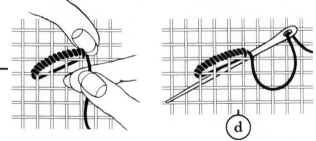

Stitch Diagram **c**: *Coax the needle through and draw up the thread. Then adjust the coils.*

Stitch Diagram **d**: *Enter the backface as in **a**. Emerge in position for another bullion in the same location or in another one.*

Bullion knots are easy and delightful to work—with a little practice. Use a long needle with a round eye, such as a milliner's needle, so that you can slide it through the coils. If you want a very raised stitch, use more coils than will easily fit in the space allowed.

BUTTONHOLE EYELET ROSETTE

b

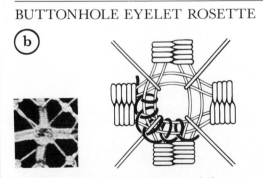

Sampler: *Buttonhole stitch around the center mesh to produce a festooned rosette.*

Stitch Diagram: *Stitch over two elements; include each vertical warp or spoke, and festoon the perimeter.*

WOVEN ROSETTE

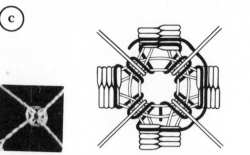

Sampler: *Weave around the center in two journeys, passing over the spokes and under the bars.*

Stitch Diagram: *Pass in and out of the center in the first journey; weave a wheel the second time around.*

REVERSE WOVEN ROSETTE

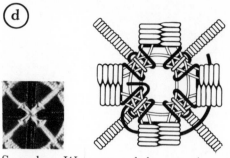

Sampler: *Weave around the center in two journeys, passing over the bars and under the spokes.*

Stitch Diagram: *Reverse the process of the previous stitch diagram.*

LESSON 10

HEDEBO EDGE

A HEDEBO PICOTS

B OPEN FOUR-SIDED EDGE

THIS lesson is devoted to describing the Hedebo edge that completes these lessons, as well as the sampler. The edge is composed of Hedebo picots, open four-sided stitches, and, in the sampler, a band of stem stitches. An unusual feature of this Hedebo edge is that the picots are worked in vertical rows. To accomplish this, you must turn the canvas every time you turn a corner. When the canvas is released and the excess canvas hemmed back with the open four-sided border, the picots project from the edge in silhouette, looking like they were worked around a folded hem.

STITCH 10A

HEDEBO PICOTS

Sampler: *Employ pairs of Hedebo buttonhole stitches to produce a silhouette of picots.*

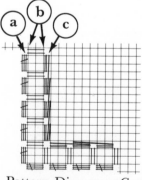

Pattern Diagram: *Complete the entire outer edge in Hedebo picots; then fold back and hem with the open four-sided stitch.*

This pattern diagram shows the various stages of work for the Hedebo edge of the sampler. First work the Hedebo picots that define the outer perimeter (**a**). You can locate them on the sampler from the master pattern in Lesson **1**. Employ a heavier working thread for these picots than for the rest of the edge, so that they will stand out. On the sampler, they are worked with two shades of blue thread in the needle. Next, fold the canvas back along the picot line and work the open four-sided border through the two layers of canvas (**b**). Next, cut away the excess canvas. Then work a row of stem stitches (**c**). Share stitch holes with the open four-sided stitch units as you proceed around the edge with the stem stitch border.

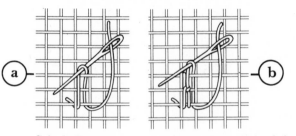

Stitch Diagram **a**: *Work the first stitch of the unit.*

Stitch Diagram **b**: *Draw up the first stitch midway and start the second stitch.*

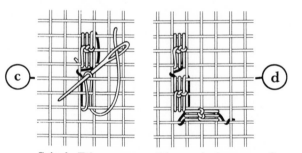

Stitch Diagram **c**: *The vertical passage from one stitch unit to another is shown in black.*

Stitch Diagram **d**: *Turn corners by passing the thread on the backface to the new row.*

To produce each picot, complete two Hedebo buttonhole stitches (see **1K**) over three and between two canvas elements (the first is shown in **a**; the second is being worked in **b**). Center the knots in each unit. To travel from one unit to the one beneath it, pass the working thread down behind three elements on the backface, pass around a vertical element between the units, and pass behind three more horizontals (**c**). Proceed around the corners (**d**) by sharing a stitch hole with the previous row and passing around an element as before.

STITCH 10B

OPEN FOUR-SIDED EDGE

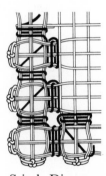

Stitch Diagram: *Fold the excess canvas to the backface, match the two layers, and hem with open four-sided stitches.*

Remove the canvas from the frame to complete the hem. Finger-press the excess canvas to the backface so that the Hedebo picots stand out from the canvas. Carefully match the two layers of canvas and work the open four-sided hem as shown in the stitch diagram. Notice that the working thread crosses just once on the backface for each unit except at the corner, where it does not cross at all. Cut away the excess canvas for each completed side when you arrive at the last two units. If you like, you can work a border of stem stitches to complete the sampler.

GLOSSARY

Terms are defined as they are employed in *The Open Canvas,* along with pertinent information and advice to help make you sharp as a needle.

acid. A chemical substance containing hydrogen. Acids are widely used in the bleaching and dyeing of textiles; they are also naturally present in some organic materials such as wood. A concentration of acids weakens fibers.

acid-free. Refers to products that contain no acid, such as paper made from cotton rags or glue produced without acids. Use acid-free paper and board for storing or mounting embroidery. Acid-free glue is a new permanent, flexible product that is harmless to textiles. It is helpful when fastening down canvas elements and working threads.

alternation. A system for organizing a pattern by repeating a particular design element in every other row or stitch. For example, the first and third rows might be worked from left to right, while the second and fourth are worked from right to left. Or, the first, third, and fifth stitches in a row might be slanted satin stitches, while the ones in between are cross-stitches.

awl. A sharp, pointed tool that is used to pierce neat, round holes in leather or fabric. Employ an awl to gently spread the canvas elements, producing openings for pulled canvas—particularly eyelets. When using an awl on fine canvas, work gently to avoid breaking the elements. An awl is also helpful when following a graphed design; by enlarging every tenth opening of the mesh, you will be able to count the elements quickly and accurately. And an awl is a convenient instrument with which to trace the path of working threads in some of the stitch diagrams of *The Open Canvas.*

A *stiletto* is a prettier antique version of an awl. Stilettos were made of ivory, bone, mother-of-pearl, or steel and were often referred to as *piercers.* Stilettos were frequently used in the nineteenth century for piercing the eyelet holes in **whitework.**

backface. The underside or wrong side of the stitch or the foundation fabric (as opposed to the **frontface**).

bars. Canvas elements or working threads that cross opened spaces, bridging two segments of work. Straight bars composed of canvas elements are either needlewoven or overcast. Bars composed of working threads thrown in diagonal lines are called **spokes;** they are generally overcast. Bars that are composed of working threads thrown in arcs, scallops, or circle segments are usually buttonholed. The bars that are typical of true lace are called *brides.*

battlement. A term used in design and embroidery, particularly in **blackwork,** to describe a steplike linear movement, the path of which resembles the notched turrets of castles.

beeswax. A thick, round wafer of wax used to strengthen thread; it is sometimes referred to as a beeswax wheel. Run silk thread through beeswax before couching down metal threads or sewing down beads to prevent the silk from being cut by the metal or glass. Use a bit of wax at the tip of a slippery thread, where it passes through the needle, to prevent constant rethreading. It is also useful at the tip end of a twisted metal embroidery thread; it prevents the twists from unraveling and helps in threading the needle. If you are practicing or demonstrating a new stitch, a thread run through beeswax will hold its shape and be easier to manipulate.

blackwork. A traditional counted-thread embroidery worked with black cotton or linen thread on a white or light-colored even-weave fabric. It chiefly employs the double running stitch. In the sixteenth century, it was worked with black silk thread on fine linen, sometimes accented with gold thread and small sequins. It has also been called *Spanish work,* because credit is given to Catherine of Aragon, daughter of Isabella and Ferdinand of Spain, for bringing it to England when she married Henry VIII. It was, in fact, known in England long before, but it became fashionable with Catherine's arrival in 1501.

Holbein work. A kind of blackwork named for the painters of the same name, who both created designs for blackwork and portrayed it in their work. Holbein work employs the double running stitch and is completely reversible.

blocking and **steaming.** Open canvas work is only slightly misshapen when it is taken off the frame. A blocking procedure that involves a thorough soaking and washing and severe stretching is not necessary if good work habits have been observed and the canvas kept tightly stretched. A simple steaming procedure is all that is required. Cover a half-inch-thick wood board that is slightly larger than the embroidery with several layers of clean cloth or a Turkish towel. Lay the embroidery on it, frontface up. Temporarily pin or tack the embroidery to the cloth, pulling it into shape. Baste it down and remove the pins or tacks. Cover the embroidery with a Turkish towel. Hold a hot steam iron several inches above it, allowing plenty of steam to collect. If using a regular iron, mist the towel and hold the hot iron over it without touching the surface. Allow the towel to dry overnight before removing it and taking the embroidery off the board.

bound edges; bind. After cutting a piece of canvas to the desired size, enclose the four sides in tape to prevent raveling and snagging of working threads. (If there is a selvage, cut it off before binding to free the elements so that they can be stretched squarely.) Use inch-wide masking tape; firmly press down half the width along one edge of the canvas frontface, then turn the canvas to the backface and press down the other half. You can also hand- or machine-bind the edges with cotton tape.

bundles. Groups of warps collected together, usually with a coral knot. Bundles are shown in *Needleweaving* and *Hemstitching*. Also see **clusters.**

buratto. A woven foundation fabric that resembles the hand-knotted netting of traditional **filet,** or the open overcast network that we show in *Filet*. This fabric is woven with pairs of warps that twist around the wefts to keep them apart. It was often used in sixteenth-century Italy as a ground for the same stitches as filet.

canvas. A starched open-mesh foundation fabric having an equal number of vertical and horizontal elements. Canvas is available in a variety of fibers, constructions, sizes, and weights; you should carefully select the appropriate one for each project. As of this writing, canvas can be purchased in cotton, linen, silk, nylon, polyester, and plastic. Listed below are the cotton and linen canvases employed in *The Open Canvas;* these are the most suitable for learning new techniques. However, each of the remaining fibers is worthy of experimentation within limited areas of open work. Canvas sizes are indicated in this book first by the number of elements to the inch; 14/inch means 14 canvas elements to the inch. Ideally, there should be 14 horizontal and 14 vertical elements to a square inch, but unfortunately, canvas is imperfect. Therefore, when accuracy is required, you should count the elements against a ruler. Always purchase sufficient canvas to provide 1½ to 2 inches of margin around the proposed work.

canvas, congress. An English term that applies to all even-weave single-element cotton canvas. The American term for this is **mono canvas.** In *The Open Canvas,* however, I use the term congress canvas to refer to a good-quality, lightweight, single-mesh cotton canvas with a mesh size of 24/inch. It comes in a variety of colors and is an excellent choice for all of the techniques shown in *The Open Canvas.*

canvas, interlock. A thin, lightweight cotton canvas in which warps come in pairs, and twine around single wefts. At each intersection, one of the two paired warps passes over a weft while the other passes under it; between the intersections the two warps cross each other. At the next intersection the one that passed over the last weft now passes under a weft, and vice versa. In weaving, this process is called twining. Due to its construction, interlock canvas does not fray easily, but elements can still be withdrawn. Choose a canvas with smooth elements; make sure it does not have too much starch. Interlock canvas is available at this writing in white cotton in 5, 10, 12, 13, and 14/inch sizes.

canvas, linen. A single-element even-weave mesh, constructed with threads spun from flax. Canvas work prior to 1800 was mainly accomplished on unstarched fine open-mesh linen fabric. Today, starched cream-colored linen canvas is available. Linen fiber has no elasticity and is particularly strong, which makes it a good choice for pulled canvas work, needleweaving, and hemstitching. It is available at this writing in 8, 13, and 17/inch sizes.

canvas, mono. A single-element even-weave cotton or linen mesh with a *basketweave* construction. This means that single warps run parallel to the selvage at regular intervals, and matching single wefts pass over and under the warps. Good-quality mono canvas is available in white and tan cotton in an extensive range of mesh sizes: 10, 12, 13, 14, 16, 17, 18, and 22/inch. All of these cotton mono canvases are suitable for open canvas work.

canvas, toile. Named after a French sheer linen cloth of single-element, even-weave construction, this cotton canvas is woven with fine, lightweight elements, usually in a peach color. The canvas itself is so attractive it is suitable for all forms of open work. It is available in 18 and 23/inch sizes.

canvas element. The warps and wefts of the foundation fabric in *The Open Canvas* are referred to as canvas elements for two reasons. This easily distinguishes the canvas thread from the working thread; it also does away with the terms **warp** and **weft,** which are interchangeable in open work.

canvas work. A term that applies to counted-thread embroidery on a firm, even-weave open-mesh foundation fabric. Although canvas work is commonly known as needlepoint, it really is not. **Needlepoint** is a handmade needle lace composed solely of buttonhole stitches.

clamps. Often referred to as U clamps, these adjust to firmly hold a wooden frame onto a work table. A pair of clamps enables you to secure the work while leaving both hands free. If the work is to be turned, the clamps are loosened and readjusted. Small 3-inch clamps can be purchased in a hardware store.

clusters. In hemstitching, pairs of elements are collected into primary groups along the long edges of the opened band to prevent the remaining wefts from floating into the withdrawn space. When the spaces are wider than three or four withdrawn elements, secondary groups of warps are collected into bundles or clusters. Clusters may also be seen in needleweaving.

coil. A kind of snug overcasting accomplished by passing around canvas elements or thrown working threads many times in a winding or wrapping motion.

compensation stitch. A stitch that is actually part of a larger one and is used to fit into a space too small for a full stitch. Sometimes compensation stitches can be anticipated and filled in as you work. Other times, they can be inserted afterwards. Compensation can sometimes be achieved more neatly by reducing the size of the stitch.

connecting thread. That part of a stitch or stitch unit that does not show on the frontface but carries the working thread on the backface between the stitches, stitch units, or rows.

couching. A system for laying a heavy decorative thread on the surface of the canvas and fastening it down with a finer working thread. The fastening thread, often silk, is referred to as the couching thread. (See couching on Sampler II of *Pulled Canvas* and on Sampler II of *Filet*.)

counted-thread work. Embroidery that is produced by stitching over a planned number of fabric elements. The foundation fabric elements are never pierced; the **up-** and **downpoints** in this kind of embroidery are the spaces between the elements. Pulled canvas, hemstitching, filet, and Hardanger are counted-thread techniques.

cutwork. An open-work technique in which all elements are withdrawn after the edges have been bound and bars have been thrown across a shape.

darning. Passing the working thread over and under the foundation elements or over and under warps of laid working threads to establish a filling or an outline. The terms *weaving* and *darning* are actually interchangeable. However, in order to differentiate between two types of darning—that in which the passing is consistent, always under or over the same elements, and that in which passing alternates with each row, creating a bricklike effect—I have called the former weaving and the latter darning. See *Hardanger*, Stitches **4A** and **4B**.

deflected element. See **pulled canvas**.

detached fillings. Repeat patterns of stitches that are fastened down to the foundation fabric only at the edges of the shape or space they occupy. For an example, see the needle lace stitches shown in *Reticello and Hedebo*, Lesson **4**.

disappearing ink. Pens using disappearing blue ink have recently become quite popular. They are used to draw designs on canvas or fabric; the blue ink disappears when it is dampened with a swab or sponge. There is also a marker with dark red ink that fades away by itself in a few days. I have found both of them helpful, particularly for marking canvas elements that are to be cut or withdrawn.

double running stitch. See **running stitch**.

downpoint. The point at which the needle enters the backface by pushing through the foundation fabric from the frontface.

drawn fabric. A term that is often applied to pulled work.

drawn work. This is a confusing term that became popular in an effort to make a distinction between withdrawn-element work (which had been popularly called drawn *thread* work) and pulled work (which had been popularly called drawn *fabric* work). All of this makes my head swim and makes me grateful to Milton Sonday and Gillian Moss (*Western European Embroidery*), who created the terms **deflected element** and **with-**

drawn element. They may sound stiff, but they are certainly clear.

elements. These are the warps and wefts of the foundation fabric. This term is frequently used in *The Open Canvas,* where warps and wefts are interchangeable. It also immediately distinguishes the canvas threads from the working threads.

embroidery scissors. See **scissors, embroidery**.

eyelet stitch. Also called an eyelet. A unit of many satin or buttonhole stitches with converging downpoints, which produce a center hole. Changing the length and angle of the converging stitches creates the many variations of eyelets. For examples, see *Pulled Canvas,* where the holes are the result of deflecting the canvas elements, and *Reticello and Hedebo,* where the center canvas elements are cut to enlarge the center hole.

faggot filling; faggot stitch; faggoting. One definition of a faggot (or fagot) is a bundle of sticks. In various forms of embroidery, faggot filling, faggot stitch, and faggoting refer to bundles of working threads or fabric elements. In hemstitching, when the long horizontal elements are withdrawn from bands and the remaining vertical elements are collected into neat clusters by bundling them across the middle, the process is sometimes referred to as faggoting. In *Pulled Canvas,* faggot fillings are shown in which the working thread draws the canvas elements together in bundles, creating even, open patterns of negative spaces.

fastening off or on. When working on a canvas that is stretched on a frame, it is often better to turn the work as little as possible and to tack threads on the frontface until you are ready to weave them into the work (see **waste knot**). However, you can also fasten off on the backface as you proceed. To do this, bring the thread to the backface and slide the needle under five or six stitches. Then, still on the backface, loop over the last stitch, slide the needle back under the same stitches again, and clip away the tail end. You can fasten on on the backface by reversing this procedure. This method of fastening on and off is particularly appropriate for the kloster blocks of Hardanger.

festoon. This term is used in two ways in *The Open Canvas.* It refers to the scalloped or swagged edge of the buttonhole stitch, as opposed to the loop part of the stitch that enters the foundation fabric (*point de feston* actually means "buttonhole stitch" in French). It also refers to a wavy or serpentine pattern of stitches, like the swags made by journeys of coral knots, seen in *Needleweaving* and *Hemstitching*.

filet. Traditionally, filet refers to a handmade lace in which a hand-knotted netting, resembling a fine fish net, is filled with darned and looped stitches. It dates back to the sixth century B.C. In *The Open Canvas,* a network is established by withdrawing canvas elements evenly from both directions, overcasting the remaining paired elements, and then filling the open squares with various darned and looped stitches. See **lacis, guipure d'art.**

fillings; filling stitches. Repeated stitches or units of stitches that fill spaces or shapes.

flat stitch; half flat stitch. A flat stitch is a unit of slanting parallel satin stitches that fill a square shape. A half flat stitch is a triangular unit of slanting satins.

foundation fabric. The canvas ground or other material on which the embroidery is worked.

frame. An open square of wood on which to stretch and fasten down the foundation fabric to prevent distortion. Stretched work stays cleaner, since it is handled less when the frame is held stationary by a weight or clamp. Also, when work is on a frame, you can use both hands for the stitching. *Stretcher strips* are suggested for open canvas work frames. Stretcher strips are matched pairs of ½- to ¾-inch-square wood strips with ends that are made to dovetail. They come in interchangeable lengths so that various size frames can be assembled. Stretcher strips are sold in needlework shops or departments, or can easily be made at home by nailing together the desired lengths of wood strips. There are many other kinds of embroidery frames, including rotating, slate, and flat bar frames, which are all excellent for controlling the tension of the stretched fabric.

    framing on stretchers. Use a tack hammer and ¼- or ⅜-inch flat-headed tacks. Hammer the tacks through the bound edges of the canvas into the wood frame no more than one inch apart. Keep the canvas taut and the warps and wefts square. Start by hammering down the first tack at the middle of one side of the frame; then hammer in a tack on either side of it. Pull the canvas firmly from the opposite side and fasten down three corresponding tacks. Work the other two sides in the same manner. Complete the fastening down, alternately tacking opposite sides.

frontface. The top or "right" side of the canvas or foundation fabric.

Gobelin stitch. Named after the famous French Gobelins tapestries, this stitch originally imitated Gobelins weaving. Today, it usually refers to a single slanted stitch taken over two horizontal and one vertical canvas elements. There are many variations of this stitch, including a small Gobelin that is taken over a single canvas element. This stitch is particularly useful in getting from one place on the canvas to another nearby, without the stitches being obvious.

ground. Short for background—the space around the design. It can be an unworked or worked foundation fabric; it can also be a small patterned (or textured) filling on which another pattern is worked.

group. A number of canvas elements that are collected by the working thread into a pattern.

    group, primary. The initial grouping of elements into simple patterns. See *Hemstitching,* Lesson **2**.

    group, secondary. After the canvas elements have been collected once, they can be regrouped to make a more complicated pattern. See *Hemstitching,* Lesson **3**.

guipure d'art. A term in filet that refers to a machine-made netting with handmade fillings, popular in the nineteenth century. See **filet.**

Hardanger. A Norwegian counted-thread embroidery that combines surface work with open work. It is typically worked on cloth, but has also been worked on canvas, as it is here. See *Hardanger.*

Hedebo. A Danish embroidery that combines surface work with open work. Curved open shapes are filled with needle lace. The Hedebo buttonhole stitch is its basic stitch unit. See *Reticello and Hedebo.*

hemstitching. A technique in which various widths of bands and borders are created by withdrawing elements that lie parallel to the long edge. The remaining elements are grouped and secured with decorative stitches. See *Hemstitching.*

journey. A single direction of travel in working a stitch. A row of stitches can be accomplished in one or more journeys. A *return journey* travels back to the start as part of the same row, often completing it.

kloster blocks. A term from Hardanger embroidery that refers to blocks of satin stitches that form squared enclosures for open-work fillings. See *Hardanger.*

lacis. A term in filet that refers to a hand-knotted netting, with or without darned fillings. The term is derived from the Latin *laquens,* meaning "noose." The earliest netting was made for hunting and fishing; it then became the foundation fabric for the earliest lace. See **filet.**

master pattern. Refers to *The Open Canvas* graphs, which position the main design shapes of each sampler.

motif. An independent design unit, usually composed of several stitches.

needles. Select the needle that is appropriate for the work to be done. Function determines its length, type of eye, and point. Use *tapestry needles* for counted-thread work; their blunt points do not pierce the elements or threads. Use *fine tapestry needles* for needle lace, so that you do not split the working thread. *Crewel needles* have sharp points and long eyes similar to those of tapestry needles. Use them for fastening down on the backface. *Sharps* are all-purpose sewing needles with round eyes; use them when fastening down a fine thread. *Chenille needles* are short with long eyes and sharp points; use them for plunging heavy couching threads into the backface. *Milliner's needles* are very long, with round eyes and sharp points; use them for making bullion knots, where the working thread must be wrapped around the needle a number of times.

needle lace. A filling of buttonhole stitches that are detached from the foundation fabric, except at the edges.

needlepoint. This term originally referred only to needle lace. However, it has gradually become an accepted term for canvas work, in which counted-thread stitches cover an open mesh ground. See **canvas work.**

needleweaving (also called **Swedish weaving, Swedish darning**). A form of embroidery well-suited to canvas, in which selected warp and/or weft threads are withdrawn, and the remaining elements are darned with a simple over-and-under stitch. Patterns are formed by changing the groupings of darned elements and also by changing the color and texture of the working thread. Needleweaving is also worked over warps of thrown working threads. See *Needleweaving.*

negative space. In *The Open Canvas,* this refers to the openings left when the stitches have pulled the canvas out of alignment or where elements have been completely withdrawn. *Positive space* refers to the foundation fabric itself. In designing open-work embroidery, it is important to realize that the negative space is as important as the positive space. Whether the work is held up to the light or placed over a colored ground, it is the shape of the openings that usually dominates the design. Consider this when selecting stitches and techniques. The size as well as the shape of negative space should also be taken into account.

netting; network. An even open-weave foundation fabric created by hand- or machine-knotting, resembling a fish net. In *The Open Canvas* it is the web of crossing elements remaining after selected elements have been withdrawn from both directions, as in the prepared ground for filet, the webs of Hardanger, and the large open grids of reticello.

open work. A category of embroidery that secures and embellishes openings made in a foundation fabric. *The Open Canvas* explores the various ways of opening a canvas and filling the spaces that result.

outlining. A method of defining the perimeter of a shape. This can be accomplished in many ways—changing stitches or using a heavier, couched-down thread, for example. See *Pulled Canvas,* Basket of Flowers.

overcast. A stitch that passes completely around the canvas elements or thrown working threads. You can also provide a neat finish for an edge by overcasting with straight stitches to prevent unraveling, in which case the overcast is called a **satin stitch.**

padding. An underlay that fills a shape or outline, producing a raised effect when that shape or outline is later covered with stitches. Padding can also serve to hide canvas elements that would otherwise show between straight stitches.

picots. Small knotted or looped stitches that accent bars or buttonhole edges. See *Hardanger, Filet,* and *Reticello and Hedebo.*

plunging; sinking. A term used in couching when a chenille needle is fed with a heavy, decorative thread and inserted—plunged, or sunk—into the backface of the foundation fabric. The tail end is then fastened down with a crewel or sharp needle and fine silk thread. See *Pulled Canvas.*

point d'Angleterre. A term that was used in seventeenth-century England to describe imported laces. At that time, there was a law against importing lace; smuggled laces were called *point d'Angleterre* to fool the authorities while indicating to consumers that the lace was of foreign manufacture. In *The Open Canvas, point d'Angleterre* is a needle lace made by throwing a grid and working small wheels at each intersection. See *Reticello and Hedebo* for a simplified version of this stitch.

positive space. See **negative space.**

pulled canvas. Other terms for this deflected-element work include pulled thread, pulled work, drawn fabric, and the Danish *sammentraeksmønstre.* In this section of *The Open Canvas,* no elements are withdrawn; the openings are produced by using the working thread to pull the elements out of alignment. See *Pulled Canvas.*

punto in aria. An Italian term for needle laces that are produced without a foundation fabric, as opposed to those made on a netting like *lacis* or filet, or those made on a fabric from which elements are cut or withdrawn, such as **punto tagliato** and **punto tirato.** *Punto in aria* laces are worked while attached to paper or cloth, and then released on completion.

punto tagliato. An Italian open work produced by first cutting or withdrawing elements from both directions of the foundation fabric. Filet, Hardanger, reticello, and Hedebo are examples.

punto tirato. An Italian open work produced by first deflecting elements of a foundation fabric or withdrawing elements from one direction. Pulled canvas, needleweaving, and hemstitching are examples.

pyramid. A triangle shape made of needle lace. See *Reticello and Hedebo.*

reticello. An early form of open work in which the barest skeleton of foundation fabric is left, forming open squares that are filled with geometric needle lace. Reticello soon evolved into a true lace, employing no foundation fabric at all. See *Reticello and Hedebo.*

reweaving. Securing a withdrawn element by darning it back into the foundation fabric, following the existing weave. Always begin reweaving by passing over the element at the edge of the unopened space. If the withdrawn element is too short to feed into the eye of the needle, weave the needle into the unopened space first and then thread it; or, use a crochet hook to pluck the element into place. Reweaving demands consistency; work on either the front- or backface, and on one side (left or right) of each element that remains in the canvas.

rivière. A band of embroidery. See *Hardanger.*

running stitch. A stitch in which the working thread weaves over and under the elements of a canvas or fabric, completed in a single journey. The length of the stitch on both the front- and backface is the same.

double running stitch. A running stitch completed by a return journey that fills in the empty spaces left by the first journey. See *Reticello and Hedebo,* Stitch **1A.**

Russian drawn ground. An opened foundation fabric achieved by withdrawing both horizontal and vertical elements in groups of threes: three are withdrawn, three remain, three are withdrawn, etc. The remaining sets of elements are overcast. The resulting ground resembles a filet or *lacis* netting. It is then reembroidered with heavy chain stitch outlines, which are filled with darning, loop, and buttonhole stitches. Similar techniques are employed in *Filet* and *Pulled Canvas*.

satin stitch. Straight overcasts worked with even tension to produce a smooth, light-reflecting surface, as in a satin fabric. Satin stitches can neatly fill a small shape or bind an edge.

scissors, embroidery. Usually 3½ inches long, with sharp pointed tips. Two pairs are needed for open work. One pair is kept very sharp and reserved for cutting canvas elements closely and precisely, necessary in Hardanger, reticello, and Hedebo; a second pair is kept handy for snipping working threads. To trim closely, rest the blades flat on the embroidered surface and cut high up on the blade. Use straight nail scissors, which are short with wide, sturdy blades, to cut metal thread or twine; these sharp, heavy threads dull embroidery scissors. General-purpose or fabric shears are needed for cutting canvas, fabric, or paper.

scooping motion. A sewing method in which the work is done on the frontface by inserting the needle into the downpoint and then the uppoint in one movement before drawing up the working thread for another scoop of fabric.

serpentine. A waving or undulating line. See *Hemstitching,* where serpentine bands are worked by grouping and regrouping remaining warps on alternate sides to produce a zigzag pattern. Journeys of coral knots can also travel across wider bands in serpentine fashion, producing waving lines.

shadow work. Embroidery that exists mainly on the backface of a sheer fabric and casts a shadow on the frontface. See *Pulled Canvas,* Lesson **9.**

sinking. See **plunging.**

spokes and **spiders.** Working threads that are thrown across an open space or over the foundation fabric from a bar or a canvas intersection to another bar or canvas intersection. They are usually overcast back to the starting point. Spokes employed as radiating warps with wheels woven around their center intersections are referred to as spiders. Spokes are employed in every section of *The Open Canvas* except *Pulled Canvas.*

stab method. A method of stitching in which the foundation fabric is firmly stretched on a frame, the frame held stationary by a weight, a clamp, or a frame stand, and the stitching accomplished by using both hands. The dominant hand is kept under the frame and pushes the needle up from the backface at the uppoint; the other hand draws the needle and working thread up and then returns it to the backface by *stabbing* it into the downpoint.

steaming. See **blocking.**

stiletto. See **awl.**

stitch. The result of passing the working thread in and out of the foundation fabric to produce a straight, slanted, knitted, or looped segment on the frontface.

What is normally thought of as a single stitch is usually a *stitch unit,* a composite of several stitches.

stitch count. The number of canvas elements over which a stitch is formed, or the number of stitches required to fill an area.

strand. A single fiber, or a number of fibers twisted into plies. Loosely twisted strands, such as three-ply persian wool, DMC Six-Strand Embroidery Cotton, and Au Ver A Soie seven-strand silk should all be separated into single plies and evenly realigned or regrouped before feeding the desired number through the needle. This is a grooming process called *stranding,* or *stripping,* which makes it possible to keep the plies aligned, allowing the stitches to reflect the most light.

stretcher strips. See *frame.*

surface work. Refers to embroidery that embellishes the frontface of the foundation fabric without adding another layer (raised work); and without opening the foundation fabric by deflecting or withdrawing elements (open work).

Teneriffe lace. A kind of lace that is worked on threads thrown within circles. See *Hemstitching* introduction.

tension. The strength with which the working thread is drawn through the foundation fabric. Whatever the degree of tension, it should be applied evenly, so that all the stitches look alike. In pulled canvas, a strong tension is usually needed in order to deflect the elements. In needleweaving and hemstitching, a moderate amount of tension is needed to draw the warps together into groups. The surface work of Hardanger, reticello, and Hedebo requires slack, even tension.

tent stitch. A synonym for *petit point,* a simple stitch taken over the intersection of a horizontal and a vertical canvas element, slanting from lower left to upper right. According to Lewis Day (*Art in Needlework,* London: Batsford, 1914), the name was derived from the word *tenture,* or *tenter*—a term that referred to the frame on which the embroider stretched the canvas (from *tendere,* "to stretch").

textiles. The end products of processing fibers into fabrics. The canvas worker, in essence, is manufacturing a textile; the open mesh canvas in its original state is not a complete fabric since it requires further embellishment to be of value. Canvas embroidery is an immensely satisfying occupation because the worker takes an active role in the creation of the fabric itself.

Many embroiderers, teachers, collectors, and curators have been deeply concerned with maintaining, protecting, and reviving both old and new textiles—so much so that we are witnessing the birth of a new science involved in the study of the conservation, preservation, and restoration of textiles. The Bibliography suggests further reading to help you care for textiles that you produce or collect.

textile conservation. The prevention of further deterioration of existing textiles by employing scientific methods and by providing proper display and storage conditions. The major causes of deterioration are pollution, dirt, bright light, dry heat, high humidity, insects, handling, and contact with acid-bearing materials such as wood and paper. Conservation requires regular inspection for damage and careful action to correct and improve the environment.

textile preservation. The maintenance of the original condition of a textile that is not in a state of decay by following the methods of conservation. Preservation begins at the inception of a work with the selection of suitable, compatible materials and the practice of clean work habits, and ends with proper mounting.

textile restoration. Returning the textile to a condition closely resembling its original state without lessening its original value.

thread. Natural fibers (cotton, linen, silk, wool) or manmade filaments (nylon, polyester, rayon) that have gone through various spinning, dyeing, and finishing processes to become the twisted yarns used for weaving, sewing, and embroidery. Listed below are the threads employed in *The Open Canvas;* most are old standards that should remain available. They are mainly natural fibers—cotton, linen, and silk. No wool has been used because finer, less heavy threads are easier to handle and produce visually clearer results. Because they are more difficult to handle, manmade fibers have been employed minimally as extra novelties. However, they should not be overlooked in creating contemporary open work. All the natural-fiber threads are described as twisted or floss. A *twisted thread* is composed of tightly spun plies and is not meant to be divided. *Floss* is composed of six or seven tightly twisted plies that are loosely twisted together in strands, and is meant to be separated and regrouped into new strands of the desired weight. DMC Six-Strand Embroidery Cotton and Au Ver A Soie silk are examples of floss.

An embroidery rule of thumb is to match the weight or girth of the working to that of the foundation fabric element. This works well when the intention is to cover the elements and to produce a smooth, even result. However, in *The Open Canvas,* the intention is to contrast the open spaces with exposed and embellished elements, producing a textured lace effect; therefore, threads of varying weights are employed. There is another rule that does apply, however. The freshly cut end from a ball or spool goes into the eye of the needle and becomes the *short end.* Remember to save wrappers and labels to aid in identification and replacement.

thread, cotton. All cotton threads employed in *The Open Canvas* samplers are DMC, because of their availability and quality. The letters stand for the Dollfus-Mieg Company, founded in 1746 in Mulhouse, France, as a weaving and printing house. By 1879, after much expansion, the company opened a factory for thread and lace making. Not long after this, it published Thérèse de Dillmont's *Encyclopedia of Needlework* and other Library Series pattern booklets. In 1934, DMC created the monthly magazine *Jeux d'Aiguilles* and opened a Paris shop of the same name. It was from *Jeux d'Aiguilles* that I purchased my first canvas work and, like other embroiderers from all over the world, I cut

my first embroidery teeth by studying the *Encyclopedia of Needlework* and the many Library Series booklets. I continue to refer to these fine old books to this day.

Brilliant Embroidery and Cutwork Thread (Coton à broder, qualité speciale). A twisted thread with a soft finish that retains a soft luster and is pleasant to handle. The *coton à broder* comes in a modest range of colors and two useful sizes, 12 and 16. Use it when you want to blend stitches together, as in eyelets, or for padding units of satin stitches and satin or buttonhole edges. To open a skein, slide off the wrapper and unfold the skein into a large ring. Locate the knot that holds the ring and cut through the entire ring at this spot. Fold the group of long strands in half and slide the two wrappers back over the fold. The wrappers serve as a record of both color and size. To withdraw a length of thread, hold the wrappers with one hand and draw a strand from the folded end. See this thread in the *Reticello and Hedebo* sampler, where it is used for surface work, eyelets, and under the buttonholed edges.

Crochet Cotton (Cebelia). A tightly twisted three-ply thread of adequate quality, Cebelia is available in twenty colors and three sizes: 10, 20, and 30. It comes in large balls. Use it for all open work, particularly for needle lace and buttonhole edges. See it on the *Hardanger* sampler, where it is used for needleweaving and fillings.

Pearl Cotton (Coton Perlé). A tightly twisted thread with a high luster. Pearl cotton has an extensive range of colors and comes in three sizes: 3, 5, and 8. Sizes 3 and 5, the heavy and the medium weights, come in both small skeins and larger quantity balls; the fine size 8 comes in balls only. Open the skeins as for *coton à broder.* Do not use pearl cotton in long lengths; the eye of the needle easily wears down the thread, and it tends to knot. Pearl cotton is traditionally used for Hardanger; see the *Hardanger* samplers, where it is used for kloster blocks, buttonholed edges, eyelets, and surface work.

Six-Cord Crochet Cotton (Cordonnet 6 brins, qualité spéciale). A tightly twisted six-ply thread of superior quality. Its only flaw is that it is now only available in white and ecru. It comes in balls that range in sizes from the heaviest (10), through 20, 30, 40, and 50. Use it for all the open work shown here, but most particularly for needle lace, as seen in the *Reticello and Hedebo* sampler. Use Cebelia Three-Cord Crochet Cotton as a substitute for Cordonnet when color is desired.

Six-Strand Embroidery Cotton (Coton Mouliné spécial). The most popular of all embroidery threads; a floss with six plies in a strand that should be separated and realigned. It must be used in several plies, as it is not very strong; if carefully kept in alignment while working, it is so lustrous it looks exactly like expensive French silk. There are over three hundred colors to choose from. Use it for surface work, filet, and needleweaving. It comes in a pull skein; do not remove the wrapper but follow the picture on it that demonstrates how to draw out the thread. *Mouliné* is used to overcast the network in the *Filet* sampler.

Soft Embroidery and Tapestry Cotton, Matte Finish (Retors à broder). A dull, soft, twisted thread in over two hundred colors that resembles a fine, prettily colored string. It provides a strong contrast to lustrous threads and is very easy to handle. It fits a 16/inch canvas. Since there is only a size 4, it must be used as a heavy accent. It comes in a pullskein; do not remove the wrapper but follow the picture on it that demonstrates how to draw out thread. See *retors* in the *Filet* sampler, where it is used for darned outlines and in fillings.

thread, linen. Those employed in *The Open Canvas* are from Sweden and Scotland because they are available from these countries in suitable weights and a wide range of colors. Linen is very strong, and from a conservation point of view, very durable. It has a soft sheen and a coarser texture than cotton thread. Linen thread is twisted and should not be separated, or it will fray. Sizes are indicated by two numbers with a slash between them. The first number tells the weight (the finer weights have higher numbers); the second tells the number of plies. Embroidery linen comes on pullskeins; hold the skein by the wrapper in one hand and pull the thread end with the other. Use linen for open work where strength and texture are desired. See linen in *Filet* Sampler I, where it is used for much of the work.

thread, silk. This beautiful natural fiber has been much appreciated by embroiderers because of its exceptional receptiveness to color dyes, its great strength, and its ability to reflect light. Listed below are five available types of silk thread that are used in *The Open Canvas.*

Au Ver A Soie. A French seven-ply silk floss with a rich, soft luster that comes in an extensive range of colors and values. Because it can be separated, you can realign the desired number of plies and obtain excellent light reflection. Use it for satin stitches to display this quality. It comes in skeins that should be opened into a ring. Cut the ring in one or two places, depending on the length of thread you require. Bundle the strands together with a loose knot and draw strands from the knot as needed. See *Pulled Canvas* Sampler II, where it is used for pulled satin variations.

Kanagawa Silk Embroidery Thread. A softly twisted Japanese thread with high luster in a wide range of kimono colors. Use it for all open work but particularly pulled work, because of its strength. It comes tightly wound on a card. If the creases interrupt your work, use a damp sponge to smooth them. See *Pulled Canvas* Sampler I, where it is employed for most of the work.

silk chenille. A high-pile thread that looks like a caterpillar but when couched down resembles velvet. It has a limited color range but texture like no other thread (there is also a wool and cotton chenille). Couch it down with a matching silk thread. See *Filet* Sampler II, where it is used for a textured border.

silk ribbon. A ⅛-inch ribbon that comes in many colors on small reels. Use silk ribbon to add a different texture to open work, where it can easily be drawn through the spaces left by the drawn elements. See the *Needleweaving* sampler, where it is used on a band of freely worked needleweaving, and *Hemstitching* Sampler I, where it is used in a band of inverted elements.

silk sewing thread. A pure silk thread that comes in a wide range of colors in a weight (size A) suitable for couching down heavy textured threads such as chenille or metals. Run it through beeswax when couching metals so that it will not be cut or shredded. See it on *Pulled Canvas* Sampler II, where it is used to couch down metals.

threads, manmade. These threads are usually more difficult to handle than natural fibers. However, the high shine or unusual textures that they possess make them useful for small areas. Dampening and rewinding onto felt-covered tubes helps to groom some of them. Use short 18-inch lengths and lightly dampen the worst offenders. This group includes the Mexican el Globo used as an accent on *Pulled Canvas* Sampler I, and the Brazilian Varicor used on bands in the *Needleweaving* sampler. Veloura, on the other hand, is a well-behaved textured thread. It can be fed through canvas mesh and has a low, smooth pile. See Veloura on the outer border of the *Needleweaving* sampler.

threads, metal. There are a limited number of metal threads that can be drawn easily through canvas mesh openings. If a metal thread is to be couched, then any of the many textures and weights can be employed. However, in *The Open Canvas,* only a narrow braided thread called Lumiyarn is used. It comes in gold and silver in three sizes, #1, #1¼, and #1½. Use Lumiyarn for needleweaving, for accents in all open work, and for couching down. See *Pulled Canvas* Sampler II, where it is couched down, and the *Needleweaving* sampler, where it is used in needlewoven bars.

throw. The stretching or casting of the working thread from one location to another across an open space or over the surface of the foundation fabric.

uppoint. Where the needle enters the frontface by pushing through the foundation fabric from the backface.

warps and **wefts.** Warps are the vertical elements that run parallel to the selvage of the foundation fabric, over and under which the wefts, or horizontal elements, pass. It is the weft that creates the fabric. In *The Open Canvas,* the two terms are interchangeable.

waste knot. A simple knot made at the tail end of the working thread that is left temporarily on the frontface of the embroidery and later cut away. It is made by twisting the thread once around the tip of the index finger about an inch from the tail end, then pushing it off with the thumb of the same hand, and pulling this bunched up thread into a knot. I like to leave a tail on the end of the waste knot; when it is time to remove the knot, I give the tail a slight tug to open it. I am then free to clip away the thread or pull it to the backface and weave it into the stitching.

web. The network of canvas elements that remains when selected elements are withdrawn from both directions; or, crossing working threads that are thrown across an open space or over the surface to act as warps for needleweaving. See the *Hardanger* sampler, where the remaining elements are overcast or needlewoven; in the *Hemstitching* sampler, the open squares at the intersections of bands are first filled with webs before they are further embellished. The network foundation of *Filet* Sampler I is also a web.

weight; weighted pillow. A sack filled with small, heavy objects such as lead gunshot, pebbles, or beans. Use it to hold the framed canvas securely on a work table to free both hands. A weight is more convenient than a frame stand or clamps because it is so easy to remove, enabling you to turn the work around or to the backface. You can use several books or a brick to raise the frame to a convenient angle, and then rest the weight so that half of it is on the frame and unworked area and the other half on the raised surface or work table.

wheels. The woven circles at the intersections of bars or spokes. There are wheels in the samplers of every book except *Pulled Canvas.*

whipping. A secondary stitch that overcasts the primary stitch without entering the foundation fabric. See *Pulled Canvas* Sampler I for whipped chain stitch.

whitework. Hand embroidery in which the foundation fabric and the working thread are both white or ecru, usually in fine cotton or linen. Most types of open-work embroidery, including all techniques shown in *The Open Canvas,* were originally forms of whitework.

withdrawn elements. The warps and wefts of the foundation fabric that are removed by unweaving and/or cutting. The foundation fabric is secured in various ways. These methods include: reweaving elements into marginal areas (as in needleweaving); binding the cut edge with overcast or buttonhole stitches either before or after withdrawing and cutting (as in hemstitching, filet, Hardanger, and reticello); tacking the withdrawn elements down on the backface outside of the opened spaces (as in needleweaving and filet); and catching the withdrawn elements on the backface while binding the edges (as in Hedebo).

It is usually easier to withdraw elements from large spaces off the frame. When there are closely placed open shapes, complete the withdrawing and the embroidery of one shape at a time to keep the foundation fabric stable. If you are withdrawing elements from both directions, as in filet, it is easier to withdraw the shorter elements first. When withdrawing an element, cut it midway first, then unweave it in both directions. Dispose of each withdrawn element as soon as possible by cutting, reweaving, or tacking.

cutting an element by mistake. This is not a calamity. A new matching element can easily be woven in to replace it. Unweave the cut element in both directions as far as possible; do not cut it. Unravel a warp and weft from an identical piece of canvas and employ whichever matches the cut element, weaving it into the space in the canvas where it is missing. Catch the old and new elements securely on the backface or fasten them behind the bound edges and trim them.

BIBLIOGRAPHY

GENERAL EMBROIDERY AND OPEN WORK

Anchor Manual of Needlework. Newton Centre, Massachusetts: Charles T. Branford, 1974.

The Dictionary of Needlework, Sophia Frances Anne Caulfeild and Blanche C. Saward. London: L. Upcott Gill, 1882. New York: Arno Press, Inc., 1972.

Drawn Thread Work, DMC Library First Series, Th. de Dillmont, editor. Mulhouse, France: prior to 1912.

Ecclesiastical Embroidery, Beryl Dean. London: B.T. Batsford Ltd., 1958.

Encyclopedia of Needlework, Thérèse de Dillmont. Mulhouse, France: Editions Th. de Dillmont, 1880.

Handbook of Stitches, Grete Petersen and Elsie Svennas. New York: Van Nostrand Reinhold, 1966.

Ich Kann Handarbeiten, Mitzi Donner, Carl Gchnebel. Berlin and Vienna: Verlag Ullftein and Co., 1913.

Introduction to Silk and Metal Thread Embroidery, Elsa Cose. New Jersey: self-published, 1977.

Jours sur Toile, Bibliothèque DMC IIme Série. Mulhouse, France: Editions Th. de Dillmont.

Mary Thomas's Dictionary of Embroidery Stitches, Mary Thomas. London: Hodder and Stoughton Ltd., 1965.

Needlework Stitches, Barbara Snook. New York: Crown Publishers, Inc., 1972.

Openwork Embroidery, DMC Library. Mulhouse, France: Editions Th. de Dillmont, 1974.

Samplers and Stitches, Mrs. Archibald Christie. New York: Hearthside Press, Inc., 1971.

The Stitches of Creative Embroidery, Jacqueline Enthoven. New York: Van Nostrand Reinhold, 1964.

TEXTILE DICTIONARIES

Caring for Textiles, Karen Finch O.B.E. and Greta Putnam. New York: Watson-Guptill Publications, 1977.

Dictionary of Textile Terms. New York: Dan River, 1976.

Fabric and Thread Collection, Kay Montclare. New Hampshire: The Needleworkshop, 1976.

The Identification of Lace, Pat Earnshaw. Aylesbury, England: Shire Publications Ltd., 1980.

The Needleworker's Dictionary, Pamela Clabburn. New York: William Morrow and Co., 1976.

Principles of the Stitch, Lilo Markrich. Chicago: Henry Regnery Co., 1976.

The Textile Arts, Vera Birrell. New York: Schocken Books, 1937.

Textile Museum Journal, "Practical Definitions for Three Openwork Techniques," Colman, von Rosensteil, Bidner, Sonday, Moss, Merritt. Vol. IV, No. 4, 1977.

Textile Preservation, Estelle Horowitz. Long Beach, California: self-published, 1982.

Western European Embroidery, Milton Sonday and Gillian Moss. New York: Cooper Hewitt Museum, Catalog No. 78-62366.

FILET

Beyers Lehrbuch der Weiblichen Handarbeiten, Bertha Schwetter. Leipzig: Verlag Otto Beyer, 1931.

Embroidery, Journal of the Embroiderers' Guild, "Lacis," I.A. Simpson. London: Sept. 1936.

Embroidery, Journal of the Embroiderers' Guild, "The Netted Laces Including Filet and Lacis," Rachel B. Kay-Shuttleworth. London: Summer 1960.

Embroidery, Journal of the Embroiderers' Guild, "Some Russian Embroideries," Stella Bird and Angela Thompson. London: Summer 1978.

Lace, Virginia Churchill Bath. New York: Penguin Books, 1979.

Le Filet-Richelieu, Th. de Dillmont. Mulhouse, France: Bibliothèque DMC, 1888.

HARDANGER

Hardanger Embroideries, First Series and Second Series, DMC Library. Mulhouse, France: Editions Th. de Dillmont, 1975.

Hardanger Embroidery, Sigrid Bright. New York: Dover Publications, Inc., 1978.

Hardanger for Today, no. 1066; **Coloured Hardanger Motifs,** no. 614. London: Coats Sewing Group.

HEMSTITCHING

Embroidery Lessons, "Lessons in Colored Drawn Work," Mrs. Isaac Miller Houck. New London, Connecticut: Brainerd & Armstrong Co., 1903.

Punti a Giorno. Milan: Casa Editrice Mani di Fata, 1978.

The Technique of Teneriffe Lace, Alexandra Stillwell. Watertown, Massachusetts: Charles T. Branford, 1980.

HISTORY

Antiques, "Two Centuries of Needle Lace," Christa C. Mayer. New York: Feb. 1965.

Catalogue of English Domestic Embroidery, John L. Nevinson. London: Victoria and Albert Museum, 1950.

Crewel Embroidery in England, Joan Edwards. New York: William Morrow and Co., 1975.

A History of Hand-made Lace, Mrs. Nevill Jackson. London: L. Upcott Gill, 1900.

A History of Lace, Mrs. Bury Palliser. West Yorkshire, England: EP Publishing Ltd., 1976.

A History of Western Embroidery, Mary Eirwin Jones. New York: Watson-Guptill Publications, 1969.

The Needlework of Mary Queen of Scots, Margaret Swain. New York: Van Nostrand Reinhold, 1973.

Samplers and Tapestry Embroideries, Marcus Huish. New York: Dover, 1970.

A Stitch in Time, Geoffrey Warren. New York: Taplinger Publishing Co., 1976.

NEEDLEWEAVING

Embroidery, Journal of the Embroiderers' Guild, "Annie Garnett 1864–1942," Gill Medland. London: Winter 1980.

Embroidery, Journal of the Embroiderers' Guild, "Needleweaving." London: Spring 1968.

Experimental Embroidery, Edith John. Newton Centre, Massachusetts: Charles T. Branford, 1976.

PULLED CANVAS

A Complete Guide to Drawn Fabric, Kate S. Lofthouse. London: Pitman, 1954.

Danish Pulled Thread Embroidery, Esther Fangel, Ida Winckler, and Agnette Wuldem Madsen. New York: Dover Publications, Inc., 1977.

DMC Albums No. 26 and No. 32. St. Gall, France: Dolfus-Meig & Cie.

Embroidery, Journal of the Embroiderers' Guild, "Drawn Fabric Work—II," A.L. London: Summer 1953.

Heimatwerk, Dr. Ernst Laur. Zurich: April 1951, August 1957.

Pulled Thread Embroidery, Moira McNeil. New York: Taplinger Publishing Co., 1972.

Pulled Thread Workbook, Mary Fry. New Jersey: self-published, 1978.

Sammentraeksmønstre, Clara Weaver. Copenhagen: Clara Weaver.

RETICELLO AND HEDEBO

The Art of Cutwork and Appliqué, Herta Puls. Newton Centre, Massachusetts: Charles T. Branford, 1978.

Embroider Now, Hetsie van Wyk. Johannesburg: Perskor Publishers, 1977.

Embroidery, Journal of the Embroiderers' Guild, "Greek Lace, Ruskin Linen Work," W.L. Raby. London: Autumn 1958.

Embroidery, Journal of the Embroiderers' Guild, "Linen Cut-Work," Oenone Cave. London: Spring 1964.

Home Needlework Magazine, "Hedebo Embroidery and Its Making," Marie M. Koch. Florence, Massachusetts: 1905.

Mary Thomas's Embroidery Book, Mary Thomas. London: Hodder and Stoughton, 1979.

SUPPLIES

In a reference book such as this, it would have been preferable not to cite brand names but to speak in generic terms. However, in the world of threads and other needlework supplies, each manufacturer or distributor carries such special products that the brand must be specified. Most of these brands, however, are tried and true, and the reader should have no difficulty in obtaining them for many years to come.

If you cannot locate any of the materials employed in *The Open Canvas,* contact the manufacturer or distributor listed here.

CANVAS

Congress: OOE/USA, P.O. Box 1467, Summerville, SC 19483

Interlock, mono, toile: Joan Toggitt Ltd., 246 Fifth Avenue, New York, NY 10001

Linen: Elsa Williams, Inc., 445 Main Street, West Townsend, MA 01474

THREAD

Cotton: DMC Corp., 107 Trumbull Street, Elizabeth, NJ 07206

Kanagawa Silk Thread and Ribbon: Yarn Loft, 742 Genevieve, Suite L, Solana Beach, CA 92075

Au Ver A Soie Silk and Chenille: Kreinik Mfg. Co., 1351 Market Street, Parkersburg, WV 26101 (east coast); Nettie's Needlecraft, 97–42 Wilshire Boulevard, Los Angeles, CA 90067 (west coast)

Linen: Frederick J. Fawcett Inc., 120 South Street, Boston, MA 02111

Metal Lumiyarn: La Lame Importers, 250 West 39th Street, New York, NY 10018

Brazilian Varicor: Casa de las Tejedoras, 169 East Edinger, Santa Ana, CA 92705

Veloura: Idle Hands, 82–04 Lefferts Boulevard, Kew Gardens, NY 11415

ACID-FREE GLUE, PAPER, BOARD

Talas, 130 Fifth Avenue, New York, NY 10011